D1071782

NIGHTFROST IN PRAGUE

Zdeněk Mlynář

NIGHTFROST IN PRAGUE

The End of Humane Socialism

translated by Paul Wilson

KARZ PUBLISHERS • NEW YORK

Published in German as *Nachtfrost*
Copyright © by Europäische Verlagsanstalt, Köln, 1978

Library of Congress Cataloging in Publication Data

Mlynář, Zdeněk.
  Nightfrost in Prague.

  Translation of Mráz přicházi z Kremlu.
  Includes Index.
  1. Komunistická strana Ceskoslovenska.
2. Kommunisticheskaia partiia Sovetskogo Souiza.
3. Czechoslovakia—Politics and government—1968-
I. Title.
JN2229.A5M5713   324.2437075   79-28591
ISBN 0-918294-08-8

The translation for the Action Program excerpts and the Moscow Protocol are reprinted from *Winter in Prague*, by Robin Remington, by permission of the MIT Press, Cambridge, Massachusetts. Copyright © 1969 by Massachusetts Institute of Technology.

Published in the United States
by **KARZ PUBLISHERS**
320 West 105th Street
New York, N.Y. 10025

CONTENTS

Page

PROLOGUE   1

Chapter
1. FROM KHRUSHCHEV TO DUBČEK   24
2. PRAGUE SPRING IN THE LEADERSHIP   77
3. FACING THE KREMLIN TRIBUNAL   146

EPILOGUE   248
APPENDIX
Zdeněk Mlynář's Resignation Address   261
Zdeněk Mlynář's Contribution to the Action Program   267
The Moscow Protocol   282
LIST OF NAMES   287
INDEX   297

NIGHTFROST IN PRAGUE

PROLOGUE

I joined the Communist party in the spring of 1946, when I was not quite sixteen. Thus I belong to the generation of Czechoslovak Communists who were around twenty in February 1948, when the Communist totalitarian dictatorship was installing itself, and my political experience is peculiar to that generation.

Those who were over twenty at that time saw many things quite differently; their experience of life and politics, not only during but just before the war years, was very different. Under normal circumstances, five years is not a long time in terms of experience. But if in those five years one goes through a world war, there is necessarily a great difference between those who were already mature when it began and those who were just growing up as it came to an end.

My generation was made prematurely aware of politics by the stormy events of that period; at the same time we lacked political experience. The only experience we had was of the war years and the Nazi occupation of Czechoslovakia, and during some of this time we were still children. One of the chief results of this was a black-and-white vision of the world, with the enemy on one side and his adversary on the other. It was either one side or the other—there was no middle ground. Thus our unique experience drummed into us the notion that the victory of the correct conception meant quite simply the liquidation, the destruction, of the other.

We opposed the enemy with all the passion of our youth. Given our Manichean view of the world, we naturally believed that the chief political virtues were consistency and radicalism. We had no patience with the pusillanimous prudence of our parents' generation that had made collaboration with the occupiers so excusable. And we perceived any argument used to counter our primitive radicalism as stemming from cowardice. There was nothing in our own experience to tell us that democracy was an entirely different order in which the victory of one concept does not necessarily mean the elimination of another. We were children of war who, having not actually fought against anyone, brought our wartime mentality with us into those first postwar years, when the opportunity to fight for something presented itself at last.

To the question whom to fight against and in what cause, the age offered a simple reply: on the side of those who were most consistently and radically against the past, who were not cautious, who made no compromises with the past but rather strove to sweep it aside, to overcome it in a revolutionary way. The Soviet Union appeared to be the force and Iosif Vissarionovich Stalin the political personality to lead the fight. Today it sounds absurd, but in those first postwar years it seemed different.

In 1945, deification of the Soviet Union and Stalin did not necessarily exclude one from the general excitement felt in Czechoslovakia concerning the prospects of establishing freedom and justice as the cornerstones of the new state. On the contrary, it was part of that excitement, and, moreover, it gave it a concrete dimension: it was a struggle for social justice and equality. The Soviet Union was, in that sense, a land of hope for those who desired a radical departure from the past after the war and who also, of course, knew nothing of the real conditions in the Soviet Union. These early political convictions of ours led us to the Communist party and its ideology, not out of a sense of political calculation or ulterior motivation, but from inner persuasion.

It can hardly be claimed that we were very familiar with Marxism in our early years as active Communists. What we did know and eagerly absorb was an ideological decoction of the Marxism of that time. The keystones of a Marxist education then were Stalin's essay "On Dialectic and Historical Materialism" and his *History of the Great Communist Party (Bolshevik)*, the *Communist Manifesto*, Engels' *Anti-Duhring*, Lenin's *The State and Revolution*, and Stalin's *Questions of Leninism*. We combined these fragments with the popular politics of various party ideological brochures to form a system of opinions.

How could I have embraced such literature as a political bible—i.e., as a deeply felt, personal view of the world? Now, many years later, only one reply seems to make any sense: the ideology contained in this literature gives someone who in reality knows very little or nothing at all the self-assurance of someone who has mastered the very laws that govern the development of mankind and the world. All it demands is belief. And those who are most susceptible to this faith are precisely those who are ignorant and most want to know. For with that leap of faith comes automatic knowledge. Your inner world is transformed; it takes on direction, and though in fact you still know nothing, you now feel in a position to pass judgment on everything. You know what is progressive and what is reactionary, what is good and what is bad for the future of mankind. And you also know what is and is not scientific without having to bother with any concrete scientific research. Among others who do not share this consciousness, who continue to grope about in obscurity, ignorant of their own future, you have become almost overnight a superior being with the correct views.

The notion that belief makes one superior to those who do not believe is nothing new and nothing peculiar to the ideological faith of communism. Christian faith also raised the believer above the heathen and the godless. The problem, however, lies in what the believer, in the name of his faith and in his feeling of superiority, feels justified in doing to the unbelievers. And the Stalinist version of communist faith that I, along with tens of thousands of my peers, embraced after 1945, justified from the outset a holy war against the infidel.

In the vast majority of cases, we accepted this faith so easily and spontaneously precisely because it seemed a very natural extension of our Manichean political worldview, which was a living product of the war. Once again, there was only the enemy and a clear goal: to destroy that enemy (this time as a "class"), radically and uncompromisingly, and thus pave the way for a new and just society (a communist society this time, where, with the establishment of equality, the sources of social tension and war would disappear, and mankind would achieve happiness). All you had to do was consistently and energetically fight that "last battle" mentioned in the "Internationale." It was an attractive ideology for our still highly-charged war mentality.

Before February 1948 and for several years afterwards, our conception of socialism was even more primitive and one-sided than that of older generations of Stalinists who, despite everything, had made minor adjustments in the dogma over the years. But this merely increased our self-assurance, comparable perhaps only to the self-assurance of West European Maoists and other tendencies in the "New Left" in the late 1960s. We were a very specific sect, and we shared

3

the traits common to all sects: we treasured the strictness of our own values and morality, and in guarding and preserving them we were reaffirming our sense of being superior to the world of unbelievers, that is, to those who did not see things as we did. Wherever the faith required unselfish and devoted labor, it could depend on us. We worked voluntarily and without pay in the mines, on construction sites, and in the fields; we worked nights, Sundays and holidays, and during school vacations. The secretariat was not just a meeting place: we lived there. The tiny political apparatus of the Communist Union of Youth in those days worked for salaries that were below the average wages of workers.

But these were not all our duties. We were also responsible young soldiers of the party, not merely serving to adorn and swell the ranks at Communist party public events but skillfully exploited by the leadership. They not only had us shouting radical slogans but, within the limits of our capabilities, we were also allowed to execute party policies. We had not yet tried or sentenced anyone to death, but we were already lending our approval when the party did precisely that. And there were other forms of repression that we personally carried out: we screened and purged people, making it impossible for many adversaries and critics of our faith, both in our own generation and in older ones, to study at the university, have normal careers, or make a decent livelihood. And we considered it natural, moral, and just to be protected and given preferential treatment by those exercising the political power, the power of the emerging totalitarian dictatorship, for this, too, was compatible with our faith and morality. It is no wonder, therefore, that unbelievers did not view our faith as at all disinterested. At that time, however, we treated criticism of us as merely an expression of "class emnity," and we repressed and destroyed those critics just as the older generation of Communists were doing.

In many private, and even in some public, discussions of the crimes committed by the political regime in the 1950s, I have often heard Communists justify themselves by saying that they genuinely believed in the party ideology. As a statement of fact this is relevant, but it is hardly valid as a defense for what went on (and still goes on to this day) under the rule of that party. We are also responsible for our beliefs. And the fact that I was a believer does not absolve me from guilt, but rather is an admission that I share that guilt. Naturally, of course, this is not the same as someone supporting or executing criminal policies without even believing that such is necessary and good "from the historical and class point of view." But that can only mean that I am not a scoundrel, someone who supports evil for financial gain or for the sake of a career.

Looking back on everything I have gone through since then, and the role my own Stalinist faith played, I have to admit that my faith, rather than exonerate me, in fact contributed to making me guilty, one of the reasons being that it was faith that kept me from drawing normal, logical conclusions from all those occasions in everyday practice and experience. After all, we, the committed young Communists, were living in the same reality as everybody else, but that reality spoke to us in a different language, and for a long time we took this to be proof of our correct views, unaware that everyone else had long since seen in that same reality much that invalidated our faith.

For in those years my communist faith was a closed system, which could not be penetrated in any fundamental way by an idea, argument, or even by any real experience from the outside. I do not want now to discuss whether this is something proper to Marxist philosophy in its unvulgarized form, for this is not important in this context. What is important here is that this closed system of logic and values *is* proper to communist ideology as it was accepted at that time (and as it is still frequently accepted to this day, in quite different conditions, by other Communist parties) by those Communists who believed in their ideology, who were "ideologically pure."

For a Communist who believes thus, the only criteria he applies to reality are the values his ideology recognizes as important in achieving its own ends. To measure or evaluate reality by other standards has *a priori* no particular significance, and criticism that derives from another value system can in no way influence his conviction that the goals of his own ideology are correct, for in the eyes of a believing Communist, such criticism is simply irrelevant to those goals.

The fundamental value of our communist faith at that time was an abstract notion expressed as "the interest of the working class." Everything else, whether it be economics or morality, was subordinated to that interest. Anything that furthers the interest of the working class is moral—that was how Lenin put it. The argument that a particular economic policy was counterproductive was meaningless to us because it was a bourgeois argument, just like the argument that a given political act was immoral because it went against the Ten Commandments.

But what, then, were the practical criteria by which we judged what was or was not "in the interest of the working class"? The democratically-determined opinion of a majority of workers? No, that was no argument for committed Stalinists because their ideological system does not concern individual, living workers, but the working class as an abstract subject of historical progress. Concrete, living workers may be, and in practice often are, politically backward; they fail to understand their own correct historical interests; they frequently take only a short-sighted, day-by-day view of their interests, for this is how capitalist society has taught them. What, then, does a Stalinist look to in order to determine the interests of the working class? In the final analysis, he looks to his own ideology and to his party, which, as the creator of this ideology, is the only correct formulator of the working class fundamental, historical interests.

As long as a Communist who possesses this kind of ideological faith remains inside his system of logic and values, his ideas have no more meaning for the rest of the world than a squirrel running inside a revolving drum has for the world outside the drum. And of course the reverse is also true: the outside world scarcely influences the squirrel, for the only solid ground he knows is the revolving drum itself.

Ideologically-committed Stalinists, of course, also noticed aspects of reality that called their faith in doubt. But no particular conflict between reality and our faith could ever have been a strong enough argument against the faith as a whole. The only thing that might have liberated committed Stalinists from the vicious circle of their ideology was the conviction that *all* reality was irrefutably in conflict with "the interest of the working class."

People who lent their support to the Stalinist type of absolute dictatorship from inner conviction and ideological faith were therefore, in a sense, a greater stumbling block to practical changes in Communist policy than those who had merely joined the party for the opportunities and advantages it provided. Changes in the attitudes and conduct of these self-seekers was only a matter of when it would be to their advantage to support the new criteria. But committed true believers had to be convinced of the necessity for change. At the same time, however, the self-seekers could hardly be expected to press for change, for that implies beginning at a time when it was not yet advantageous to one's career to do so, when it might even have involved risks and dangers. Committed Communists, on the contrary, could be active bearers of change, but they had first to go through a long intellectual process full of inner conflict.

I was a member of the Communist Party of Czechoslovakia (CPC) for 25 years, from 1946 until my expulsion in 1970. Of that time, I spent twenty years undergoing this slow and painful process as my own ideas developed. And even after being expelled from the party, it still took me another few years to complete its final phase.

In September 1950, when the machinery for mass-producing political trials—now no longer of non-Communists, but of leading function-aries of the CPC itself—was getting into high gear, I went off to Mos-cow to study law. Everyone studying there belonged to the elite of the young generation of Communists; they had already worked for sev-eral years as functionaries in the CPC, and they were naturally all believing Stalinists. And the wave of suspicion and the witch hunt for "class enemies and agents of imperialism" that was beginning to rage at home spread among those of us in Moscow as well. The Central Committee in Prague appealed to all Communists to help in exposing "criminal bands of wreckers" in the party, and help we did.

A letter of mine, which I had sent to the party commission for in-vestigating the activities of Otto Šling and Marie Švermová, already arrested, had a quite unusual fate—not at that time, however, when it was only one of thousands in the party and police files, but twenty-six years later. On March 1, 1977, *Rudé právo* published quotations from that letter to demonstrate that I was an unscrupulous informer who had no right, under the Husák regime, to talk about human rights and that my signature under Charter 77 must be judged as merely another act of opportunism.

But my contribution towards uncovering the "wreckers in the party" did nothing to advance my career even back then, in 1951. In the hot-house atmosphere among the young party elite in Moscow, it was inevitable that attention soon turned to finding "wreckers" in Moscow itself: and here we only had each other to suspect. According to the logic then prevalent in Prague, any decent wrecker was to be found hiding among the upper ranks of party functionaries, and at that time I was the party leader of the Czechoslovak students in Moscow.

Thus, before long, letters from strict Stalinists began arriving at party headquarters in Prague warning that I too was very likely one of the "wreckers in the party." Friends suddenly began to find simi-larities in my working methods and those used by the chief "agent of imperialism," the secretary-general of the CPC, Rudolf Slanský, who was under arrest in Prague. They discovered that my public utterances on the Soviet reality revealed an insufficiently-conscientious attitude. I was removed from office and awaited a verdict from Prague. And naturally I was not alone in this: several other equally-conscientious Stalinists in our midst were accused by the rest of similar sins, the main one being an insufficiently-correct attitude to the Soviet Union.

I still recall very clearly my own private reaction to this situation. It was quite clear to me that the friends who had accused me were acting from the same motives from which I had accused others. Only in a few cases did I suspect personal vindictiveness—but in most cases, I understood what they had done and considered them to be correct Communists. I looked within myself for the reason why I had been accused—and I even found some cause: it was true that my work methods in the party were those that were common at that time—but until only very recently that had been in my favor. I even dissected all my thoughts and statements about the Soviet Union, and here too there were things that conflicted with the standards of ideological purity, things which derived quite simply from the fact that our experience of everyday life in the Soviet Union mercilessly shattered all our preconceptions about "Soviet Man."

At the time, therefore, I made a quite sincere self-criticism in which I admitted to all these shortcomings, but refused to confess to any antiparty intentions or motivations. And I calmly awaited the decision from party headquarters, convinced that I was safe because it was quite simply a mistake and a misunderstanding. And I quite seriously and sincerely believed that, even as the trials against Rudolf Slanský and others, eleven of whom were condemned to death, were going on in Prague. And of course I had no idea at the time that those eleven were also correct Stalinists who, even after their arrest, had continued to believe that it was all a big "misunderstanding" and that it would eventually be cleared up.

Unlike them, however, I really did live to see my naive trust fulfilled. In December 1952, two of the most highly placed members in the CPC—Antonín Zápotocký and Viliam Široký—came personally to a meeting of Czechoslovak students in Moscow to put an end to the affair of "unmasking the enemies." Zápotocký more or less made public the contents of the letters sent to party headquarters and asked their authors to stand up. He then looked them over like a school teacher and made a short speech to the effect that anyone could write letters like that and that the party had not sent us here to learn that kind of thing, and we were not to go around suspecting one another but rather to trust each other and study. In a style for which he was famous when addressing mass rallies, he told us a story about how he built an addition on his house but didn't know how to calculate the slope of the roof so it wouldn't collapse. And the party needs people who can do just that, he said, because the roofs of socialist construction will not be held up by political speechifying. And that is your task, he said, to finish your studies and genuinely learn how to do something. On the subject of "incorrect" and "anti-Soviet attitudes," Zápotocký declared: "Living here you can see for yourselves that our people could not nor would want to live in the conditions the Soviet people live in. So don't make a problem of it when discussing it among yourselves, but try to understand it and arrive at a reasonable solution." Then he declared the matter closed and said that there should be no more letters to Prague and there was no cause found in any of the accusations to justify punitive action. And this, he said, was Comrade Gottwald's opinion as well.

Thus direct personal experience confirmed my party faith: everything had been examined in the spirit of justice and found to be a misunderstanding. For some time afterward, I could not believe that the same Zápotocký who had intervened so positively on my behalf could ever have consented in the execution of his long-time colleagues and friends were he not convinced of their irrefutable guilt. It was not until many years later that I learned it was scarcely a month before his little pep-talk to the Moscow students that this same Zápotocký had raised his hand in support of the eleven death sentences knowing full well that the whole trial against the "centre of intrigue led by Rudolf Slánský" was based on fabrications, but that it was Stalin's will. And a year before his level-headed speech to us, the same Zápotocký invited Slanský to his home for a party knowing that on his way home Slánský would be arrested. When Slánský was getting into his overcoat after the party, Zápotocký telephoned the police officer responsible for making the arrest and, according to a prearranged agreement, told him: "He's on his way." Today, I have no doubt in my mind that Zápotocký personally found his role as a fatherly dissuader of our youthful and overactive imaginations in Moscow more pleasant than his role as an accomplice of the police or as a self-appointed judge. Nevertheless, he was capable of playing both.

It was not until years later that I came to understand how special my situation was in 1952. At that time I belonged to a group of elite young party members in which the party leadership itself had placed so much hope that it set us apart from the consequences of its own policies. This up-and-coming generation was not to be split into accusers and the accused just yet, and it remained for the future to decide who would be given what role. In the meantime, we were to study. My experience of Stalinist terror, consequently, was quite exceptional for that time and embarrassingly sheltered. What I lived through then differed so diametrically not only from the experience of the purge victims but even from what a huge majority of the nation went through, a majority that huddled in fear hoping only to somehow survive, that it took several years before I could begin to understand what that period had meant for ordinary people in Czechoslovakia.

But even more than the climax of Stalinist terror in Czechoslovakia, it was my five-year stay in Moscow that gave rise to my first serious ideological doubts.

My doubts were not the result of those things that usually shock Western visitors to the Soviet Union: the wretched living standard of Soviet people, the poverty and backwardness of their everyday lives. The problem was not chiefly the fact that Moscow was a huge village of wooden cottages, that people scarcely had enough to eat, that the most typical dress, even then, five years after the war, was old military war-issue uniforms, that most families lived in one room, that instead of flush toilets there was only an opening leading to the drain pipe, that both in the student residences and on the street people blew their noses into their hands, that what you didn't hang onto tightly would be stolen from you in a crowd, that drunks lay unconscious in the streets and could be dead for all the passers-by knew or cared, and that there were dozens and dozens of similar phenomena.

All these facts seemed somehow explicable by the past. We did not go to the Soviet Union expecting to find a consumers' paradise, and, in any case, such was not to be found anywhere in Europe five years after the war. On the contrary, we considered the poverty and wretchedness we saw in Russia as a direct consequence of the war and of the terrible backwardness of czarist Russia, and the way in which the people bore these material hardships was seen as evidence of the human strength to be found in the "new Soviet man." No, it was not the negative aspects of Soviet life that presented a challenge to our Stalinist faith: that was undermined far more by the absence of anything positive in its place, the absence of values that the faith itself considered as primarily necessary to the future of communism.

Whereas we considered devotion to public causes as an almost fundamental characteristic of the "new man" and never questioned the need to fuse our entire personal life with the struggle for grand social goals, to submit ourselves to the "demands of history" and the "interests of the working class," most Soviet people whom we came to know tried to keep politics utterly separate from their personal lives. They satisfied the demands public affairs made on them by formally pronouncing their "political point of view" according to the prescribed rituals, and then resumed dealing with the problems of their own lives quite without regard for this "point of view." While we took it for granted that what we said in public we also thought in private, this was not so in the life of the Soviet people.

When I came to Moscow to study, a considerable percentage of university students were demobilized soldiers who had fought at the front, and, therefore, Soviet student life at that time differed considerably from that of the standard (in terms of age, social structure, life experience) student milieu. One of the habits these ex-soldiers had was vodka. In student residences, there was drinking at every conceivable occasion, from personal birthdays and name-days to state holidays. But the most frequent occasion for celebration was simply the presence of a bottle of vodka.

The basic dosage was a jar full, which, on being drained at a single gulp, signalled that the drinking had begun. As greenhorns from a non-Russian background, we at first simply got very drunk. It was only after a while, when we had learned to take it in our stride and were on a more equal footing with those experienced war-time soldiers, that I began to understand the significance vodka has in the life of Soviet people: it allows them to forget reality for a time and creates the illusion of freedom. It is only under the influence of alcohol that normal, human communication can begin.

As far as the political aspects of drinking were concerned, these were directly expressed in a symbolic ritual performed in the room I shared with six former soldiers from the front. A framed poster was hanging on the wall depicting Stalin sketching the wind-breakers on the steppes of the Volga basin on a map of the USSR, and thus, in fact, also sketching in the concrete outlines of communism. When vodka appeared on the table, the poster was turned face to the wall and the room was then dominated by an amateur portrait of a courtesan from czarist Petrograd painted on the other side. At the same time the door was locked, thus opening the door to several hours during which duplicity was unnecessary and people whose intoxicated tongues became increasingly tangled still managed to make more and more real sense.

In such situations I first heard stories of the war that were utterly at variance with the picture we had formed in Prague from Soviet films and literature of conditions in the Soviet army. Suddenly I understood that if I were to express my highly correct opinions aloud in front of these people, they would see me, not as a revolutionary, but as a fool in the same class as Kadet Biegler in Hašek's *Good Soldier Švejk*. Here, a member of the Soviet Communist Party told me how, on his *kolkhoz* in the Ukraine, they had looked forward to the arrival of Hitler's army and what they expected would be the dismantling of the *kolkhoz,* the returning of land to the peasants, and the inauguration of paradise. When the Germans finally did arrive, they burned the village to the ground and shot everyone who didn't manage to get away. Those who escaped to the forests found a party secretary there organizing a unit of resistance fighters. And so they became partisans. Now they really did fight for all they were worth, knowing that it was a matter of life and death and that no paradise was awaiting them, now or ever.

Most often, however, vodka drove Russians to introspection. Contempt for their own moral weakness and self-pity for being powerless to change the things that aroused the contempt in the first place—all the qualities familiar to us from classical Russian literature and considered as problems of prerevolutionary Russia—suddenly surfaced as fundamental, vitally important practical problems in the thoughts and lives of young Soviet students. The classic question asked by drunk Russians: "Am I a human being or not?" was echoed here in many different forms, but it never ended with the cry of Maxim Gorky: "Man—how proud that sounds!"

"I'm a swine—go on, tell me I'm a swine!", a drunken functionary of the Bolshevik party cried on my breast after he had voted at a meeting to expel a friend from the university for running through the corridors of the student residence in his underwear to win a bet. From the viewpoint of the official puritanism then reigning in Moscow, this had the same shock value as if he had done it anywhere else in the world completely naked. And the contrite Bolshevik was not content until I told him that yes, he was a swine.

Inebriated as I was, it still puzzled me why a confirmation from me, of all people, should help him, and so I asked him about it. "Because you're not a swine—you believe in it," was his reply. I tried to explain to him that I certainly did not believe that it was proper to expel someone from the university simply for running around the corridor in his underwear, especially since in Czechoslovakia it happens all the time. "Nonsense," he interrupted me, "that's not the point. You actually read Lenin. You understand it because you believe it."

Obviously the problem was far deeper than I had at first suspected. But the penitent Bolshevik slept it off, having ventilated his self-contempt; and, as far as I can recall, he went on behaving in more or less the same way right up to the end of his studies, when he bacame a military prosecutor. It is quite likely that to this very day, after many a trial, he still gets drunk and then compels someone to confirm to him that, yes, he is a swine. And he is probably quite unaware that his example helped to undermine my ideological faith, a faith that he himself, in his own way, respected.

For us, the writings of Marx, Engels, Lenin, and Stalin were the last word when it came to solving our personal problems. The Soviet students simply treated them as compulsory reading. Most students prepared for tests in Marxism-Leninism by learning long passages from these writings by rote. This meant that the examiner could not censure them for incorrect formulation—nor was anything more than that required. Like us, the Soviet students knew how to make a "correct Marxist evaluation" even of things they knew nothing about. But whereas we believed in the correctness of the "evaluation," most Soviet students merely treated it as a learned, habitual schematic mode of expression that had nothing to do with personal conviction. The fact was that they had little concern for political and ideological matters. It was other matters, in altogether different intellectual and value systems, that were vital to them.

It took me five years of living in Moscow to discover that if you want to understand the inner world of the Soviet people, it is far more important to read Tolstoy, Dostoyevsky, Chekov, and Gogol than all the literary productions of socialist realism put together; that even all the deeply positive characteristics of this people have far more substantial roots in the old Russian form of general human values than in the Soviet form of industrial civilization in which they are living; and that the traits which can in fact be attributed to the Soviet system are frequently negative characteristics whose common denominator is ultimately a schizophrenic splitting of life into two spheres:

the official, public, ritually-formalized sphere, where the ideas and values of "Marxism-Leninism" are held to be valid, and the private sphere, where entirely different intellectual and value systems are adhered to, systems rooted in ancient Russian history.

And yet in the early fifties there was one significant point where, in a very odd way, the real thoughts, convictions, and faith of the Soviet people became wedded to the official ideology of "Soviet patriotism." Countless occasions convinced us that a vast majority of Soviet people genuinely believe that elsewhere in the world, in the capitalist states, working people live far worse than they do in the USSR—and in the material sense of the word, as consumers. At the same time, however, they had no actual knowledge of the rest of the world on which this conviction was based.

One night I was awakened by students from another room who wanted me to come and arbitrate a dispute they were having. They disagreed on whether Czechoslovak villages really were full of stone and brick (and not wood and clay) houses with tile-covered roofs (and not straw thatching). A soldier who had been there during the war claimed that it was so; a student from a *kolkhoz* somewhere whose only travel outside his birthplace had been to Moscow did not believe it. The rest were uncertain. There were perhaps ten people in the room ranging from 20 to 30 years of age. When I told them it was the soldier who had seen this miracle who was right, the debate ended, but I could tell from the main antagonist's face that he was not entirely persuaded. He most likely suspected me of using the situation for national self-glorification and that I was probably lying.

People with such limited horizons found it easy to reconcile their true convictions with an official ideology and propaganda that daily reassured them that their country was a model for the entire world in all things. But even better educated people with more concrete and accurate ideas of the world generally accepted the Messianic role ascribed to their country; and here traditional Great Russian Messianism combined with the official Soviet Marxist-Leninist Messianism to produce a strange concoction of ideas. What lent credibility to this notion at the time was the conviction that the Soviet Union had played the decisive role in saving mankind during the Second World War at incredible sacrifice to herself and that therefore she had a natural claim to reverence from other nations. Soviet people with such views often treated criticism as ingratitude and disrespect for their war victims, and in this sense they were very much like their own government, which in many other ways they were inclined to view critically.

There was another important area where official ideology combined with the real attitudes of the Soviet people to produce a strange outlook. Many Soviet people have a genuinely fatalistic view of the world, which has traditional roots in Russia. Whereas we took Marxist ideology, with its thesis about the deterministic nature of social development, as the basis for an active radicalism, which attempted to remold given conditions, in harmony with that determinism, they, quite naturally, combined these vulgarized Marxist-Leninist "precepts" with a fatalistic passivity: there is nothing one can do to alter destiny. In practical terms, they viewed the Soviet bureaucracy as the framework of that destiny. This work-a-day philosophy of the Soviet people is well captured in some popular turns of phrase in colloquial Russian: *"Nichevo nye padyelayesh"* ("There's nothing you can do about it"); or, *"Nyet nashevo uma dyelo"* ("It's not for us to judge"); or, *"Na vyerchu vidnieye"* ("The ones on top know best"); etc. What official ideology claimed to be the product of politically-conscious socialist-collective living, of politically-conscious subordination of the individual to the whole, of politically-conscious social discipline on the part of the "new Soviet man," we saw in everyday practice as a consequence of the fatalistic Soviet view of the world: man is always more or less subject to limitations and the given order is wiser than the individual.

Studying in Moscow, however, meant more than just meeting real Soviet people; it also meant coming in contact with real Soviet institutions, with the day-to-day operations of the gigantic all-controlling bureaucratic machinery of the Soviet state. We all encountered it, regardless of what we were studying, but for me the study of law made this encounter possible to an unusual extent. The functioning of this machinery was in fact the proper subject of my study and for my field work I spent several months right inside the Soviet state apparatus itself.

Despite all this, after five years of study, I still had no idea whatsoever of the extent and forms of Stalinist political terror. I felt that mass political terror was something of the past, of history, and, as far as I know, the other students felt the same. The fact is that the young generation of that time had, as a whole, not been affected by the terror—even less so those selected for university education. It was something that had touched the acquaintances and sometimes the relatives of people I knew personally—but the victims belonged to the generation of their parents or grandparents.

Sometimes, however, the young people themselves were unaware of how tragically and profoundly they had been influenced by the Stalinist terror. The story of one of my fellow students is an extreme example. He belonged to the youngest wave of students, those who, because they were at the top of their class, had gone directly to the university from the Moscow junior high schools. He was active in the *Komsomol* (Union of Communist Youth) and was one of the few Soviet students who actually believed the ideology. In seminars on Marxism-Leninism, he would very militantly and with great conviction declaim everything he had learned about the Trotskyists and other diversionists and agents of imperialism. After 1956, during the Khrushchev rehabilitations, he suddenly received official notification that his parents, both of whom had died in Stalinist concentration camps as Trotskyists, had been rehabilitated. This was the first he had ever heard of his real parents or of his adoption as an infant by people who were party members and who he had assumed were his real parents. The only consequence for him of Khrushchev's rehabilitation, however, was that he became an inmate in a psychiatric hospital.

As a trainee in the public prosecutor's office, I was present at several interrogations in Moscow jails, including the Lefortovo prison. At the time, I never dreamed that in another wing of the very same prison things were taking place that Solzhenitsyn afterwards wrote about. The Lefortovo itself is a depressing old nineteenth-century prison building, but what I witnessed there were entirely routine interrogations of criminal offenders conducted according to forensic procedure. Nor did these delinquents strike me as having been unjustly jailed or in any way degraded or maltreated. Criminals in the Soviet Union are often brutal and in many ways have more in common with American gangsters than with the criminals of Central Europe. The police who deal with these men often carry scars from knife or bullet wounds, something quite exceptional in Prague. One could come into very close contact with this part of the Soviet police and judicial apparatus and not have any notion of the reality, or the extent, of the neighboring kingdom of the Gulag.

In the actual university course on law, the theme of antistate (i.e., political) crimes was touched upon in only very brief and general terms. There was nothing complex about it, as long as you accepted the fundamental principle that political activity upsetting to the government was comparable to any other form of criminal activity. And that axiom was accepted both by the instructors and the students in the Moscow Faculty of Laws.

I recall once how during a seminar on anti-state crimes I embarrassed the professor by saying that for such crimes the presumption of innocence before guilt is proven did not apply, and my example was the political trials in Prague, where certain kinds of behavior, points of view, and ideas were first politically qualified as an expression of emnity towards the working class, and only then did the judiciary, bound by the preceding qualifications, preside.

This, of course, was true and it was difficult to dispute. As a sincerely convinced Stalinist, I considered the procedure to be correct. Under the dictatorship of the proletariat, law is "the will of the working class codified," which was how the Soviet legal textbooks put it. The Communist party is the interpreter of the will of the working class, and therefore it is natural that if the party organs interpret certain activity as being inimical to the working class and the state, then this decision is binding on the organs of class justice as well.

The professor naturally knew the truth about the presumption of innocence in political trials, but he could not admit I was right because he ran the risk of being criticized himself: it was true, but it could not be admitted. He knew why, but, at the time, I did not understand this. Why not admit it openly? The experienced professor, however, declared the discussion out of bounds and referred the issue to the Marxist-Leninist seminar, where of course it was never raised again.

Not until a later phase of my liberation from the charmed circle of Stalinist-communist faith did I finally understand that my study at the University of Moscow's Faculty of Law had only very little to do with actually understanding the law and its significance for human society. For Stalinist legal theory (and the same applies to official Soviet doctrine even today) had no other criterion for determining what is and is not law than this tautological statement of legal positivism: Law is that which the state (its constitutional organs) declares to be law. According to this "Marxist-Leninist doctrine," the Nuremberg laws issued by the Nazis were also legal—but in a bourgeois, fascist, imperialist context. Stalinist doctrine does not criticize the Nuremberg laws because they are a denial of legality, but because they are an expression of bourgeois and racist conceptions. Such an argument, therefore, leads only to the conclusion that the class content of these laws is unacceptable; should, however, the class content be different (that is, should it embody the "interests of the working class"), there are no grounds for criticizing them. According to this way of thinking, the feudal lord's right of the first night with newly-wed women is also within the bounds of law, but reprehensible since it serves the interests of the exploiters. The notion that such a "right" is unwarrantable rape and quite simply outside the law no matter what the circumstances (even if, for example, it is a question of an entire workers' council having the "right" to sleep with the factory owner's daughter), because the relationship it creates between people makes one of the parties involuntarily an object to be used at will by the other—such an idea is not contained at all in official Soviet legal theory. Thus law becomes merely a formal means of applying and exercising power. Except for the problem of "class content," therefore, Stalinist and fascist legal thinking are in essential agreement.

For this reason, Soviet law schools do not educate people to think in terms of the concepts and values embodied in the law; rather they turn out "legal specialists," people who know what regulations the authorities have laid down for given cases and where to find those they don't know and how to deal with petitions. In effect, Soviet law schools produce qualified bureaucrats. From the viewpoint of the people they rule over, however, such qualified bureaucrats have one important advantage over the unqualified variety: they know what can and cannot be done to people; they know the boundaries for applying at least the kind of arbitrary measures not endorsed by the authorities and not entrenched in the regulations or valid legal norms. Given the arbitrary conditions that exist under a bureaucratic tyranny, this is often a not insignificant advantage for the people dealing with that bureaucracy.

In the five years it took me to become a "legal specialist," that is, a qualified, Soviet-style bureaucrat, I therefore had the opportunity to learn what was and was not permitted in various aspects of life in the USSR. In this mirror, distorted though it may have been, I gradually came to know the outlines of life on the *kolkhozes* and in the factories, the family and property relationships of Soviet citizens, the world of government agencies and civil petitioners. The overall effect was to provide me with a concrete idea of how Soviet bureaucracy administers society.

On the one hand I was rather impressed. Everything was relatively well thought out and, above all, regulated in great detail. Many of the questions I brought with me to Moscow—about how, practically speaking, this or that problem in everyday life would be dealt with under socialism, how the work process, and other processes, would be regulated (things that neither Lenin nor Stalin ever wrote concretely about)—seemed to receive answers here. Many answers seemed correct to me, and I felt that I would return home equipped to deal with many things, "in the interest of the working class." But on the other hand there were many of those real Soviet experiences which I simply could not accept as ideal and as something to be introduced in Czechoslovakia.

However Stalinist our communist faith may have been, it was at the same time in sharp conflict with the fundamental tendency of the Soviet state to bureaucratically regulate everything that goes on in society. We saw ourselves as radicals, not bureaucratic conservatives; yet, through a process of ideological sophistry, we managed to convince ourselves that something, at least, in these bureaucratic practices was revolutionary, because it was in the "interests of the working class." But this kind of sophistry had its limitations.

Just as our Soviet friends were more like people from Chekov's stories than like the heroes of Fadeyev's *The Young Guard,* many of the bureaucrats with whom we had daily dealings seemed more like characters out of Gogol's *Government Inspector* than the embodiment of ideas from Lenin's "The State and Revolution." It was not just the absence of any self-administration from below, an idea that was part of our ideological faith, that bothered us; the essential problem was that the insolence of Soviet bureaucrats—their undisguised contempt for the petitioners in line for the required *"bumazhky,"* or rubber stamps— their crudeness, incompetence, and arrogance were phenomena that we had simply never experienced in Czechoslovakia.

In my final year of study, in the winter of 1954, I spent some time in training at the city prosecutor's office in Moscow. One day in the week was set aside to hear oral "complaints by the working people": hundreds of people would crowd into the building to present the prosecutor with their own personal legal difficulties. The prosecutor on duty heard the complaint and then rendered an immediate decision as to which side was in the right. Each case generally took between five and ten minutes. The "new Soviet people," these "creators of history," stood before him cap in hand and, with timid deference, stammered out their feeling of injustice and injury, while the prosecutor, who was usually doing some other paper work at the same time, sat behind his massive desk listening with only half an ear. Invariably, he would dismiss 99 percent of the complaints as groundless. These elderly workers and wasted peasant women seemed like figures straight out of films I had seen on the October Revolution only without fist shaking and demands for justice; the verdict of this potentate, who again reminded me of the bureaucrat from Gogol's play, was awaited timidly.

In the fall of 1954 I moved to a new Moscow University building on the Lenin Heights that had been opened with much pomp and ceremony. Until that time I had lived in an old student residence called Stromynka, which had originally been a barracks for Peter the Great's Preobrazhensky Regiment. The Soviet state had added two extra floors to make room for 10,000 students, there were from seven to fourteen students a room, and for the several hundred on each floor there was only one collective latrine with a washing area and a single common kitchen. For everyone in the building there was a single Russian *banya* (bathhouse) in the courtyard. The new university residence, in contrast, radiated comfort: the students were given single rooms with modern furnishings and conveniences, and there was one flush toilet and shower for every two students. Even we felt that it was a civilized and modern residence, and for the majority of the Soviet students it must have been the most luxurious accommodation they had ever experienced before or since. It was from here that I commuted each day to the city prosecutor's office.

One day a delegation from a *kolkhoz* situated about 20 kilometers from the new university residence came to see the public prosecutor with a complaint. It turned out that because of the limited capacity of the power plant the new university could not be opened without cutting the electricity to their village and several others. A year had gone by and the villages were still without electricity, although they had been promised that it would only be a temporary, short-term measure.

You have no legal right to electricity, was the public prosecutor's explanation. There is no law that says you have to have electricity. That is something which depends on the economic possibilities. No law has been broken and the prosecutor's office has no just cause to intervene in this instance.

The deputation then tried to explain that they had written and visited everyone from the power plant to the city court, but no one had answered any of their letters, and no one would talk to them. This made no impression whatsoever on the prosecutor, and he stuck to his original position. On an inspiration, one member of the *kolkhoz* then spoke up that it ought to concern the public prosecutor because the villagers were compelled to light their dwellings with the highly inflammable kerosene lamps and rush-lights.

This artful piece of cunning only angered the prosecutor.

"How long have you had electricity in your village?" he asked the rebel.

"Since 1938," was the reply.

"There, you see?" said the prosecutor. "And what did you use to light with before?"

"Rush-lights."

"So then you know how to use them. Should there be a fire, prosecution proceedings will be instigated. And the guilty party will end up in the cooler."

The representatives of the *kolkhoz* peasants, the ruling class in the Soviet state second only to the workers, said no more and respectfully left the office. When the audiences were over that day, I raised the subject again with the prosecutor and said that perhaps something might be done about it. He explained to me that were he to take any action in the matter the chief prosecutor would give him a dressing-down, because he in turn would receive a dressing-down from the municipal party committee for not considering the difficulties they were having with the problem. And then he defended his position from his own personal feelings: "The *muzhiks* know very well how to use rushlights," he said, "and they merely wanted to annoy me."

After that, I could not turn on the lights in my luxurious room on the Lenin Heights without thinking of that scene. And that scene was far from being an exception. Not even with my high degree of ideological consciousness could I see this as a model for dealing with people under socialism and to be adopted in Czechoslovakia.

Most of the young Communists who studied in Soviet universities in the first half of the 1950s returned home with their ideological faith shaken. We had gone to Moscow hoping to see our own future. But we failed to see that that was precisely what we had seen: yet our communist faith still refused to yield to our experience. Nevertheless, for most of us a fundamental article of that faith had been shaken: we no longer believed that the USSR was the embodiment of our ideals, that it was a model we were bound to follow without reservations.

What the party leadership had sought by sending young party hopefuls to study in the Soviet Union for the most part did not work out. Instead of being even more faithful and highly-qualified Stalinists, the returning people, though still Stalinists, carried within them the seeds of future heresies; they were beginning to doubt one of the party's most powerful incantations: the mandatory authority of the "Soviet model." And in order to rescue our Stalinism we subscribed to the paradox of ideologically downgrading Stalinist reality. It was in fact a small foretaste of the approach later taken by the party itself—both the Soviet party under Khrushchev and the Czechoslovak party under Novotný.

At the same time, however, our Stalinist communism was not entirely contingent upon our own experience and ideological image of socialism, but was also contingent on a certain ideological image of capitalism and the world in general, which our experience could not verify.

But regardless of how imperfect a model the Soviet Union may have seemed to us in terms of our own future socialism, it remained in our eyes the only world power that defended the prospects of socialism and the only one capable of doing so against attacks by the international class enemy—world imperialism.

True, our ideas of the world were not as primitive as those of the young Soviets, but they were formed by the same ideology. And, in any case, it was impossible for us at that time to test these ideas against reality: trips to the West were quite impossible for a vast majority of young Communists. And if the truth be known, we were not particularly interested in such trips: we had enough revolutionary tasks here at home without looking for class enemies out there in the world. Thus we lived in the world presented to us by the Communist press as though it were the only real one. That, of course, does not excuse us, but that is how it was.

Whatever faults the Soviet Union may have had, there was no private capitalistic exploitation, there were no people who became rich by virtue of being factory owners or hereditary members of a propertied class, there was no unemployment and—so we thought at the time—there was no government policy of aggression, no power faction set on instigating a new war. We quite simply accepted the atmosphere and propaganda of the cold war as a truthful picture of the world. In our minds conflicts like the Korean War completely justified the production of arms and the evident militarism in the USSR and Czechoslovakia at that time as an attempt to increase our defensive capabilities against the imperialists. It genuinely seemed to us that Nazism was on the increase in West Germany and that the foreign policy of the US was an entirely unwarranted policy of imperialist aggression.

We imagined the conditions in the capitalist states of Western Europe to be somewhat analagous to those we remembered from the Nazi *Protektorat* and the final years of the First Czechoslovak Republic, before the Munich Agreements were signed. The propaganda predictions that a great depression with its attendant poverty and unemployment was only a matter of time therefore spread easily. Even older people found such prognoses believable as far as their own experience from just before the war was concerned.

We were convinced that the only way, on a world level, to prevent a repeat of the 1930s and another world war was through the gradual victory of socialism, as we understood it, in other countries. All of this considerably blunted the impact of those things in our own domestic political experience that called some of the articles of our communist faith into question. Such international problems, on the contrary, were a large imperative to fortify that faith.

CHAPTER 1

FROM KHRUSHCHEV TO DUBČEK

The year 1956 began with Nikita S. Khrushchev's secret speech to the Party Congress in Moscow on the personality cult and crimes of Iosif Vissarionovich Stalin. Khrushchev's revelations, which hit the entire Communist movement like a bombshell, overwhelmed me as well. But—owing to the paradoxical consequence of my "Soviet schooling"—I was more mentally prepared for them than most of my comrades in Czechoslovakia. My final two years in Moscow after Stalin's death had already given me occasion to suspect that Stalin would eventually be criticized "from above," by his inheritors in Moscow.

I was in Moscow in March 1953 when Stalin died. And it was then that the Soviet people's view of Stalin essentially as both a feared and beloved czar—nothing less, but hardly anything more either—was clearly displayed.

When the radio announced that Stalin's body was lying in state in the House of Trade Unions in Moscow, many of my fellow students, Czechoslovak and Soviet, and I joined the huge crowds to see Stalin. No instructions about which streets to the House of Trade Unions would be open had been issued and therefore hundreds of thousands of people thronged chaotically into the center of Moscow. The streets on the outskirts of the city were still relatively empty and nothing much was happening there, but as one came closer to the center, more and more streets and lanes were cordoned off by large trucks and guarded by the army and militia. When the crowds came up against such barriers, they searched about for an open route. And, thus, by trial and error, they at last reached Moscow's inner circular road, where they could go only one way. By now, the crowds had become a mass of people several kilometers long, slowly inching forward to the coffin.

This scene of the crowd converging into a formation that was expected to form roughly into ranks of four recalled the czarist Cossaks handling of workers' demonstrations in St. Petersburg. Long cordons of soldiers and militiamen simply forced the crowd to one side of the street, thus creating a corridor between the middle of the street, where a line of trucks were parked bumper to bumper, also occupied by soldiers and policemen, and the walls of the buildings where the crowd was supposed gradually to form up.

Occasionally the crowd would break through the cordon of soldiers and force their way through the protective wall of trucks, at which point mounted militiamen would appear to restore order. They neither fired arms, nor used swords as their Cossak predecessors had done, but that was unnecessary. The wall of police horses pushed slowly against the crowd, already packed together, and because a horse is, after all, stronger than a man, the animals pushed the people back. If there was any resistance, the horses would rear up on their hind legs. The menacing sight of horses' hooves thrashing in the air above one's head evokes quite atavistic survival instincts, and so the crowd retreated. And where not even that was enough, the riders beat them back with truncheons.

The density of the crowd became that of a streetcar full to bursting at rush hour. At the same time there was a continual influx of tens of thousands from behind, in front were the horses and soldiers, and on each side the barrier of trucks and the buildings. It was cold and the slush was slippery underfoot; anyone who fell down had little hope of ever getting up again, and help was impossible. Naturally, no statistics have ever been released about the number of people trampled to death or wounded, and it is difficult to estimate the total toll. But that night I myself saw dozens of wounded and unconscious people, and some I saw were dead. The casualties were loaded into trucks and gradually taken away.

Wherever the line was to be forcibly narrowed, or where "order" was being restored after a rupture in the cordon, the density of the crowd reached unimaginable proportions. Such places were marked by a column of white mist rising into the darkness and were visible from a distance. The crowd referred to them as "corks" and it mounted spirited attacks on them by increasing the pressure from the rear, at first chaotically and then rhythmically, shouting orders to itself like "heave ho!" I navigated the first of such "corks" without incident and in the next few hours went through about five more. The following one, however, which was far from being the last, I did not manage so successfully. By this time I had been forced to the outer fringes of the column right next to the wall of trucks, where it was no longer soft bodies I was being squeezed against but the hard metal bodies of the trucks. My leather coat was already giving out at the seams and was being ripped against metal protruberances. I was no longer moving of my own will, but being rolled helplessly and dangerously along the sides of the trucks like a piece of flotsam. There was only one hope left: to wait until I was rolled next to the hood of one of the trucks, then climb over it to the other side. That meant, of course, abandoning any hope of seeing Stalin in his coffin, but it also insured not ending up in a coffin myself. The plan worked.

The crowd with which I had just spent several hours and which was moving slowly over dead bodies towards Stalin's coffin, had no thought of Stalin. It was not possessed by a spirit of mourning, which usually imparts a sense of self-discipline to masses of people and makes certain crowd reactions highly unlikely. Here, wherever the press of the crowd was slackened, people talked and joked like those on their way to a football match. There were also thieves and pickpockets among them, men felt under women's skirts, and vodka was drunk straight from bottles hidden in pockets. It was a crowd united by determination not to miss a spectacle, whether it be a funeral or a public execution. I had gone into the streets expecting to see something from one of those Soviet films where disciplined crowds, overcome by grief, made their way to the coffin of Lenin. Perhaps such scenes existed only in those films and that in reality Lenin's funeral had been something like this one—but I still believe there must have been some difference. What I had experienced, however, was almost certainly the same crowd that might have been seen long ago in Russia during public executions, the coronation of a czar, and similar occasions. This was a crowd attending the czar's funeral.

When I got back to the Stromynka residence sometime after two next morning, four of my six roommates were sound asleep and there were two empty vodka bottles on the table. One of the students, awakened by my arrival, looked at my torn overcoat and remarked, "You're a fool. Get some sleep and tomorrow morning take your passport and go by subway to the city center. When you get there, pretend you don't know a word of Russian except for the word "chief" (*"nachalnik"*). The police will take you to their chief and he'll take you to Stalin." Heeding this advice, I made it to Stalin's coffin after all.

In the days following Stalin's death, the atmosphere in Moscow was filled with more than mourning. There was also a feeling of shock, accompanied by concern, even fear, for the future. Conversations with Soviet friends led me to conclude that they actually had no idea what would happen next. But it was clear from their private forebodings that they felt some very fundamental changes would take place. All this intensified in the next few months, but by the end of the year—after the arrest and execution of Beria—symptoms of a change in the general atmosphere began to appear. The original fear of the future gradually disappeared and the dark reasons for that fear began to take on clearer outlines.

It became more and more obvious that even the Soviet people I knew personally sensed and knew far more about the reality of Stalinist terror in their country than I had gathered from them while Stalin was still alive. In 1954 and 1955, such things were spoken of more and more openly. Even the tone of the press changed: newspapers began to write about the need for "collective leadership," methods of the Soviet bureaucracy were criticized, and the question of the need for criticism was broached. Likewise, the campaigns against "cosmopolitanism" gradually died out, and the atmosphere of suspicion relaxed. The climax of it all came when Khrushchev flew to Belgrade and, immediately upon disembarking from the plane, addressed Tito, who until recently had been called "an agent of imperialism" and a "bloody dog," as "Dear Comrade!" And from the party apparatus, information began increasingly to filter out among Communists, and even down to the general public, suggesting that conditions were changing "on top" as well.

What overwhelmed me most of all in Khrushchev's speech on Stalin were the concrete details of crimes committed by the Soviet security organs, of torture and forced confessions in political trials. That was something that had never crossed my mind, and it had direct implications for Czechoslovakia: the recent political trials in Prague were revealed in a light in which we, highly-conscious Stalinists, had never seen them before, though every thinking person had. In other respects, however, the political line set down at the Twentieth Congress of the CPSU on the whole conformed to what our stay in Moscow had, in part at least, prepared us for, and therefore it did not strike me like a bolt out of the blue.

For faithful Communists living in Czechoslovakia, however, the situation was different. When President Gottwald died a week after

Stalin, as though even in the act of dying he was continuing his disciplined subservience to Moscow, it left Zápotocký and Novotný at the head of the CPC; the composition of the politburo remained unchanged, consisting of people who three months before Stalin's death had sent eleven people from their midst to the gallows. Two years after his death, a huge, bombastic monument to him was unveiled in Prague. And the wave of political trials continued unabated in Czechoslovakia; as late as 1954, Gustav Husàk was sentenced with a group of "Slovak bourgeois nationalists" and the last execution in a whole series of political-judicial murders was carried out. In 1955, Novotný laid down a hard-line policy for completing the collectivization of agriculture, and the machinery of police and judicial repression was unleashed against the peasants who resisted. The Stalinist ideology of "intensifying the class struggle" in direct proportion to the successes achieved by socialism reigned in Czechoslovakia at that time. For the CPC, Stalin's death was in fact a challenge to continue in his footsteps and complete the work of the defunct "generalissimo of the world proletariat."

Returning to Prague in the summer of 1955, I suddenly found myself in a world very different from the one I had left five years before, and also from the one I had just left. The *esprit de corps* of a happy sect of young, ideologically-pure Communists had vanished. The secretariats where we had once lived, debated, and campaigned had been transformed into much larger bureaus, staffed by well-paid employees, ruled by a bureaucratic hierarchy, and were churning out various directives and memoranda. I knew hardly anyone there any more, nor did anyone know me. Many of my former acquaintances were no longer in the upper echelons of the party, and some had been affected in various ways by the purges of the past few years. An atmosphere of fear reigned, even among young Communists. They no longer talked freely, except among their closest friends. The expression of civic, political loyalty had become a formalized ritual, and the disagreements that in 1948 had been openly discussed among Communists were now deeply submerged and could only be surmised.

It was paradoxical, for my homecoming was very much like my arrival in Moscow five years before: what had shocked me then in Moscow had since been successfully imported into Czechoslovakia; while in Moscow, in the meantime, some of these things were being discontinued, under the influence of a slow but very real subliminal movement. Dedicated Communists in Czechoslovakia were trying desperately to convince themselves, with the help of ideological sophistry, that the change in their lives was in fact revolutionary progress because it had brought them closer to the Soviet model. While in Moscow, people were beginning, *sotto voce,* to discuss these very same phenomena as "deformations of the personality cult." In the beginning, friends and I found it hard to understand each other, to explain what we had lived through in that period, I in Moscow and they at home in Czechoslovakia.

Given this atmosphere, Khrushchev's speech on Stalin genuinely hit the CPC like a bombshell. The shock waves were felt throughout the party, and this stimulated discussion among Communists. It was in fact the first real discussion to take place within the party since February 1948, and it clearly demonstrated how much the CPC had changed since then: it was no longer a party that brought people together, in the words of its own statutes, voluntarily and on the basis of their belief in the party program. It was now an organization that united people on the basis of their involvement in power.

The discussions provoked by the Twentieth Congress of the CPSU gave rise to three main groupings within the Czechoslovak party. The first consisted of both believing Stalinists and careerists who were so closely associated with the realities being criticized and bore such direct responsibility for them that they could only maintain their positions if they silenced the wave of criticism, at least for the time being. Their attitude was shared by many convinced Stalinists who, although they often bore no personal responsibility for the political terror, still identified so deeply with all of Stalin's policies that desertion was simply unthinkable. They felt that criticism of Stalin would turn out to be just another "deviation," orchestrated by the "class enemy" to weaken the party.

Against this group stood believing Stalinists for whom Khrushchev's criticism had provided the impetus they needed to express their already-growing doubts about the party's policies and their own positions. As a rule, these people bore no direct responsibility for the policies for which Khrushchev had criticized Stalinism. On the contrary, some of them had suffered from such policies.

The third group consisted of CPC members who took little part in the discussion, but merely awaited the outcome. Most of this group were in the party for reasons of personal advantage, but they differed from careerists who were often overly zealous about accepting personal responsibility for the state of affairs being criticized. Even in the past they had kept to the sidelines, doing only what was necessary to show their loyalty to the authorities and thus buttress their very ordinary careers. This group inclined to sympathize inwardly with Khrushchev's criticism, but they were unwilling to get their fingers burned for it.

On the whole, then, support for Khrushchev's course predominated in the CPC. The balance of forces varied in the different components of the party. In the higher party organs and apparatuses, the first, pro-Stalin, group predominated, and it was also very strong among Communists holding important positions in the power apparatus. Among the intellectuals and among the younger party cadres in general, the critical group was stronger.

In the course of CPC discussions in the spring of 1956, however, it was usual not to express any doubts concerning the fundamental features of the party dictatorship. It was presumed that the absolute rule of the CPC in the state was essential for the "construction of socialism and communism." Likewise, it was generally accepted that the class struggle presupposed a political dictatorship, although certain practices were cast in doubt, especially when used against Communists themselves.

Only very seldom did the discussion go beyond these bounds, and then it was most frequently among intellectuals, who argued that the essential problem of Stalinist ideology was the false picture of reality it created. This opened the way to a debate on problems that were fundamental to the very system of totalitarian dictatorship, but such debates took place for the most part only on an abstract, theoretical level. Even the most radical of Communist circles at that time were not yet demanding the elimination of the dictatorship but merely freedom for a radical Marxist critique of its theory and practice.

The most significant radical political demand to come out of that discussion was the request to convene an extraordinary party congress. As a congress, it would have had authority to elect a new Central Committee, and thus it was opposed by the ruling party elite. As a result, a state-wide conference of the CPC was called instead. Naturally, the conference voted to support the new line in Moscow, and it resolved that several ideological and political theses of Stalinism were no longer valid in Czechoslovakia, but it did not produce any qualitative change in the leadership of the CPC nor in any of the important political apparatuses.

The CPC leadership managed to soften some of the political impact of the new Khrushchev line, but none of the measures taken could have prevented the main thrust of Khrushchev's critique from affecting the Stalinist faith of Czechoslovak Communists. I think that Khrushchev's main blow to that faith was this: by shifting all the blame and responsibility onto Stalin, he in fact raised the question of the personal responsibility of Communists for their words and deeds.

To this day reform Communists generally have one main objection to Khrushchev: his critique of Stalinism was directed at Stalin's personality rather than at the system itself. And they see no redeeming value in this critique. In reality, however, the matter is far more complex. A systemic critique would be more radical and more essential in the sphere of rational thought, but it sweeps the moral problems, the question of the personal responsibility of those who make the system, under the rug, just as Stalinist ideology itself did. Khrushchev's critique may have been more primitive on a national scale, but it did highlight, whether intentionally or not, the question of the guilt and responsibility of the individual.

We convinced Stalinists did not worry a great deal at the time about our own responsibility. The final court of appeal regarding the correctness of a given opinion or action was not my own personal judgment but the objective significance of that opinion or action, the extent to which it furthered "the interests of the working class," and thus the interests of the revolution, socialism, communism and so on. In practice, the party was the final judge of objective significance, and this meant, again, its organs and leaders. At the top of the pyramid stood Stalin: his point of view was therefore frequently the decisive factor.

But Stalin, Gottwald, the party politburo, or the party itself were never for me what God is to the believing Christian. They were rather what the Pope, the cardinals, the concilium and the Church itself is to a devout Catholic. The God of the believing Communist is the Objective Law of History, which leads to the fulfillment of the "interests of the working class" and to human progress, as understood by the communist faith. Like the Catholic who is loyal to the Church, a devout Communist assumes that his Pope and the cardinals also submit themselves to the will of that God, that their thoughts and actions are the product of an encounter with God. As a faithful Stalinist, moreover, I had always allowed that my Pope—Stalin—might not be infallible, that he might possibly even sin and that his cardinals and concilia might sin even more. But what I in my original faith could not admit was that the hierarchy might not acknowledge the primacy of their God—the Objective Law of History—and that the "interests of the working class" might not in fact be something which they continually, and in the best possible conscience, used as the measure of their thoughts and actions.

Khrushchev's criticism of Stalin, however, was unequivocal: the Pope acted only on behalf of himself and frequently showed himself to be a pagan. He did not kill because the Objective Law of History demanded it, but to maintain his grasp on power. He, consequently, even murdered faithful sons of the church. We, the cardinals, knew this or at least suspected it, but could do nothing. We have already taken measures, however, and the worst cardinal, who directly aided and abetted the Pope and corrupted him even further, has been executed. We have talked everything out thoroughly together and concluded that we no longer need a pope. From now on we shall study collectively what the Objective Law of History genuinely requires, and in this matter we shall even seek the guidance of you, the faithful. Therefore, continue to believe in us and in the Objective Law of History, and thus we shall see the fulfillment of the "interests of the working class"; this time genuinely and without "deformations." The Objective Law of History exists, and the Church, "in essence," has always perceived and followed it correctly.

To continue this historical analogy (which like all analogies is imprecise), one might conclude that Khrushchev's critique of the "personality cult" would be, on the whole, about as effective as his cardinals declaring themselves a "collective pope" after the death of Pope Alexander VI in order to avert a schism in the Church and ultimately the whole Protestant "deformation." They too would not have succeeded, and not only because they lacked a systemic critique, but because once believing Christians had discovered that the Pope and his cardinals were in fact godless men, they would begin to search for a direct, personal relationship with God unmediated by the hierarchy (which is the essence of the Protestant Reformation). To put it more generally: when believing Christians discovered that it was impossible to depend upon the Pope, the cardinals, and the Catholic Church for their relationship with God, the question of their own, personal responsibility before God for their faith and their actions was raised.

Khrushchev's critique of Stalin necessarily raised exactly the same question in the minds of believing Communists, without any systemic analysis. And many Communists began to provide answers to this new question. But from the very beginning, the situation of believing Communists fundamentally differed from that of believing Christians, who can fulfill the basic values of their faith inwardly and be at one with God in their individual lives. In contrast, the basic values of the communist faith cannot be realized without transforming supraindividual, social conditions, without changing the external circumstances of one's own individual life. The believing Christian can survive with his own soul and his own conscience; he can even get along without the Church. The believing Communist requires an instrument of change that goes beyond himself, and therefore the party is essential.

Thus for a Communist, the question of personal responsibility for one's own thoughts and actions is from the outset linked organically to the problem of reforming a "deformed" party. A Communist can avoid dealing with the party as such either at the price of renouncing his own faith or by having that faith entirely theoretical (that is, by becoming an independent Marxist Communist intellectual, content with fleshing out his ideas in literary form). These paths notwithstanding, there is only one course left to a believing Communist: he must reconcile personal responsibility with the party.

But in 1956 I had only just begun to suspect the existence of this whole complex of fundamental problems, and I had not as yet grasped them clearly. However, my rather insouciant attitude had been shaken. Up till then, I had been convinced that if I obeyed the party, I would be acting in the "interests of the working class," with no personal responsibility for any eventual errors because the party bore that responsibility before history. Now Stalin had been clearly called to account by that very same party: he was to bear the responsibility himself. Where, then, did that leave me? Was I any different?

Another reason why the problem of personal responsibility was of such primary importance to me in 1956 was my particular position. From the fall of 1955 on, I had served as a department head in the Office of the Public Prosecutor in Prague, having been appointed as a promising young cadre member with Soviet schooling. My department had nothing to do with political trials or even with penal policies, but was rather concerned with supervising the legality of state administration activities. The fact was, of course, that the state administrative organs were also instruments of political repression: favoring some citizens and discriminating against others according to their political attitudes. It was the organs of state administration, for example, that confiscated people's flats and furniture, and the national committees executed forced collectivization of farms, to mention only two instances. So that even in this area I had occasion enough to contemplate personal responsibility for my decisions. Moreover, the prosecutor general's office had been involved in the political terror of the recent past, and the problem of illegal repression, political trials, and judicial murders was literally hanging in the air here.

Who concretely was responsible for these things in Czechoslovakia? It was a question the Communists in this institution could not avoid, once they were apprized of Khrushchev's critique of the "personality cult of J. V. Stalin." At the time, the prosecutor general was V. Aleš, who had been one of the state attorneys in the Rudolf Slanský trial; the chief prosecutor, J. Urválek, was now chief justice of the Supreme Court. The deputy prosecutor general for criminal matters, E. Švach, had prosecuted the case against M. Švermová. In Slovakia, the acting prosecutor general, L. Gešo, had been prosecutor in the Gustav Husák trial. In such company, raising the question of responsibility for the "deformations" and unlawful repression meant, not an academic debate, but a direct conflict with these high officials and with those even more highly placed who had appointed them.

In discussions, both in and outside party meetings, I gradually received a very concrete view of a terrifying reality. Yes, these and other people either knew or could deduce that they were sending doubtfully guilty, and even quite obviously innocent, people to prison or to their deaths. Nevertheless, their attitude was unequivocal. Are *we* responsible? We were just acting on orders from above, on party resolutions, on oral instructions from party dignitaries. So either the "party" is guilty—or no one is; those illegalities and "deformations" quite simply "took place." It was precisely the same logic on which Nazi war criminals usually based their defense: they were merely carrying out the Leader's orders.

I recall a conversation I had with V. Aleš on discovering that both the prosecutors and the accused in the Slanský trial had learned their roles by heart from tape recordings and merely recited them in court as actors in a play. Aleš made no attempt to deny it; quite the contrary, that was his defense. After all, he argued, the one who wrote and directed the scenario is the one responsible. I admitted there was nothing he could have done to stop the whole thing, but I asked him why he had allowed himself to be used in such a tragicomedy? After all, he could have refused to take part. "Well," replied the man whom the constitution declared the supreme guardian of legality in the state, "that was theoretically possible all right, but in practice it would have meant ending up in the dock along with them." Fear for one's own life is an argument too, even though it carries no moral weight. So I acknowledged that and asked him why, if that was how he looked at it, he hadn't tried a way out that would not have exposed him to personal danger: for example he might have deliberately injured himself and thus made his participation in the trial impossible. He replied that it had never crossed his mind.

During the several months that I worked in the Office of the Prosecutor General, I was able to observe Aleš in different situations. He didn't strike me as an unprincipled man like Urválek, who had risen to his supreme role, thanks to the political police, from being an undercover cop in the South Bohemia justice department. Nor was he evil like Švach, a ruthless careerist dazzled by power who had been appointed to his job in the "worker's cadre" of the justice department after a timely departure from the Bata shoe manufacturing enterprise to become a "revolutionary." He was not even a primitive man like Gešo, who had no distinguishing attributes and no backbone, perfectly suited to execute any service his masters might require.

Aleš had been a district magistrate before the war, and he had the mentality of a petty bureaucrat. In his own way, he believed in the ideals of communism, which had justifiably made "room at the top" for workers and petty bureaucrats like himself. He was personally a rather ascetic man who was not interested in gaining power for personal advantage but as a means of lifting himself out of the grayness of the district court into the role of a co-creator of history. I have no doubt at all that as a district magistrate he had once served on the bench correctly and according to the law, and that in those days he would have rejected as absurd the idea that a judge and a public prosecutor might one day learn their parts by rote from a scenario provided by someone else.

Later, when he actually found himself in such a situation, he may well have had no idea how to get out of it—but, if so, it was because he had never given it any serious thought. Very likely he was genuinely afraid, yet he didn't fear his own conscience. From the moment he began to "create history" instead of respecting the law, his conscience failed him. For he had once assumed responsibility for passing judgment on someone accused of stealing chickens, but in those eleven death sentences passed against "traitors of the people, agents of imperialism, and destroyers of socialism" he was easily able to shift the responsibility and blame from himself to the "party." He felt quite safe in this, and it caused him no fear; he never bothered to contemplate ways of avoiding it because he never imagined he might one day be called personally to answer for it: after all, it had all been done in the name of "higher ends."

But how did Aleš differ from the prosecutor or judge who tried and sentenced people in the name of the "higher aims" of Nazi ideology? In the sense that Aleš did not believe in "the superiority of the Germanic race" but rather in the "interests of the working class"? I suddenly became aware of this terrifying analogy during that discussion about guilt in the prosecutor general's office in 1956, and no ideological argument could expel it from my mind. This was a rather new element in my thinking. After all, only a month before I too had judged the political trials from the viewpoint of the "higher interests" of the class struggle and thus tried to still my various doubts. True, I was now more familiar with what went on behind the scenes, and it was obvious that in no sense had these been normal trials. But was it not also true that three years before, in a Moscow seminar, I had made precisely the same claim, that they were not normal trials, that the presumption of innocence did not apply, and that the party itself was responsible for dealing with such matters? What was new and different—what led to my change in thinking—was Khrushchev's critique of Stalin. It was a primitive critique, clearly calculating, and far from being "systemic," but it was effective nonetheless in introducing normal human morality in politics. And this came to pass because of one simple fact: the party would not accept the responsibility even for Stalin. He himself was responsible. And who, therefore, would take the responsibility for my acts?

There was nothing left to do but try to act in a way that permitted me to be answerable for my own actions. This was far from easy at the Office of the Prosecutor General in Prague, then or at any time afterwards. Alongside the official laws published in the *Legal Gazetteer* (*Sbirka zakonu*), there was another set of decrees that applied in the prosecutor's office and in the courts, called "mimeographed laws" in the local argot. These were confidential and secret directives on how to proceed in certain categories of cases and were in the keeping of every prosecutor, department head, and deputy of the prosecutor general. These directives, issued for prosecutors by the prosecutor general and for the courts by the minister of justice or the chief justice of the Supreme Court, quite openly set out the procedures to be actually followed. In my department, for example, there was a binding order that citizens' complaints against certain decisions (such as eviction from flats, confiscation of property, measures taken against the "kulaks" once their land and property were expropriated, etc., etc.) were not to be examined on their merits at all, but rejected out of hand by the prosecutor as groundless. Thus hundreds of cases were dismissed with a single sentence: the prosecutor's office simply informed the citizen that it had "found no grounds" for altering the original decision. Date and signature. But whose signature? Usually that of one of the clerks, but even then there was the rider: "For XY, department head." In other words: in the name of *my* function. And in some cases, where the clerk himself hesitated, he simply sent the document directly to me, saying that with regard to the "complexity" or the "importance" of the matter he requested that I make the decision. If finding an alibi was all there was to it, I might occasionally have done the same thing myself, passing the case on to my superiors. But, even so, I could only have done so in exceptional cases, and, besides, I did not consider looking for alibis as a solution.

In the atmosphere following the Twentieth Congress of the CPSU, people who had been the victims of various unlawful acts in the past began to seek redress *en masse* and present petitions of complaint. To proceed according to the "mimeographed laws" meant perpetuating the old politics, now generally criticized by the party. Yet the prosecutor general refused to rescind the instructions and secret directives, which had been dictated by party resolutions, until they were countermanded by a party resolution. In the meantime, the resolutions still in force, having commonly been passed during various campaigns to "intensify the class struggle," were on the whole legally untenable. There was only one way open to me, therefore: to point out specific instances of conflict between the secret directives and the Twentieth Congress of the CPSU, thus necessitating the rescinding of those directives, and then begin examining citizens' complaints on a very concrete basis, providing redress wherever possible.

One of the best places to start, it seemed to me, was with "Operation B," as it was called. This had taken place in the early 1950s in Prague (and later in Brno, Pilsen, and other district towns and cities), and it involved evicting hundreds of people from their apartments. The apartments were expropriated "in the public interest," and their

37

tenants forcefully relocated in the dilapidated cottages, vacated by the exiled Sudeten Germans, in the border regions. In this same "Operation B," vacation cottages and villas in the environs of Prague were also expropriated. The owners were branded as "class enemies," and the whole operation was justified in terms of "the interests of the public and the state" and the requirements of the "working class." The unlawfulness of this operation was obvious, both generally and in the particular ways it was carried out. But, owing to the limited number of persons affected (especially when compared to other problem areas, such as the collectivization of farms), it was considered a minor problem. Some of the cases had already been settled in the meantime: older people had died, younger ones had married and moved elsewhere, and so on. Those who registered complaints were often not even demanding their original apartments back, but were only asking for a reasonable solution that would lift the stigma of "class enemy" and end what amounted to forced residence in the border villages. Such solutions were not impossible.

I compiled a dossier of available material on the whole question, and what clearly emerged was that not a single apartment confiscated "in the interests of the working class" had actually been allotted to workers in need of a place to live. They were all given to officers in the army and security services, or to employees of the CPC apparatus and other political administrative bodies. The vacation cottages and villas were taken over by the Central Committee, which divided them up with the Ministry of the Interior. I also discovered that the original apartment owners were, "from the class point of view," often far from being members of the bourgeoisie: many came from the middle classes—doctors, lawyers, and white-collar workers. The victims were in fact chosen, not according to their "class" qualities, but according to the quality of their apartments.

Armed with this dossier and a plan for dealing with the matter, I went to see J. Harus, the chairman of the Central Commission of Supervision and Auditing, at the CPC headquarters. He was neither for nor against. He gave me a lecture on the nature of the class struggle and promised to review the whole matter. The result? Until the autumn of 1956, none, and after the Soviet intervention in Hungary, I was accused of "promoting the interests of the class enemy." This accusation was made after my resignation and was not made public at the time, but it was published after my expulsion from the CPC in 1970 and once more when I signed Charter 77 in 1977.

In the meantime, however, I was also involved in other matters. In the instructions and circulars that I issued for the regional and district prosecutors' offices under my jurisdiction, I tried to formulate a line of approach that, although it did not radically disturb anything, obliged them to strictly observe the legal norms in force. In those days, of course, this was an out-and-out revolution for the regional and district headmen. I also submitted a number of protests on my own authority against ministerial decisions, something that was theoretically possible but simply never done by the prosecutor's office. Gradually I discovered that resistance to this approach was being organized, indirectly, through the party apparatus. But the general atmosphere of uncertainty in the party bureaucracy after the Twentieth Congress, combined with respect for my own "Moscow-bred convictions," meant that my measures usually got through without a great deal of commotion. Until one day I did something quite unheard of.

The minister of the interior at this time, Rudolf Barák, who was also a member of the party politburo and possibly the most influential party functionary next to Novotný, had had a personal conflict with someone from a very unpopular department of his ministry, the press censorship bureau, and had fired him with an hour's notice. This person then brought his complaint to me during official business hours, and I saw that what Barák had done was clearly unlawful. In an attempt to avoid the scandal of a court case—for I was well aware of Barák's exceptional position—I tried to solve the matter through cabinet methods as it were, and I sent Barák an official protest originating in the prosecutor's office. This would have made a quiet settlement possible.

About three days later, however, the storm broke. Barák telephoned the prosecutor general and told him that there had clearly been some kind of misunderstanding on the part of one of his minor officials who was trying to interfere in his own spheres of competence as minister of the interior, and he demanded that the prosecutor general straighten things out. Naturally, the prosecutor general humbly complied. I was summoned by his deputy, who, in a generally friendly tone, tried to explain the enormity of what I had done and suggested that things might be smoothed over if I were to withdraw my protest. This gave rise to a discussion, which developed into an argument, since I refused. What was surprising about the case was that my superiors had the option of annulling my protest on their own authority, which, however, they were none too eager to use, for it was clear even to them that Barák had proceeded unlawfully. So they chose another course: they ordered me to withdraw my protest. According to the regulations governing the prosecutor's office, however, a prosecutor has the right to refuse the order of a superior should the content be unlawful. I invoked this article and refused to obey.

Something like that had happened only very rarely in the entire history of the prosecutor's office, and it always had unpleasant consequences. In the end, the deputy prosecutor general annulled my protest on his own authority, but both I and my superiors felt that the matter would not end there. Barák, however, was satisfied. Five years later he had a run-in with Novotný, who suspected him of trying to engineer a putsch in the party leadership. Barák sought support in Moscow, but despite his contacts in the Soviet security forces, his gambit failed. Khrushchev gave Novotný a free hand in the matter, and Novotný had Barák tried for "abusing his function." The prosecuting attorney was the chief military prosecutor, J. Samek, one of the deputies at the Office of the Prosecutor General at the time of my own little incident with Barák. When I read about the trial in the newspapers, I was curious to know whether or not Barák, confronted with the chief military prosecutor, had recalled how he had taught the prosecutor's office a lesson in the law. I had an opportunity to ask him about it in 1968 when I was secretary of the Central Committee, and Barák, having just been released from prison, had requested an audience with me. He had learned a few things, he said, some of which he passed on to me. His main advice was never to get involved as a party functionary with the Czechoslovak and Soviet security forces. "I could have wrapped them around my little finger"—Barák complained—"and look how I wound up." But he could recall nothing about that incident from 1956.

My problems with the Office of the Prosecutor General were finally resolved when the leading Central Committee administrators willingly agreed to my suggestion that I resign. Although at a party plenary session, K. Innemann, a department head in the Central Committee, moved that I be expelled from the party along with several other rebels, the whole affair ended in a conciliatory compromise. The report that went into my dossier stated that in view of my inexperience I had not understood the class situation in Czechoslovakia and had perpetrated a "mechanical transference of Soviet experience." However, I was released on the understanding that I could work at the Institute for the Study of the State and Law in the Czechoslovak Academy of Sciences, in the field of political theory.

I came to the Academy of Sciences on October 15, 1956. Three weeks later, the Soviet army moved against the "counter-revolution" in Budapest. But even before that, during the Polish "October," as a result of which Gomulka, who was then a revolutionary critic of Stalin, became the head of the Polish party, conditions in Czechoslovakia got tougher. After the Hungarian events, however, there was a clear and abrupt change to the offensive on the part of all the CPC forces whose positions were threatened by any criticism of Stalinism. Inside the party, the repressions were directed against many Communists who in the preceding months had been particularly outspoken in their criticism of existing conditions and who had tried to induce changes. In the Office of the Prosecutor General, too, critical opposition was swept away, and even one of the prosecutors was himself prosecuted for statements, allegedly made at a party meeting, that "defamed an allied state," i.e. the Soviet Union. Some zealots in the prosecutor general's office and in the Central Committee even took retroactive action against me to have me expelled from the Academy of Sciences. But there was, after all, that written report prepared by the party organs, scarcely a month old, and in the Academy of Sciences at the time there were several who had made far more heretical statements than I had and, moreover, had done it publicly in the press. So I sailed safely past those dangerous reefs and worked in the Academy of Sciences for the next twelve years, up until the Prague Spring of 1968.

The shooting in the streets of Budapest and the intervention of the Soviet army in Hungary naturally played right into the hands of those in the CPC who opposed the wave of criticism and wanted to maintain the status quo and thus their positions of power. Yet the pacification of critical tendencies inside the CPC was not simply a consequence of the repressions unleashed by these forces. In various memoirs and essays by former Communists, one very fundamental circumstance is always passed over in silence, or at least lightly, one that in late 1956 facilitated the ending of greater tolerance inside the CPC: we Communists were quite simply afraid.

Naturally I can't say to what extent this applies to particular individuals who later went on to represent reform communism in the

CPC, but I would be lying if I said that at the time I was interested only in the general political and ideological problems raised by the "Hungarian events," as they were referred to. For apart from these problems, there was the quite concrete image of a lynch mob hanging Communists from the lampposts. And from the conversations I had at the time with various Communists of different generations, I recall that they were all preoccupied with the same thought as well. This was an important assistance to Novotný in subduing the wave of criticism precipitated in the CPC by Khrushchev's critique.

Of all the assessments of the Hungarian revolt, the one that impressed me the most was by E. Kardelj. It was circulated illegally in Prague, and it even inspired me to start learning Serbo-Croatian. I felt that here was someone formulating ideas that had occurred to me as well, but which I had neither the skill nor even the courage to think through for myself. For here were the essential elements of a much needed systemic critique of the "personality cult" and which, at the same time, derived from an ideological faith in communism. But regardless of how dazzled I was by Kardelj's theories, I still felt that armed mobs overrunning the streets of Prague now would hardly be shouting "all power to the workers' councils." It was far more probable that if all those petitioners who over the years had been told by the prosecutors, the courts, and the government and party offices that "no grounds have been found to reexamine the original decision" were to march on these institutions, more than just the official files would end up flying out the windows.

The problem of personal responsibility took on a new dimension in the form of a feeling of collective responsibility, or complicity. Moreover, this sense of shared personal guilt for the past existed despite the different degrees of our individual guilt which a mob never bothers to distinguish, nor could it even if it wanted to, though it never does. Given the euphoria of the preceding months, this was a rude awakening. Out of fear, I had been brought closer to those I had despised. When Karel Kuehnul, one of my friends from that naive, sectarian era in the Union of Youth, was expelled from the party in the fall of 1956 for his radical criticism of Stalinism, he said: "But what could I do if they burst in off the streets and said they were going to hang the Communists? Tell them I'm not one of that lot any more? They won't care: I was one a month ago. My next-door neighbor is a Stalinist whore! I don't want to hang on the same tree as him; so I'll have to tell them: fine, gentlemen, go right ahead, but would you mind hanging me a couple of trees down from this man here?" And years later I still think that he was expressing exactly just how little significance our distinctions in 1956 between formerly united Stalinists had for very many people who had never been Stalinists. What was for us a recent discovery had been the tragedy of their lives.

But the streets of Prague and of other towns in Czechoslovakia remained quiet and orderly, and the party leadership became more confident and relaxed. Czechoslovakia and the CPC thus entered what seemed on the surface to be a decade of peaceful development. But it was precisely that calm exterior which ultimately enabled the hidden, critical powers of reform inside the party to emerge as a great, organized force, with relatively clear direction, in 1968, during the Prague Spring. By this time, it was no longer afraid of lynch mobs, nor did it have any reason to be. But it is interesting to note that those who opposed democratic reform during the Prague Spring tried consistently to revive that fear from 1956, and that the same approach was used by the Soviets and their Czechoslovak allies after the military intervention in August 1968. This indicates that the "realistic socialists" knew very well what had played an important political role in suppressing the critical currents inside the party in 1956.

At the end of 1956, after all I had been through, I found myself mentally incapable of taking part in party political activity. Too many elements of my original faith had collapsed, and I did not know what ought to be or might be preserved after all that. Of course my political activity had always been motivated exclusively by ideological convictions and therefore my inability to act politically followed from my inner uncertainty. Moreover, I was a party member who had just barely escaped punishment by the party, and therefore there was nothing for me to do inside the party but remain silent. I had just come into a new and unfamiliar working environment; as a candidate of science I was on the bottom rung of the ladder in the Institute of the Academy of Sciences, and I was expected to become a theoretician, a research worker; that is, I was expected to work at something I had never done before.

But, in the end, all of these apparently unfavorable circumstances worked to my advantage. For the first time in my life, I was able to study literature previously unknown to me and which, moreover, related directly to the fundamental concerns of my life: politics and ideology. I had three years ahead of me, and my only requirements were to pass a few tests and complete a dissertation, whereby I would gain the title of Candidate of Legal Sciences in the general theory of the state and law.

I soon learned how flimsy in many ways my education at Moscow university had been. Here I was twenty-six years old and for the first time in my life reading pre-Marxian authors, including such classic political philosophers as Plato, Aristotle, and Machiavelli; authors of social utopias such as More, Campanella, and others; and ideologists of bourgeois revolutions such as Hobbes, Locke, Montesquieu, Rousseau. It was my first encounter with non-Marxist intellectual concepts, with the opinions of Max Weber and G. Mosca, with the legal theoretical conceptions of the normative school, with legal sociology and in fact with sociological literature altogether. Even Marxism itself suddenly began to appear very different from what it had at the Moscow university. Wide though our exposure to Marxist literature may have been there—from *Das Kapital* and all the main works of Marx, Engels, and Lenin through to the writings of Stalin—it was nevertheless considerably censored. Marx's early writings were missing, nothing was mentioned either about Gramsci or Luxemburg, and it was only from an anthology of Lenin's critical articles and polemics against the bourgeoisie that students learned anything at all, not only about social democrats like Kautsky, Hilferding, and Bernstein but even about some of the Bolsheviks like Trotsky or Bukharin.

Thus it was not until the late 1950s that I finally studied what every Marxist-oriented university should teach its political science students as a matter of course. But I did not read Plato and Machiavelli, the young Marx and Gramsci merely to strengthen my academic credentials: I plunged into my reading with a deep sense of personal involvement, seeking answers to problems of immediate importance to me. Authors ancient and more modern, Marxists and non-Marxists, all helped me to reconstruct my own view of the world. My former system of Stalinist ideology was destroyed, and upon its ruins there began to grow the conviction that Marxism was a rational, open-ended theory of social development with inner contradictions, and that it was not identical with the political ideology of the Communist movement.

As my world view was undergoing this regeneration, however, so was my ability and desire to take part in active politics revived. Once, right after the war, politics had been a powerful force and I had simply been swept into it. However, at that time I didn't think of my Stalinist faith and activity as politics, but rather as taking part in making revolutionary history, a new world. In 1959, when I again stepped into the waters of practical politics, it was something quite different. This was an entirely conscious step, a carefully-considered decision. And I also knew that I was entering a political arena that had well-defined relationships, conditions, and laws which could not be disregarded if progress were to be made. I was also aware that human moral problems were involved, as they always had been in politics.

What were my opinions at this time? I shall stop to deal with them now in more detail, for they clarify many of my political positions and actions in later years, including the Prague Spring of 1968.

After 1956, intellectual Communists, who had originally been oriented toward Stalinism, achieved a new stage in their thinking, which paved the way for what is called reform communism. Through their study of Marxist literature, they discovered that in Marx, as well as in Lenin, there are many ideas which basically contradict the way Marxism is presented by the official party interpreters. Impressed in particular with Marx's humanism and his unequivocal stand in the cause of freedom and the emancipation of man—the class struggle being only a necessary instrument to attain these higher ends—critically-thinking Communists came to set Marx (and, in some cases, Lenin as well) against official ideology, which they felt had abandoned Marx's scientific methodology and his commitment to truth. This was the basic point of departure at this stage in the development of reform communism.

Though I essentially shared this viewpoint, in politics I came to adopt another view. These intellectual Communists, insofar as they stood for the preeminence of Marxist theory, limited themselves to an academic and theoretical critique; in such a conception, Marxism necessarily became a matter for intellectuals. It enclosed itself in the libraries, and its influence was restricted to university departments and specialized periodicals. As a result, it could have little bearing on the party ideology as a whole and could not dispel the prevalent Stalinist conceptions from the minds of the faithful Communist masses. The humanistic interpretation of Marx was simply not comprehensible enough for most Communists in terms of actual political practice and their concrete problems. What these people wanted from theory was "a guide to action," which was something the theoreticians of

Marxist humanism were unable to provide. Their criticism of Stalinist practices was convincing, but they could not come up with a sufficiently comprehensible and concrete alternative.

Unlike many reform Communists from the social sciences who were not directly involved in party politics, I supported the view, in the late fifties, that the contradiction between Marxist theory (understood as an attempt to arrive at objectively-truthful knowledge) and Communist ideology (understood as a guide to practical political activity) could not be resolved simply by rejecting the ideology as false and distorting and therefore unnecessary. I was convinced that in the interests of the new politics, it was necessary to replace the old ideological constructs with others equally ideological. This new ideology would, of necessity, not be identical with scientific theory and would once again simplify and distort complex reality in the name of its political aims. This new distortion, however, should not conflict with the truth to such an extent that the truth would be altogether unrecognizable in it, and certainly not such that the forces trying to suppress truthful knowledge would in practice be supported.

My study of pre-Marxist, and especially revolutionary, political theories led me to believe that a similar contradiction between theory and ideology has always existed and that it has never been resolved simply by rejecting the ideology, for that was practically impossible. For example, it was the rational and, in their time, controversial theories of Locke, Montesquieu, and Rousseau that formed the basis for Robespierre's thinking and the mood of the "third estate" and even of ordinary Parisians during the French Revolution, all of which replaced Rousseau's notion of a democratically-created "general will" with the religious cult of reason and the practical cult of the guillotine.

Rousseau's philosophy persisted as an intellectual system but practical political thought did not develop as it would have had it been based on a return to the "authentic" Rousseau.

Napoleonic generals no longer read the writings of Jean-Jacques Rousseau at all, yet it was they who consolidated the results of the social upheaval formulated by these writings. Those who then wanted to go further, not only in political thought but also in political practice, had first of all to confront the concrete results of the revolution rather than simply dust off the original intellectual conceptions.

In the process of being implemented, ideas themselves enter into a different state of being. In this dimension, the value of ideas is based not on their objective truth but on their ability to organize and unite people politically. It is on this basis that theories are altered by ideologies. There may very well be ideas that are quite essential for a truthful picture of reality but inappropriate for political and organizational purposes. Rational scientific scepticism, for example, is always *a priori* inappropriate where a fanatical faith based on emotion rather than knowledge better serves the need to mobilize and organize. Thus when theory is transformed into ideology, things like relativity and scepticism get pushed into the background and for the most part disappear entirely, to be replaced by absolutism and belief. The economic, social, and political interests of the people alter the theory according to their own requirements. This is the necessary price that ideas pay for becoming a material force in the form of a mass social movement.

In the 1950s, when I studied the relationship of Marxist theory to the practical ideology of the Communist parties, I could not help seeing historical analogies in that the evolution of Communist politics could not be furthered by a return to the "authentic" Marx (quite apart from the fact that it is extremely difficult to determine what is understood in politics by this notion: Marx's works contain contradictory views on serious questions concerning the economic, political, and social processes of the "transition from capitalism to communism"). I was convinced that active Communists would continue to be influenced by ideology shaped in part by their political interests and not by the most objective and scientific theoretical knowledge, and that therefore it was necessary, alongside the theory, to have a new rational ideology that would resolve many of the concrete social and political problems in a way consonant both with the political interests of Communists and with the needs of society.

I think that the intellectual development of many reform Communists brought them precisely to this conclusion, that communist ideology, and the political work of the whole party, ought not to be simply rejected from the position of "authentic Marxism," but rather it should be realistically changed and reformed. In the CPC from the late 1950s on, a considerable number of functionaries and party members began to think this way. And for a large majority of these Communists, the main impulse for such a change in orientation did not come from any profound theoretical and ideological considerations, but rather from their everyday, practical experience. On evaluating objectively their experiences in production, state administration, social services, and elsewhere, they discovered that reality was essentially different from the Stalinist ideological picture of it, demonstrating the need to adjust the ideological picture of reality itself.

Reform Communists who thought this way were somewhat of a pleasant surprise for non-Communists, that is, for the vast majority of Czechoslovak citizens. That majority had by now come to be thought of by reform Communists as a group whose interests and needs had to be taken into consideration, and therefore reform Communists were compelled to think about a governmental system in which others as well might express their interests. The main problem for reform Communists, however, was still how they, their party and ideology, were to correct their errors and properly "express the needs of the whole of society." They could not accept the idea that society might itself find a solution not predicated on the orientation of their ideology and their party, because they still believed that their ideology and party ultimately expressed the "genuine historical and objective" interests of the working class and of all society better than any other ideology or party.

Consequently, from a democratic political viewpoint, reform communism was still very limiting. From the viewpoint of real change in the dictatorial system, however, that same reform communism was the prime political impetus, and it opened the way to a political democracy. In practical terms it was not itself a solution, but it paved the way to finding a practical solution. Looked at by noncommunists, reform communism thus remains trapped inside its own vicious circle. Yet it does create for its adherents a situation in which they gradually become aware of the existence of their vicious circle, and of its untenability.

When I took up active reform politics in the late 1950s, I was far from being fully aware of all these limitations. And of course this was equally true for all the others as well.

My conviction that reform communism was going in the right direction, however, did not derive only from general ideological beliefs. Like hundreds of thousands of other Communists who were trying to critically reevaluate the past, I also tried to determine what in fact developments after 1948 had contributed to society, to working people, to the working class in whose "historical interest" these policies, with my own active assistance, were carried out. I came to the conclusion that by no means all the results of this development were bad; on the contrary, I felt that the essential changes were positive and therefore reform of the system was not only necessary, it was also possible.

By the late fifties and into the sixties, the new economic and social conditions in Czechoslovakia had become stabilized. Some of the essential ideas of our communist faith had genuinely been realized, and society had, by all appearances, accepted them. There were no longer any private capitalists, nor the old class and social division based on private property relations. Poverty as a social phenomenon had disappeared. People going about in rags, beggars in the streets, slums in urban peripheries—things I could still remember from childhood (and what I had seen in Moscow)—had disappeared for good and were known by the younger generation only from movies. The fear of sickness or old age that comes from material insecurity also vanished from everyday life. It was taken for granted that the specter of economic depression and unemployment was no longer a threat. The average standard of living, of course, was by no means an affluent one, but it was decent and the main thing was that it was steadily, if slowly, rising. The housing crisis—clearly the most sensitive spot in that living standard—seemed to be soluble in time by stepping up housing construction, which the Stalinist emphasis on developing heavy industry had eclipsed.

Of course these purely material advantages were little compensation to those whose interests extended beyond the private-individual and family; i.e., who were political and were personally concerned with economic efficiency, cultural development, and freedom of thought. For the great majority of people, however, material security was a basis for generally peaceful and contented lives.

In everyday life, the exhausting rat-race of competition, common in capitalist industrial society, disappeared from the lives of working people. Of course there were other, negative features in everyday life: inadequate public services, an utter lack of labor-saving household appliances, and a shortage of consumer goods meant that life outside the workplace tended to be a ceaseless scramble after the necessities of life. But the more relaxed pace of working and living on the whole made many of these negative features more palatable. In social relationships—such as between employees and superiors, between the sexes, the generations, and various nationalities and ethnic groups—there was visibly more equality in everyday life. These relationships were more egalitarian than they had been in the capitalist past. In general, this nonpolitical, grass roots democratism held true to a far greater extent in Czechoslovakia than in the Soviet Union; the political and social regime, however, was on the whole just as bureaucratic and dictatorial.

In addition, marked changes had taken place in popular attitudes since the beginning of the fifties. In the first few years after February 1948, dissatisfaction with the new conditions invariably led to comparison with pre-Communist days. Now it was different. You could no longer hear remarks like, "That would have been impossible before nationalization." Nor was it common any more to compare Communist policies with those of the non-Communist parties before 1948. Criticism and opposition continued, of course, but they were directed toward change on the basis of the new economic, social, and political conditions and not of turning back the clock to the capitalist past. This could be observed even in the villages, where collectivization had been completed scarcely a few years before. Here too a return to private forms of farming was no longer a dominant theme, particularly among younger people. At the time, I felt that the social reality did not fundamentally contradict its ideological depiction in official party resolutions: the "foundations of socialism had been built," and it was no longer a matter of turning back but rather pushing ahead to the "construction of an advanced socialist society." In the political sense, "the class struggle for power in socialist society" was over. The issue now was a "deepening of socialist democracy."

Today, after what I have lived through since 1968, I know that my estimation of the state of affairs at that time was considerably oversimplified. It was still a view from the world of the privileged, who see the life of the unprivileged only partially and with distortion. What seemed to me then like acceptance of existing conditions was very often in reality only the resignation of a people weary after years of Stalinist violence. In a situation where there could be no critical approach to social and political problems, people simply withdrew from such concerns. And the suppression of their interests, needs, and opinions was only prolonged by the reform Communists and their many political compromises.

The "contentment" of the "average citizen"—who had in fact ceased to be a citizen and had withdrawn from public, civic life into the world of his own private needs and interests—therefore, far from being essential to successful political reform, was, in fact, a bulwark of the totalitarian dictatorship. This "average citizen," whose needs and interests had already been diminished by the dictatorship, was, in fact, the aim of the dictatorship: someone who feels the dictatorship is inevitable and adapts to it entirely, and thus, in his deformed life, makes it possible and reinforces it. In return, the dictatorship provides him with average food, average clothing, average entertainment on state television, and average health care.

Regardless of these negative features, however, a vast majority of the society were, in fact, materially secure and able to satisfy their basic needs. This is why they did not seek ways to restore the social and economic conditions under capitalism, which, in the past, had not provided this security. This fact was finally borne out in the course of 1968: despite the eruption of a wide variety of contradictory social and political tendencies, the attempt to return to capitalism simply never became a political factor. Even in the villages, not a single agricultural cooperative was dismantled, and only a few individuals went back to being small private farmers.

The weakness of reform communism, therefore, did not lie in the fact that it was a socialist tendency and that it unequivocally rejected the possibility of restoring the social conditions of capitalism and private ownership. In this, it based its position on a consensus of the absolute majority of society, and it expressed their genuine perceptions of how things ought to be. The weakness of reform communism was far more probably the fact that it had an overidealized conception of these attitudes of the absolute majority. It was only later developments, however, that made me realize this. At the end of the 1950s and during the 1960s everything seemed to indicate that the politics of reform communism would triumph. I saw the main problem as getting reform communism accepted as the official ideology of the CPC and insuring that power would be exercised according to it. Above all, that meant working in this direction inside the CPC and winning over the center of political power.

This was not a simple task, but neither was it impossible. Thousands of Communist party functionaries had been thinking in similar terms since the late 1950s, and it was this that made the reform policies in 1968 possible. During the 1960s, this trend gained support among the rank-and-file of the party.

However, given the nature of a political dictatorship, these intergovernmental goings on were not very evident to outside observers. In Czechoslovakia, before 1968, people had very little opportunity to distinguish between the various rulers hidden in the grayness of the party secretariats and the government apparatuses. Who could have known, for example, in what way Alexander Dubček differed from J. Lenárt, or O. Černík from Alois Indra, before the Prague Spring? And was anyone really much interested anyway?

And so for several years before the Prague Spring, public attention was drawn to the differences between those Communists in the visible sphere of the arts and journalism. They too were among the elite, but the very nature of their work demanded that they appear before the public in their own right. Despite all the censorship and self-censorship, ideas and opinions were expressed in this public forum from which quite definite political views could be inferred. People sympathized with those who became increasingly critical of the reality around them, and who thus put their careers on the line and were, from time to time, singled out for punishment in the various campaigns waged by the regime.

Those who wrote critical articles in the cultural and political journals and spoke openly at writers' congresses, and were persecuted for their opinions, quite naturally and deservedly gained authority among wide sectors of the population. The authors of various critical ideas and proposals who remained behind the walls of government buildings were for the most part anonymous, and their victories or defeats went virtually unknown outside a narrow circle of professionals.

In reality, however, both were part of the same front: those who were familiar to the public could not have functioned without these anonymous people and, in general, vice versa. Nevertheless, during Novotný's rule, this situation reinforced a tendency that is a powerful factor in politics anyway: the tendency to judge the importance of things according to public pronouncements. This tendency remained, and in many respects was intensified, in those few months of the Prague Spring of 1968. And the political proclamations, consequently, played a more important role than the practical steps taken in the sphere of political power, despite the fact that the potential realization of such proclamations often depended on such steps.

Personal accounts of the Prague Spring published abroad after 1968 by reform Communists are usually by those who belonged to the publicly visible front: journalists, writers, social scientists, and so on. The other part of the front still remains largely hidden, to the detriment of a more complete understanding of the period and to an evaluation of the future. The question as to whether there can be another Prague Spring cannot be answered without dealing with the question of whether there can be another situation inside the governing elite like the one that existed during the final years of Novotný's rule.

In the 1960s my work as a reform Communist was conducted both publicly and in the party apparatus; I thus was myself a part of that hidden world of power. It was my whole life in 1968, and this had a far more profound impact on my life afterwards than my activity as a publicist for reform communism.

When the central newspaper of the CPC, *Rudé právo,* published my first ideological article, sometime in 1959, the director of the Institute for the Study of the State and Law, Academician V. Knapp, summoned me to his office and talked to me about it. I told him that I would be happy if some of my ideas about ideology reached a wider circle of readers. "You mean a narrower circle, don't you," remarked Knapp, and laughed knowingly.

He was right. The real significance of articles like mine was not that they might be read enthusiastically by a community of millions of readers. On the whole the readership paid little attention to such articles, but, rather, preferred the sports page. Ideological articles were read by those to whom politics and ideology were of professional or semiprofessional concern: people in the political apparatuses, CPC functionaries and activists. For them, opinions in *Rudé právo* could be taken as political directives; they had official approval. For *Rudé právo* was also required reading for a circle which, although it was very narrow, was very influential and powerful. It was read by members of the politburo itself, by secretaries of the Central Committee, and circles close to them. These people, of course, did not read everything, nor did they read particularly attentively, but, even so, the entire political apparatus beneath them could consider anything printed in black-and-white in *Rudé právo* as having their approval.

And thus, not through the main door, but through the pages of *Rudé právo,* I gained entry to the sanctuary of political power in Czechoslovakia. Yet for a long time I had no official political function. One of the big mistakes uninformed people make is to judge real political influence only, or chiefly, by formal position. Such observers believe that a government minister is more important than a department head in the apparatus of the Central Committee, which is dead wrong. A department head of the Central Committee is, practically speaking, independent of the minister and closer to the real center of power, that is to the party politburo. He also has a decisive influence on the appointment, promotion or demotion of all the ministers' subordinates, and ultimately of the minister himself.

For anyone unfamiliar with these things, common occurrences in the world of power in Eastern Europe are incomprehensible. If, for example, one were to see a general who was inspecting a regiment of soldiers suddenly ignore all his colonels and majors and rush with outstretched arms to a captain standing in the ranks on parade and engage in a very friendly chat with him, one might think that the general was either eccentric or mad. In fact, however, that captain is an officer in the defense department of the Central Committee who is just doing his thirty days of compulsory military exercise. And both the general and his colonels and majors know that this captain is only apparently their subordinate and that, in fact, he can have a far greater say in their ranks, functions, pay scale, promotions and demotions than they themselves do.

But it would also be a mistake to think that among all the institutions of political power, the CPC apparatus is the most important and that this provides the key to understanding the world of power. It may be true that head physicians in hospitals and even the minister of health himself would defer to a party *apparatchik* in charge of the health service, but that same party worker must beware of a State Security officer who lives in his apartment building, even though this officer does not work for the party. This same State Security officer and even his superiors, in turn, try to insinuate themselves into the good graces of officials in the defense and security departments of the Central Committee, the secretaries of the Central Committee and their assistants, and, in some cases, even some other very particular person working in the party apparatus. They often defer to them more than they do to their own minister, the minister of the interior: for, after all, he is only a minister, even though he is more than just "rank-and-file."

Inside the party apparatus itself, the formal hierarchy is often far from being decisive in determining real influence. In the 1960s under Novotný, for example, an important criterion of genuine influence was whether or not you belonged to the narrow circle of people who played cards with Novotný. The regional party secretary or minister who played *maryáš* with Novotný often had more influence and power than Central Committee secretaries who did not. But those who did and those who did not, and ultimately even Novotný himself, all behaved very deferentially toward some apparently ordinary and insignificant apparatus officials. I first encountered this phenomenon in regard to a normally outspoken and authoritative secretary who suddenly hesitated to do something against the advice of an ordinary apparatus official. When I expressed surprise, the secretary openly told me a revealing thing: "When you speak with some comrades in the apparatus," he said, "it's like speaking directly to Moscow."

Knowing who these particular comrades were was more important than having a doctorate from the Party University, in terms of getting along in the upper levels of the party apparatus and avoiding quite a bit of unpleasantness. For those who knew such things, there would be no mystery concerning why, just before August 21, 1968, some rank-and-file party *apparatchiki* went on sudden vacations in the USSR or the German Democratic Republic. Neither would the sudden promotion of the Central Committee official responsible for running the Academy of Sciences to minister of the interior be a surprise; nor an official in the international department of the Central Committee suddenly appearing to be best qualified to head the cultural department in the party headquarters. Everyone else gropes about in blind uncertainty and is always being surprised.

High-ranking official functions, therefore, do not always bring power and influence. I did not play cards with Novotný, nor did I work for the KGB, but I belonged to that infrastructure or mycelium of power, invisible from the outside but nevertheless vitally important for the life of the visible structure. Without that mycelium, those proud mushrooms of power, the official organs, could not exist. Both individuals and entire organs of power are utterly dependent on that infrastructure: they literally derive from it vital nourishment, which otherwise they would not get.

The very proposals considered by an organ of the party, and even, at the highest level, by the party congress and by the Central Committee, are formulated, not by the secretaries or the department heads, but by their administrative apparatus. It is true that the higher organs alter these proposals in many ways, certain things are changed during discussion, but in essence they contain what these faceless (even for the party "public" as well as the general public) subordinates put there. In many cases it is they who determine the wording of certain resolutions of the Central Committee, the party congresses, and the government as well as the wording of laws, even in the constitution: for even constitutional laws are approved by the presidium as proposed, formulated, and revised by the apparatus and its various committees and "working groups."

The struggle for genuine influence in the decision-making process, therefore, also involves a jockeying for position in the lower, apparently less important, sections of the apparatus. Even secretaries of the Central Committee try to have their own personal "agencies"—that is, a group of people who are loyal to them personally, or friends of such people—in the various departments of the apparatus. It was also particularly valuable to have such an "agency" in the personal secretariat of the highest governing official, the first secretary, who in the 1960s was Antonín Novotný. The genuine influence enjoyed by individual secretaries, department heads, and other higher functionaries depended on how many people loyal to them or in their personal debt they had in the various lower-level departments. And there too, are various informal and, to the uninitiated eye, invisible groups and cliques united by a shared outlook.

All this can serve only to enhance the personal careers of the mutually supportive members of such cliques. However, in the 1960s these personal and bureaucratic ties contained a confrontation of differing political viewpoints and conceptions, and thus, paradoxically, made it possible for an antibureaucratic, democratizing trend in politics to be contested. Some groups and cliques inside the power apparatus gradually became tools of the reform Communists, whereas others were instruments of conservative forces trying to slow down and frustrate the reformist policies.

Thus my public appearances in *Rudé právo* on questions of ideological theory were in fact the beginning of my nonpublic, pragmatic political activity inside the power structures of the party apparatus. Until 1968, I was not employed by the party apparatus; I still continued to work in the Academy of Sciences, but my real activity in the 1960s shifted increasingly towards the sphere of the party apparatus.

As soon as I began to appear in print more regularly as an author of theoretical, ideological articles, I was also selected with increasing frequency to participate in the various "working groups" that prepared documents for the party organs and their apparatuses, relating both to problems of party ideology and to problems of the political system in general, and of the state, law, and social organizations in particular. In the 1960s, the party apparatus increasingly employed these "working groups" to deal with the widest possible variety of problems. The importance of the groups varied but, on the whole, the practice gradually led to a strengthening both of the party intelligentsia outside the apparatus and of reform communism. Officially speaking, the working groups were the expression of a trend in the party that demanded a higher degree of scientific management in society; in actuality, they often reflected the inability of the apparatus itself to carry out any form of analysis or generalization whatsoever.

Gradually, for almost all important discussions, the party apparatus prepared documents by setting up "working groups" of people from outside the apparatus: from state and economic organizations, universities and scientific institutions. The documents they prepared were then revised by the various sections of the party apparatus in a way that would make them acceptable to the party leadership. Thus the party apparatus itself fulfilled a double and contradictory role: it assembled reports that often quite critically pointed out genuine problems, and then it censored these reports, revising the proposed solutions, sometimes fundamentally. The resolutions and decisions that the organs of the party and government then passed were often quite different from the original proposals. But even as compromises they nevertheless reflected genuine problems. Essentially the same system applied to the preparation of speeches and various public addresses made by the highest party and state officials in Czechoslovakia in the 1960s.

Thus my participation in "working groups" gave me an ever greater opportunity to insert some of my ideas into the resolutions of party organs and the mouths of high party and state dignitaries, even if the ideas were highly edited and distorted. I was then able to take such passages in resolutions and official speeches and interpret them in a way that created even more room for critical analysis and reformist ideas. Thus the two levels of my activity—in the public, political forum of journalism and in the nonpublic domain of the working groups—complemented each other: the things I wrote as a journalist found support in political resolutions and official speeches and, naturally, vice versa.

Of course, the situation went both ways. And those of us academic specialists who thus gained a certain influence within the mechanism of bureaucratic power inevitably paid a penalty for it: the power that we were trying to influence at the same time influenced us and our reformist concepts. For power to serve our needs, we in turn had to serve it.

I recall many concrete situations in which I had to weigh all the pros and cons to decide what to give up for what gain. The issue was not only being sometimes unable to formulate problems in draft resolutions as openly and fully as I thought they deserved. These were, after all, usually only problems of a general nature. What was worse was, because of my position in the party mechanism, having to clearly and publicly "defend the party line," even when I was far from convinced of its correctness.

In 1961, for example, when Antonín Novotný again announced that the problem of the 1950s political trials was now "definitively settled," I was unconvinced. Even so, at meetings and in print, I defended Novotný's claim that Slanský would never be rehabilitated, because he had a share in the crimes of the 1950s, like Jezhov, Jagoda, and Beria in the Soviet Union, who also were not rehabilitated. In 1962, as a Central Committee spokesman at party meetings, I defended the official position on the arrest of Rudolf Barák. The indictment against him was for alleged abuse of his position as minister of the interior to enrich himself, squandering foreign currency, and so on. Novotný even had an exhibition set up of expensive suits and shirts along with foreign banknotes, pictures, and art objects to demonstrate Barák's guilt to ordinary people. It was quite embarrassing. I knew the whole thing had a political basis, that Novotný had simply suspected Barák (clearly with some justice) of planning a putsch in the CPC leadership. Yet I "defended the party line."

For the most part insincerely, I also engaged in a number of polemics against "revisionism," particularly against certain Yugoslav conceptions, which, in fact, I believed to be somewhat relevant for our own political transformation in Czechoslovakia. It was a time when the "critique of revisionism" had a high priority in the CPC's ideological line, and to deviate from this at such a time would necessarily have meant losing all the ground I had gained over the years, losing the opportunity to struggle for the reform of party policies from inside political power itself.

From the viewpoint of political pragmatism, such actions were not difficult to justify. I was certain that they would allow me to influence and help create a conception of party politics that would facilitate the further evolution of the entire political system, and that I would also assure myself a place in the party mechanism that would enable me to go on doing so. And I considered that most important. After all, I had written my dissertation in 1959 on Machiavelli, and I knew that power politics had been that way four hundred years ago and that Machiavelli had had the courage to see it openly. I concluded that a successful politician cannot always base his decisions on the principles of individual human morality (concretely, on Christian morality) and that, in this sphere, people ultimately recognize as moral and correct what is in their own interests and is successful.

From the viewpoint of my conscience, and the sense of personal responsibility that I had developed since 1956, however, it was not easy. I resolved the conflict by setting myself concrete limits to what I would do in the interests of political expediency. On the one hand, this included illegal, criminal behavior, and, on the other hand, conduct where the political damage would outweigh the possible political usefulness. I do not think I ever breached these limits while I was inside the power structure after 1956. There were only two occasions when there was any danger of this happening. The first was a minor but nonetheless clear case. In 1966, at a time of intensified ideological struggle (several magazines were banned and various people in the arts were persecuted, etc.), I concluded that any further "support for the party line" would necessarily take me beyond limits I could justify by political expediency. I resolved the situation by interrupting all my ideological journalism, resigning from several functions, and devoting myself exclusively to theoretical work. The result was the founding of an interdisciplinary research team for questions relating to the political system, whose work I directed until the spring of 1968. The second time came after the Soviet military intervention in August 1968, in response to which I resigned from all my political functions 3 months later. But I shall be dealing with this in more detail later on.

For reform Communists in the political power structure as well, the limitations on the whole became a way of life. Even when seeking to objectively analyze and determine what the society required and desired for its development, they first determined what would be realistically acceptable to the party. This produced self-censorship not only in what they said but in the very way they thought. If any questions were clearly unacceptable to those in power, they would, as a matter of course, not give them a second thought but assume they were unrealizable until such a time as they could at least be broached.

For this reason, these reform Communists often differed quite distinctly from those groups operating outside the apparatus of power politics. Those reform Communists who were only active in cultural life—writers, artists, journalists, scientists and other academics—did not perceive the inability to realize certain ideas through these organs and apparatuses as a limiting factor in their thinking. Naturally they continued to persevere in practical politics, but they expected results to come from another direction, above all from outside pressure on the power structure: from public opinion, expressed through various social groups (usually from the ranks of the intelligentsia) and through various organizations only very loosely connected with the power structure, such as the unions of writers and artists, and scientific, academic, and other educational institutions.

Thus the general political orientation of this group of reform Communists was more democratic and radical than that of groups inside the power structure itself. The contrast between *Literární noviny* and the party press in the 1960s is a good example of this. And it often led to conflicts between this more radical group and the political authorities, with the reform Communists inside the power structure caught in the middle. But such differences between the reform Communists were more a matter of style than substance.

What did my internal political efforts actually accomplish in the 1960s? The legal commission, to which I was the secretary after 1964, did not alter existing conditions in the state apparatus, nor did it have a great influence on the creation and application of the law.* Between 1964-67, however, it did help to focus increasing attention on problems of law and legality—raising questions that came to the forefront in 1968—and it had even managed to have certain legal norms democratized, and so on. As a leading functionary in this commission, I and my opinions received official blessing, as it were.

Apart from this, and from acting as advisor to the highest organs and functionaries and participating in dozens of different "working groups" that prepared the documents upon which various decisions and resolutions were based, I was also an official interpreter of ideology and policy, insofar as matters of the state, democracy, law, and the political system in general were concerned. I lectured at hundreds of different training courses and meetings (between 1964 and 1966 I

---

* The legal commission was one of several commissions in the Central Committee set up in the 1960s to act as advisory bodies. There was also an economic, an ideological, an agricultural, and a youth commission. The commissions were chaired by Central Committee secretaries; in the case of the legal commission by V. Koucký. Members of the commissions included leading functionaries of the Central Committee apparatus in the given field and employees of scholarly and scientific institutes and universities. These commissions dealt with practically all the important proposals passed on to the presidium. Among other things, their importance lay in the fact that they stood between the presidium and its own apparatus in the Central Committee, for it was the commissions who would transmit, with their own interpretation, Central Committee proposals directly to the presidium.

often gave twenty such lectures a month) for party archivists, for regional and district functionaries, and for workers in the state apparatus, including the police and army. I wrote dozens of brochures published by the party and state for internal use. Thus thousands of party and state functionaries knew my opinions, and most were received with sympathy.

The ideological and political concepts that I tried to propagate in all these ways among party and state functionaries, and which, at the time, the mid-60s, in fact became officially propagated in the CPC, can be summarized as follows:

The experience of the USSR has showed that the victory of socialist relationships in society creates a great many new problems. With the end of the class struggle—i.e., with no one left to repress as a class—and the dictatorship of the proletariat transformed into an all-people's state, the main problem becomes how to give proper expression to the needs and interests of the whole of society and to ensure that the partial, particular needs and interests of people are not given precedence over their overall, general needs.

Formerly, it was a very simple matter to decide what was in the interests of socialism: it was the limitation and liquidation of private ownership and the class relationships associated with it. No special knowledge or experience was necessary: "class consciousness" was enough. Anyone could recognize an unnationalized factory or an uncollectivized farm. But how were we to decide whether it is in the interests of society as a whole to increase chemical production by 5 or 15 percent? Is it in the interests of the working class to produce more corn or more peas? Which serves the general interests of socialist society better, the waltz or jazz?

Such questions are nonsensical, and attempting to govern society in such a way is harmful. What is and is not genuinely in the interests of the whole of society under socialism can only be determined if two conditions are met: all decisions must be made on the basis of qualified expertise, and society itself must have the opportunity to say what it thinks its own interests really are. These two principles must be applied throughout the political system as a whole.

In economics, as in culture, we must allow specialists to make their opinions felt. Without education, without expertise, it is almost impossible today to determine what "the interests of the working class" are. And, at the same time, it is essential that all organizations in the political system have the opportunity to express their points of view on what they think state policies should and should not include. The main point here is to insure that the trades union, the youth organization, and other special interest groups and organizations have a genuine say in what they consider to be in their interest. The interests of society at large can only be determined properly if partial and particular interests are taken into consideration. This is also true for local interests, and therefore the role of local government must grow as well.

Each individual must also have the chance to express his interest, his needs, and thus his opinions. In this regard law plays an essential role. Law cannot be understood as a collection of arbitrary decrees; it must guarantee that those with certain interests (both groups and individuals) can express those interests: if this possibility is suppressed, the law will have been denied. This principle cannot be upheld, however, in cases where the particular interest goes against the interests of society at large, but such cases will be expressly laid down in the law. Only those limitations which are enshrined in law can limit the people's rights.

The Communist party was the leading social force during the class struggle. But this leading role is not something, ipso facto, guaranteed for all time. The Communist party had to continually reearn and reestablish its leading role in the new conditions. If it makes mistakes, if it fails to push for the interests of the whole of society, then it weakens its leading role. The party itself must make it possible for people to express as well those needs and interests that the party does not consider relevant for society at large. It must be ready to explain why it does not agree. Ruling by decree is not sufficient in the long run. It is equally wrong for the party to attempt to usurp the roles of the state and the social organizations, which must remain independent. The role of the party is that of a conductor, and the conductor ought never to try to play instead of the orchestra.

I had no illusions about these being particularly scientific ideas, not even when I was propagating them inside the Communist party. This collection of ideological and political theses is wide open to attack from any consistently democratic position as well as from the standpoint of Marx's own theory. But that was not the point. What was important was the fact that those thousands of Communist functionaries on whom the totalitarian dictatorship of Czechoslovakia in the 1960s depended gradually became critical of the dictatorship and began to turn against it. Ideologically inconsistent though this attitude may have been, it was still critical, after all. And precisely because it had been presented in a form accessible to those people who had served that dictatorship for years, it was effective. The idea that development along the old lines was no longer possible, that political reform was essential in the very interests of socialism and communism, gradually became generally accepted inside the structures of political power.

I could not see myself devoting so many years of my life to disseminating that kind of ideology today, among the functionaries of the Husák regime. Such an effort would be doomed from the start, for the vast majority of those people today care nothing about socialism, nor the interests of society at large, nor even about the "historical mission" of the Communist party: they are only concerned with their own power and the benefits derived therefrom. Clearly in time they too will be compelled to reform the system, but it will be out of concern to maintain their power and benefits rather than out of a faith in the communist ideology. Before 1968, however, I was convinced that it did mean something to those tens of thousands of Communists that they were genuinely looking to solve the problems not only out of self-interest but also out of commitment to socialist and communist ideals and to their possible realization in society. I was ultimately proven right about this in 1968, and then further in 1970 when about half-a-million Communists refused to surrender their reform ideas and had to be expelled from the party.

Had it not been for the fact that a considerable number of CPC functionaries and members had already, several years before 1968, seen the necessity for reform from their practical experience and, moreover, from their intellectual and ideological development—in other words had they not been prepared for a gradual democratization of the political system—those few months of the Prague Spring could never have occurred. For the political success of the Prague Spring was possible only because both the movement of society "from below" and the movement of the CPC "from above" coincided and to a certain extent combined. And without those several years during which the ideas of reform communism were active inside the very power structure of the Communist party itself, that would have been impossible.

The reform Communists who were exerting an influence within the power structure naturally could not have done so without the knowledge of the top party leadership, led by Antonín Novotný. I think to discuss the entire period of Novotný's rule as one of Stalinist darkness to which Dubček's reform policies suddenly brought light after January 1968 distorts the actual situation in the CPC in the sixties. It becomes particularly paradoxical if the Novotný era is evaluated in the black light of Husák's leadership, which has employed methods in society and even in the CPC itself that Novotný, in the final years of his rule, could never even have considered, let alone used. Moreover, many publicists in the West oversimplify matters. For example, they consider the present state of affairs in Hungary the pinnacle of liberalism, while associating the entire Novotný era in Czechoslovakia with the dark ages of Stalinism. In reality, however, even the most liberal fruits of "Kadarization" in Hungary in the late 1970s do not diverge from the character of the Novotný regime in 1964–1967.

The economic reform called "the new system of economic management" and associated chiefly with the name of Ota Šik was not, in Novotný's time, some form of heresy conducted surreptitiously, but had the blessings of the party leadership and was implemented as official party and state policy; though the policy of economic reform was inconsistent, out of fear that it would lead to political complications and things would then "get out of hand." It was Husák's leadership of the CPC that condemned the entire reform as "revisionist Šikism" and banned all discussion of it, despite the fact that for pragmatic reasons some of the elements of Šik's reform remain in effect to this day.

After 1956, Communist intellectuals were periodically exposed to various forms of harassment: they were criticized in various campaigns and a few were occasionally prohibited from publishing or working in cultural or academic institutions. But even that, for the most part, was only temporary, and the victims of such harassments returned to public life after a time, and even when they were under the heaviest fire they were never, with a few minor exceptions, excluded from doing some form of intellectual work for which they were qualified. Although limited by censorship, *Literární noviny* and other magazines whose political line was unequivocally critical of the regime and in favor of reform communism came out. Hundreds of writers, artists, historians, sociologists, economists, lawyers, and philosophers—who since 1970 have been supporting themselves as stokers, laborers, window-washers, and God knows what else—were sitting in the cultural, academic, and scientific institutions working away on various aspects of the one grand theme: a critique of the Novotný regime. And all that was taking place during Novotný's rule.

Does this mean that Antonín Novotný was himself a reform Communist? I think not. He was a genuine leftover from the Stalinist period, but his role was not unequivocally negative. It was rather more complex and contradictory than it might at first appear. And the same can be said of some other people in the party leadership and in the party and state apparatuses during the sixties. After January 1968, the reform policies became clearly linked with the names of some top party leaders from the Novotný era, in particular with Alexander Dubček and O. Černík. Yet 1968 also swept others in Novotný's leadership from the scene—men like J. Hendrych and V. Koucký, both Central Committee secretaries—who, I am personally convinced, were more responsible for making the development of reform communism inside the CPC possible than some of those whom the reform elevated into leading positions or left there. Like every political coup, the Dubček reform of 1968 did not always settle its accounts on the basis of merit—far from it—but very often according to personal animosities, or personal indebtedness. And that too was one of the reasons for its ultimate downfall.

Antonín Novotný belonged to the "old guard" of Communists. He had been a member of the CPC since its foundation in 1921 and a regional party functionary before the Second World War. He survived the war in one of the worst Nazi concentration camps, Mauthausen. And, according to prisonmates, he resolved there to have nothing whatsoever to do with politics when the war was over, but rather devote himself to his family, house, and garden. Needless to say, he did not keep his resolution, and in 1945 he became leading secretary of the regional party committee in Prague.

I remember Novotný from that time, in 1947–1950. Most district functionaries of the CPC saw him more as an administrator than a politician. The chairman of the regional organization, J. Krosnář, was an authoritative figure, and Novotný was surpassed in political insight and organizational abilities by Krosnář's deputies, among them František Kriegel. There were many minor everyday incidents indicating that Novotný was not a man of penetrating intelligence.

Novotný's ascent to the secretariat of the Central Committee was connected with his activity in "uncovering the enemies within the party" and his zeal in the preparations for the trial against the secretary-general of the CPC, Rudolf Slanský, in 1951–52.

Novotný may well have been born without some basic human

qualities. During my brief period in the procurator general's office in Prague, I saw some official documents that indicated an incredible thing: after the execution of the defendants in the Slánský trial, their property was sold off cheap to surviving high-level functionaries, and on this occasion the Novotný family (Mrs. Božena Novotná personally) bought the bedclothes and china tea service belonging to Vlada Clementis!

The thought that the first secretary of the ruling party and the head of state slept between sheets belonging to a man whom he had helped send to the gallows is something quite incredible in twentieth-century Europe. Nevertheless it was true. And it was not as if the Novotný's did not know what they were doing. I talked about this matter to Lida Clementis in 1956, and I learned that Božena Novotná had admired the Clementis's china tea service when she and her husband had been for a visit back in the days when Clementis was foreign minister.

I am not bringing this literally dirty linen into the light of day after twenty years merely to make Novotný look bad. I do think, however, that it says more than a lengthy political analysis would about the kind of moral responsibility Novotný might have felt regarding the political trials of the Stalin era. What kind of human background could a man have had who in 1954, as head of the party, oversaw several political trials, including one in which the death sentence was handed down?

At the same time, in 1954, Novotný's niece, who was then a student in Moscow, told some close acquaintances how Novotný, having coffee with her father, had held his head in his hands and sobbed complainingly: "I'm not up to this job, I can't do it, I haven't got what it takes." I believe he was sincere and that he was tormented by fears that he might be harming socialism and the working class by occupying a function for which he did not feel sufficiently qualified. Purchasing Clementis's sheets, however, had nothing to do, in his mind, with the interests of the working class, and, consequently, he never gave it a second thought.

Novotný may have been a bureaucrat capable of criminal acts, but originally, at any rate, he had been a working class functionary. He represented a highly specific combination of true belief in the correctness of communist doctrine and its advantages for workers, with political hucksterism and a talent for bureaucratic intrigue. He never lost the former but it was the latter that increasingly dictated his conduct.

When he was at the height of his power he had a "recreational center" built on an artificial lake on the Vltava river near the Orlík castle. In an area of land surrounded by fences and guarded by police, there are modern villas outfitted according to Western European standards for the recreational use of individual presidium members, the Soviet ambassador, and other potentates. Standing apart, on a stretch of higher ground off by itself, is a house, then referred to by members of the apparatus as "the Eagle's nest," built for the personal use of Antonín Novotný. But it is not modeled after the mansions of Western capitalists: it is an imitation peasant's cottage. In front of the cottage stands a gigantic beer barrel with a table and chairs inside. And at this table Novotný used to spend his Sundays with his closest associates (not in terms of their official positions but in personal terms), and he passed the time after his own taste—playing cards. This was, of course, a form of inverse snobbery.

In the final years of his rule, Novotný was convinced not only that he was up to his job but that he was doing it exceptionally well. Once in a private conversation, he formulated his political credo thus: "People have to like you. They needn't agree with you—but the important thing is that they respect you. And in the party the main thing is: don't let any opposition form to your left. Opposition on the right doesn't matter, but don't let any groups form on the left."

It is extremely simple, but given the realities of power in "real socialism" it is by no means stupid. In such a system, it is clear that one can govern undemocratically, without regard for people's opinions, but it is also clear that there are certain limits to the people's toleration, limits beyond which the people would lose their respect for power, either because it has proven incapable of guaranteeing their most elementary needs, or because it has proven weak and unable to defend its own interests. And the ideological credo of that party bureaucracy—not to permit opposition from the left; in other words, to be itself the only possible variation of leftist politics in the eyes of the people—is merely an old idea of Machiavelli's adapted to new conditions: states maintain themselves by maintaining the idea that gave rise to them.

Novotný was undeniably a pragmatic politician who made no pretense of contributing to theory or ideology. Nevertheless, he viewed party ideology as a kind of general criterion for conducting practical politics. What this ideology's "laws and lessons" amounted to in his mind, however, is another question. It was undoubtedly a conglomerate of the vulgar, official brochure dogmas. But the important thing here is that this primitive, essentially authoritarian person did not ultimately set himself up as the final judge of the correctness of ideas or actions, but rather he acknowledged the existence of criteria that were above him, the criteria of certain ideas and principles, and not merely the criteria of power. He was still an old-fashioned Communist functionary for whom party ideology had a deeply personal significance: his whole life, the formation of his personality, everything he valued personally stemmed from his subjugation to party ideology. I know personally many functionaries like that, people for whom "the party is everything" and who, even after their expulsion from that same party, still declare: "I am what the party made me" (a statement full of unintentional charm, of course, for in the ironic sense it is profoundly true).

People of this type, however, will only accept the actual contents of an ideology as binding when they become official and are entrenched in party regulations and directives. In the name of party ideology, people like this can behave like criminals and not consider it a crime because they have absolutely no value system beyond what is implicit in their ideology. When the ideology officially changes, they, likewise, change with it and are sincerely surprised at the notion of their being censured for their former conduct. Ladislav Kopřiva, an old Communist functionary (in my opinion akin to Novotný) who as minister of security actively prepared the staged trials of the early fifties, declared before a party commission in 1956: "Yes, those arrests [of the early fifties] were against the law, but you didn't worry about that in those days. It wasn't until later that they got round to making the regulation that the laws had to be obeyed."

If, however, a person of that type stands at the top of a power hierarchy, he will be in a position to prevent changes in the ideology that might damn his own past. Even so, this may not always be the case. And there were several such instances that influenced Novotný.

Under Khrushchev the new, anti-Stalinist ideology became the official ideology of the Soviet Union, and both Novotný and the entire CPC were at the mercy of this higher authority. Even Novotný the bureaucrat was under pressure to change his orientation. While at the end of the 1950s he had not been able as party leader to shift the blame for the political terror on others without jeopardizing his position, this factor too changed in the early 1960s. Two important members of Gottwald's leadership, A. Zápotocký and V. Kopecký, died. Rudolf Barák, who tried to exploit Novotný's involvement in the political trials to his own advantage during a power struggle inside the presidium, was sent to prison by Novotný with Khrushchev's blessing. Novotný replaced these men in the presidium with supporters—J. Hendrych, D. Kolder, and M. Chudík—and in both the new secretariat secretary, V. Koucký, and the new minister of the interior, L. Štrougal, he had supporters. Thus the situation in the CPC leadership changed to the detriment of those personally responsible for the political trials of the 1950s, and it freed Novotný to conduct a more thorough critique of those years and a more thorough rehabilitation of the political trials victims, with the hope that his personal position would, as a result, be strengthened rather than weakened. Thus, in 1963, blame was squarely placed on the three remaining members of the Gottwald leadership: V. Široký, K. Bacílek, and B. Koehler. And the three new functionaries who replaced them in the presidium of the party were Alexander Dubček, J. Lenárt, and M. Vaculík.

It was consequently not until 1963 that Novotný managed to establish the kind of power base in his own leadership that Khrushchev had already achieved in Moscow by the late fifties when he disposed of the "anti-party group" of Molotov, Malenkov, Bulganin and Kaganovich, that is, the majority of Stalin's former politburo. Thus, however paradoxical it may sound, the height of Novotný's power coincided with his eliminating the old Gottwald-Stalinist clique in the party leadership, and it was only then that Khrushchev's policies ceased to pose a threat to his own position, thus ending what must have been a long nightmare of seven years (1956–63). Now he had his own leadership, composed not of people who had brought him to power but whom he himself had appointed.

This new party leadership, thus quietly installed, took its most important political step when the third five-year plan collapsed in its first year (1963). It dealt with the economic crisis not by attempting to return, as before, to the old, discredited methods, but by trying to be more consistent and go further in implementing the "new system for managing the national economy." The essence of the new line consisted in dismantling bureaucratic centralism in favor of a more independent state enterprise, which would enable the mechanism of the marketplace to work and increase productivity and efficiency. In this way, the dictatorial system in the field of economics was effectively disrupted, fostering gradual reforms in other areas of social life. Even the personnel in the party leadership itself changed to the advantage of people who supported economic reform: O. Černík was appointed to the presidium and L. Štrougal became the secretary of agriculture to the Central Committee.

Thus several years before 1968, Novotný's leadership already consisted of a majority of people who were not closed to the idea that further development required changes and reforms. And the same applies to many in the party apparatus whose job it was to serve those leaders. The very idea that reform was necessary, the very conviction that the old system of directing society must change, dominated the atmosphere of those years inside the political power apparatuses as well. Of course, the very necessity of reform did not mean it was viewed positively. In fact, reform was viewed as something that could, if not properly limited, pose a threat either to the power of the leadership and their apparatus or to most of their members. On the whole this presented a considerable barrier to the implementation of any practical reforms, and it led to a state where the reforms were merely deliberated (as far as possible not in public) rather than actually executed. Most frequently, the main effort went into assembling arguments to demonstrate the impracticality of certain reforms, either at a given moment or in the form proposed. But neither the leadership of the party nor its apparatus really doubted the inevitability of reforms, even in the political system itself.

I believe that Antonín Novotný himself shared this conviction. As soon as he had managed, not merely to survive, but to strengthen his position as party leader on the basis of Khrushchev's ideological and political orientation, he became genuinely committed to this orientation. It, and no longer his Stalinist ideological past, was his sole criteria for action. His conversion to the Khrushchevian ideology and policies, however, had come too late. In late 1964, Khrushchev was deposed.

It is a well-known fact that, at the time, Novotný and his presidium did an unheard of thing: they expressed critical objections to Brezhnev's handling of the putsch against Khrushchev. This protest is still frequently presented today as more of a comic curiosity than a serious political act. My personal view, however, is that this "revolt" of a vassal as traditionally obedient to Moscow as Novotný was demonstrates Novotný's personal commitment to Khrushchev's line.

After 1964, a paradoxical situation thus arose. At a time when Brezhnev's camarilla was increasingly abandoning the Khrushchevian line, forcing it into the background and restoring more and more elements of Stalinism, it happened that under Novotný's government, generally considered to be a willing puppet of Moscow (there was a popular rhyme that went, "I'm Antonín Novotný, I'll do what you want of me"), anti-Stalinist reform Communist criticism was first fully developed not only in Czechoslovak society but also inside the CPC and the power structure. This necessarily reinforced the hidden conflicts between Novotný and Moscow.

Novotný instinctively felt Brezhnev's disfavor to be dangerous, and in 1967 he probably sought independent support in Moscow: he became close to the group of marshals around the commander in chief of the Warsaw Pact, Jakubovsky, who stood closer to Shelest in Moscow than he did to Brezhnev. Brezhnev's own position in Moscow in 1967 was uncertain, and therefore some of the vassals were backing other groups in the Moscow power hierarchy. Once again, self-preservation began to outweigh Novotný's ideological commitment. He attempted once more to "tighten the screw" in domestic politics, and from the summer of 1967 he moved against writers, reform Communist intellectuals, and his own critics in the Central Committee.

There was a group of functionaries in the army and the security forces under Novotný who took their lead from the "hawks" in Moscow. These people were represented in the Central Committee by Miroslav Mamula, head of the armed forces and security department, and their influence was beginning to grow. Brezhnev was clearly following these developments with growing disapproval, and when he went to Prague in December 1967 on Novotný's invitation—presumably to support Novotný against opposition in the Central Committee—Brezhnev pronounced his famous *"Eto vashe dyelo"* ("It's your business"), thus giving free rein to those forces opposing Novotný. Since it's unlikely that Brezhnev had any intention of facilitating the Prague Spring, we can only assume that his concern was to have Novotný ousted simply because Novotný was no longer a sufficiently pliable and suitable instrument for his personal policies.*

---

* High potentates are naturally always accompanied on such visits by a group of their aides. From conversations of Brezhnev's aides with Novotný's aides, I know that before his departure for Prague, Brezhnev had asked his advisor on Czechoslovakian affairs, "Who is really Number Two over there?" The aide, though relatively well-informed about conditions in Prague, could only say that in the given situation it would be impossible to name anyone in particular. "Very well," Brezhnev replied, and there the matter ended. He obviously concluded that ultimately it didn't matter who succeeded Novotný. Nor did he change his mind on this even after personal conversations with CPC leaders in Prague. That is the source of his condescending comment: "It's your business."

Novotný was an uneducated man who, as compensation, possessed a wide range of practical knowledge, acquired in the course of his work. Foreign words in his speeches had to be written into the text phonetically so that he wouldn't cause embarrassment by mispronouncing them. This gave Novotný an inferiority complex of a kind quite frequent in uneducated people. He was vengeful towards anyone who remarked on his lack of education. Nevertheless this complex had its positive side: he respected education and was convinced that learning and science were indispensable to communism. He could be crude to the intelligentsia, and he could even use his position of power to bully them, but on the whole he respected them. It also flattered him to associate with top members of the intelligentsia. He held meetings with writers and artists—and it was clearly no accident that he did so in Lány, where President T. G. Masaryk had met with intellectuals before the war.

Novotný was often the enemy of reform Communist intellectuals, particularly when they were disobedient and didn't respect his political power. At the same time, however, he made an effort to win them over rather than suppress them, to have them join forces with the "politics of the party" rather than exclude them from political activity altogether. He wanted the intellectuals both to adorn his government and to be an "instrument in the building of communism." And his policies towards intellectuals would swing from praise, preference, and bribery to threats and repressions, depending on whether he felt they were assisting his aims or thwarting them.

There were two secretaries of the Central Committee who were chiefly responsible for executing his policies toward the intellectuals, Jiří Hendrych and Vladimír Koucký. Unlike Novotný, they had a certain education—both of them were university drop-outs. They also possessed a greater natural intelligence. In my opinion, Koucký was by far the most intelligent member of the party leadership under Novotný: he had once studied logic and mathematics and was capable of abstract thought, and he had command of several languages and was more cultivated and worldly than anyone else around him. Both men had begun their Communist careers as journalists, Hendrych before the war and Koucký in the illegal *Rudé právo* during the war. They were about thirty in 1945, and in the 1950s, under Stalin, they were not yet members of the party leadership. They gained a more independent influence on party policies after 1956, and they gambled their political careers on Khrushchev's ideological and political line.

Both men were among those who in the 1960s formulated No-votný's policies with all their contradictions, but they certainly had more responsibility than most for those policies evolving as Khrush-chevian policies. Naturally, they were "Novotný people"—he had appointed them to their functions in the upper party bureaucracy—but they were not without a political future if Novotný were to leave the scene. On the contrary, in terms of age and politics, they could only have gained by Novotný's demise, provided, of course, that the general political continuity in the CPC had remained unbroken.

The ideology of reform communism in the CPC was spread during the 1960s not only with their awareness but also with their support. Without Hendrych's direct patronage, Radovan Richta and his re-search team could never have developed the ideological vision of the scientific and technological revolution, thus influencing official party ideology in the spirit of reform. Without the support of Hendrych and Koucký, I too could never have propagated my notions of re-forming the political system, and official support for the work of the team that developed the general conceptions of political reform in 1967 would not have been forthcoming. The ideas developed by these two teams in fact formed the basis for the CPC Action Program in the spring of 1968; hence, had it not been for the work of Hendrych and Koucký during the Novotný years, this program would not have been created in the form that it was.

Why then did the Prague Spring sweep Hendrych and Koucký off the stage while leaving untouched men like D. Kolder and L. Strou-gal—two other secretaries under Novotný—and J. Lenart, who was Prime Minister, and raising Alexander Dubček and O. Černík to the role of national heroes? I think the answer is a simple one. The first phase of the coup inside the party, in which Novotný was deposed, took place in a manner appropriate to a dictatorship and its cabinet politics: behind the closed doors of the secretariats. It was a power struggle at the top levels of the party bureaucracy. Like all such coups, those people most objectionable to the public had to be sacri-ficed for the sake of those who, because of their unfamiliarity to the public, were less objectionable. Hendrych and Koucký had worked for years in the area of official party ideology. Unpopular restrictive measures taken against the press, writers, and culture in general, and publicly known cases of suppressed criticism were all directly con-nected with their names. It was clear that the new leadership would not gain the confidence of the oppositional intelligentsia in the party—and that included in part the journalists—if it failed to get rid of these publicly discredited individuals. Moreover, the political fall of Hendrych and Koucký distracted attention from the career profiles of several others—men such as Vasil Bilak, Alois Indra, and M. Jakeš—whose ascension did not arouse opposition from those who considered the fall of Hendrych and Koucký as their personal triumph.

I came to know V. Koucký quite well during my four years on the legal commission of the Central Committee. I recall a number of incidents where he was quite obviously acting against his own opinions and conscience. This man, a great admirer of playwright Vaclav Havel's work—I remember particularly his praise for *The Memorandum*—not only publicly condemned to death many literary works and films in the name of official ideology but before the opening of several exhibitions he personally removed "ideologically unsound" paintings from the walls. Yet the walls of his flat were adorned not with the work of the socialist realists but of modern artists.

Koucký was perhaps the only man in the CPC leadership who as early as the mid-sixties had great expectations for developments in the Communist Party of Italy, and he hoped that in association with what today is known as Eurocommunism, reform communism in Czechoslovakia might gain strong support. Mutual support among European Communist parties, regardless of whether or not they were in power, was for him connected with greater room for reformist developments within the CPC. For the public, however, Koucký was the standard-bearer of pro-Moscow "proletarian internationalism."

Koucký sacrificed everything, his character and his personal conscience, to his political career. For years he worked at becoming a full member, rather than merely a secretary, of the presidium. In order to reach that final rung on the party ladder, he played the flunky to Novotný and did the dirty work in culture, science, and among the intelligentsia. His notion of politics was so fused in his mind with cabinet politics that he no longer saw the limits beyond which it was impossible to make amends for what he had done in the interests of his career. It was the limit beyond which the public ceased to care about what someone's real convictions and conscience were, since he was willing to do practically anything against them.

People who conducted themselves in politics with an obvious regard for their own consciences looked upon Koucký as an extrovert, whereas he thought of himself as an introvert. His was a closed personality, but the decisive motivations for his actions were largely external, which is precisely what characterizes the extrovert type.

In April 1968, before the Central Committee session that was to decide on his removal as a secretary, Koucký talked to me about whether he ought to resign voluntarily. From what he said it was clear to me that he did not comprehend his situation: why now, when reform was the big issue, something that he too had desired and helped pave the way for, should he resign? Why now, when the international aspects of CPC policies would be far more important than before, should he, with his experience and contacts in that very field, be the one to leave? He spoke with great insight on the importance of the international context of the new Dubček politics, and he, indisputably, saw the fundamental problems in that direction more clearly than anyone in the new leadership, including Dubček himself. He quite genuinely did not understand why he could not stay on as secretary for international affairs only because Communists in scientific institutions, writers, artists, and journalists had an aversion to him, or that he rubbed a few Slovaks the wrong way (for even in his former positions on some of the Slovak questions he had served as an instrument of Novotný's policies).

I advised him to resign, but I did so with mixed feelings. I knew that he wasn't a die-hard Stalinist and that he might well work hard for reform. But I also knew that his secretary position was untenable. He resigned, and he was shifted onto a side-track as ambassador to Moscow, which, because relations between Prague and Moscow were not handled through the embassies, and because he did not have the necessary confidence of either side, meant being shunted out of political life altogether.

But it was clear that even after 1968 Koucký still understood nothing essential about his own past. In the Central Committee session in January 1969 he was the first to move for the annulment of the presidium resolution of August 21, 1968, condemning the Soviet military intervention as a contravention of international law. I am entirely convinced that he did *not* view the intervention as conforming with international law. But in this way he was hoping to buy his way back into politics. However, denying his own morality again did not gain the support of those who had likewise denied theirs, if they had any to begin with, but who, unlike him, already held power. For such people, Koucký could only mean more competition in the struggle for the upper echelons.

Like Koucký, J. Hendrych also ended up a victim of his own scheming. He was a master of political compromise—but in the corridors of power, not in public politics. In the party apparatus he was known as a man who could "make a billiard ball out of a hedgehog," someone who knew how to blunt and round off the sharp edges of conflicts. In public, however—and that includes the party public—Hendrych was the main buttress and implacable representative of Novotný's rule in the CPC. And after January 1968, he could no longer blunt the sharp barbs on which he found himself impaled. But Hendrych understood his situation better than Koucký, and in his own way he reconciled himself to it and retired from public life. And the Soviet invasion didn't change this.

Now, when former associates—reform Communists who are now window washers, laborers, and invalid pensioners—meet Hendrych on the streets of Prague, he stops to chat amiably with them but never fails to end the conversation with some little dig, such as, "Still cursing the sixties?" During the savage campaign against the signatories of Charter 77, one of the signatories met Hendrych on the street. Hendrych's appraisal of Charter 77 was very succinct: "Haven't you had enough yet? You're all a bunch of Don Quixotes!"

Life is more colorful and paradoxical than it appears later in simplified, schematic accounts. Reform communism in the CPC in the 1960s was not a unified, undifferentiated trend, nor was it a movement defined by opposition to Novotný's party leadership. The reform orientation of the party semiofficially governed the atmosphere of that time inside the very power structures of the dictatorship as well.

I experienced the Prague Spring inside those structures of power. I not only saw them from up close and inside, but I also tried to reshape them. That world of power had a hand in the Prague Spring, but in reality it was a less dignified role than one might suppose from the words that were being bandied about in the press and on television.

CHAPTER 2

PRAGUE SPRING IN THE LEADERSHIP

Journalists in 1968, having to interpret history in the making in time for next morning's edition, devised an easy shorthand to identify and classify the Communists: they were either progressive, centrist, or conservative.

I was usually classified along with the centrists, which didn't particularly bother me because I knew why: I defended the right of the state to intervene in the freedom of the press when the interests of state policies required it and it was in accordance with the law as determined by the courts. I was also against the formation of new political parties in the spring of 1968. I wanted a party congress called as soon as possible and elections held, although many felt this would prematurely bring the stormy development of the democratic movement to an end and thus should be postponed, and so on.

Later, shortly after the Soviet tanks had steam-rollered through the Czechoslovak political scene and more than one apparent boulder had proved to be a heap of mud, I suddenly began to follow with amusement the development of some of the men who, a short while before, had been universally recognized as "progressivists": Oldřich Černík, Čestmír Císař, Gustav Husák, and also Radovan Richta and Jiří Šotola, not to mention many "progressivists" in Slovakia.

It bothered me then and it still bothers me today that there is so little understanding in Bohemia for politics as the art of the possible, precisely in a situation where the native soil, befouled by long years of misgovernment, could scarcely be transformed overnight into an "earthly paradise to human eyes," as the national anthem describes it. It's upsetting to see so many intelligent, honest, and diligent people squander the opportunity simply to make what improvements are possible, having their sights set on an impossible utopia. And then in the aftermath of all this, they sift through the ruins of their hope, wondering remorsefully whether things might not have been different, if only. . . .

But at the outset I would like to say frankly that today, almost ten years after the Prague Spring, I really have no delusions about having had the right recipe for everything at the time. I am not at all persuaded today that my goals were feasible even had things gone as I then thought they could. Chances are that Czechoslovakia would have become less a political democracy than I had hoped was realistically possible, and reform communism would have proven to be a less than ideal solution. But, even so, perhaps Czechs and Slovaks would now be in a better position to seek real solutions—of course only over a long period of time. And their lives—their normal, everyday lives in which, after all, problems of world-shattering historical significance are by no means the only ones—might perhaps conform more to life in late twentieth-century Europe than it does.

One never knows. Perhaps even limited reforms would have provoked the same "fraternal assistance" from Moscow. Had that been the case, however, things would in fact be even worse than they are today, for the nation would have no memory of a time when the impossible seemed within reach. It would only be quite clear that Moscow would use force to crush not just attempts to create a pluralistic democracy in which Communists would have to submit to democratic electoral laws but even the kind of reforms where Communists would remain securely in power, but without the kind of totalitarian dictatorship they endorse in the Kremlin.

But enough prophesying and back to reality. In any case, I want to present 1968 as I have the years leading up to it—not from an objective analysis, but from a personal perspective. As it has up to now, my angle of vision will only take in a small segment of the social and political reality of that time, and I will select, from an entirely personal perspective, only those things that seem important to me.

The fall of Antonín Novotný came as a surprise to me. I was not expecting any changes in the leadership to take place until sometime before the next party congress, which was scheduled for 1970. Decisions were traditionally made just before the congresses, and the congresses themselves merely ratified these changes and allowed the newly-established ruler to create a new Central Committee in his own image. With this idea in mind, then, I planned the work of my research team in the Academy of Sciences in early 1967. I reckoned that by the time the congress came round in 1970 the team should have completed conceptual proposals for the new leadership that would stimulate the development of the political system in the direction of democratization.

In January 1968, this important team had not quite a year's work behind it. Nevertheless, it had already developed certain general conceptions of the problems that were to be theoretically, and ultimately politically, dealt with as accompaniments to the already-initiated economic reforms.* It was clear to me at the time that if political reform were to have any real meaning, it had to dismantle the system of totalitarian political dictatorship, and yet this could not be accomplished, practically speaking, unless the hegemony of the Communist party was maintained until the mechanisms of a democratic system were already secured. And that, of course, was no easy task.

I realize that some people see such a task as *a priori* impossible, an absurd attempt to square the circle. However, I consider, to this day, such a task generally possible: if Franco's fascist dictatorship could be reformed into a democratic political system without a popular uprising, then it must also be possible in the case of an originally-Stalinist dictatorial system. It requires, however—as it did in the case of Spain—a very favorable constellation of domestic and international conditions. And from the economic, sociological, legal, and historical viewpoint, very many of the domestic conditions in Czechoslovakia in 1967 seemed to promise the success of such an enterprise.

From the economic viewpoint, the economic reforms already introduced had created conditions for changes in the political system at four main points. For one, a gigantic state apparatus for directing every aspect of economic life was no longer necessary and could be gradually converted, except for the organs responsible for long-term central planning, into an administrative apparatus for enterprises and interenterprise associations. Closely related to this was the possibility of phasing out the ruling party's regulation of the economy. On the one hand, that would vastly reduce the mammoth party apparatus, whose command of the economy through directives comprised about two-thirds of its activities, and, on the other hand, it would

---

* There is no room here to expound the theoretical considerations that emerged from the team's activity. I discuss them in my book, *The Czechoslovak Attempt at Reform, 1968 (Československý pokus o reformu 1968)* (Cologne: Index, 1975), see especially pp. 54–107.

reorient Communist party activities as a social organism toward political policies and programs. Third, by transforming socialist enterprises into independent economic units bound to the laws of the marketplace, the economic reforms created incentives to increase productivity and the role of professionally trained and qualified personnel. Professional qualification became more useful than "political reliability," something which must eventually subvert the mechanism of totalitarian dictatorship at its very foundations. If the dictatorship were no longer able to tie people's livelihoods and security to "political reliability," one of its basic pillars of power would be gone. And, finally, with wage earners directly exposed, under the new system, to the negative consequences of bad management, insofar as the size of their premiums (their share of the profits) is at stake, they had to be given the right, in some form or other, to have a say in the management. Thus there was pressure for new roles for the trades union and for the development of workers' self-management in both the enterprise and interenterprise components of the economy.

From the sociological viewpoint, there was no longer any social class or stratum that, by virtue of its status, was in fundamental conflict with any other class or social stratum and would therefore require a totalitarian dictatorship to defend its interests. This includes the bureaucracy, taken as a whole, even with its privileges. The bureaucracy would have survived equally well under a democratic system, and, in some respects, with the criterion of "political reliability" eliminated, it would be better off. The only parts of the bureaucracy obligated to the totalitarian dictatorship were those directly related to political power, and they were a relatively significant social force only because of their power, certainly not in terms of number or their importance to the social system. The relative social equality provided far more favorable soil for a political democracy than ever before. From the demographic viewpoint, the population was mostly from a generation formed in the post-1948 social and political conditions. The pre-1948 generation of social and political leaders (i.e., those who were in their forties in 1948) were by now at retirement age. This considerably reduced the possibility of old conflicts between the former victors and the vanquished being revived with the end of the CPC's dictatorial reign. In any case the share of the different social strata in political power was about equally small, so that by democratizing the political structures all strata would gain, excluding the small segment of the bureaucratic elite.

From the historical viewpoint, too, everything seemed to indicate success for the democratic reforms. Totalitarian dictatorship was an alien system imported from the USSR, whereas the domestic political traditions of the past fifty years lay mainly in the struggle to create a pluralist democracy.

And from the viewpoint of constitutional law and political science—in other words, from the legal and political structure of the system—things looked favorable for democratic reform. Important steps could already be taken toward establishing the rule of law, on the basis of existing constitutional and legal norms. The norms themselves were usually formulated so broadly that, in practice, often contradictory interpretations, favoring either the dictatorship or the rule of law, were possible. This is a general characteristic of legal and constitutional norms in Soviet-type totalitarian regimes: unlike fascist dictatorships, they try to pass themselves off as democratic systems and therefore formally codify in law many of the basic, general principles of democratic order. In fact an entire system of division of power and checks and balances might have been instituted within the framework of already-existing representative, executive, and judicial bodies. According to the letter of Czechoslovak law, the courts are independent and all the executive bodies, including the government, are subordinate to and derive their authority from representative bodies of the parliamentary type. By realizing such formally-valid relationships and by reforming the electoral laws, it would have been possible to disrupt the dictatorial system without, for the time being, touching on the problem of having only one political party.

There was also the related area of civil rights. Here too the already-existing legal norms could be used as the basis for change. The main problem was applying the legal rights of individual citizens against institutions, which had, in practice, been favored over individuals for years. There were some questions, however, relating to freedom of expression and freedom of movement that required a modification of the laws (for example certain sections of the Criminal Code limiting freedom of expression and information and the absence of the right to a passport, and so on).

Political reforms such as these, complemented by a system of self-management in the socialist enterprises and in the economic sphere in general and by the development of independent trade-union activity and other special-interest groups, seemed to me both realistic and a quite effective way out of the situation. I assumed that once the political system was thus reformed and had been working for a certain length of time, it would be clearer where and how to go from there.

But very serious political problems arose when our research team began to consider freedom of the press and freedom of association, which were undeniably essential in the whole process of transforming a totalitarian dictatorship into a democratic system. The problem, however, was how to introduce these freedoms in the transitional period, when it was not yet practical to raise the question of government by more than one party. It was somewhere here that our thinking about political reform began to run up against two fundamental problems that we never fully clarified: the problem of a single ruling political party and the problem of the international repercussions of any eventual reform in the other countries of the Soviet bloc.

The participants of the team discussions were not only aware of both these problems, but they debated them as well. For the most part, however, such talks took place in the corridors, and there are no written records of them. In 1967, officially raising such questions meant exposing the entire study team to the danger of being disbanded.

What was my own attitude to these two problems?

I was a reform Communist, not a non-Communist democrat. I didn't try to hide it then, and there is no reason why I should try to do so now. This meant that I quite naturally had neither the political interest, the ideological reasons, nor the personal desire to see the CPC stripped of its political power, nor did I work towards that end. However, this did not preclude thinking it proper—in harmony with my understanding of socialism and communism—to dismantle the system of totalitarian dictatorship in which the CPC held a monopoly on political power. I wanted the political power of the Communist party to be achieved not in such a dictatorial system, but in a pluralistic political democracy.

It was clear to me that in all this the question of other political parties competing with the Communist party according to democratic rules (i.e., in general elections) for a share of that power could not be avoided. In theory I did not see the problem as being particularly complex, and, summarizing the results of the team discussions in 1967, I wrote:

In my opinion, of course, there is no scientific argument against a two-party political system in socialism. On the contrary, in principle such a solution would appear to be optimal for a pluralistic socialist society: it could provide firm guarantees against the tendency towards monopolization of political power by a single body; it could create an instrument for dealing with the conflict between the hypothetical goals of communism and the empirical reality of socialism (the Communist party as creator and bearer of the Communist hypothesis would be modulated by a party, most probably, deriving its program empirically from the socialist "status quo"). A two-party system would generally create and guarantee the necessary "balances" against any further monopoly of power, as takes place in a multi-party system through the formation of coalitions. At the same time, it makes the extension of political decision making beyond the state bodies (its representative organs) impossible, in contrast to the multiparty system (either through a coalition or, for example, through a permanent platform like the National Front in Czechoslovakia in 1945–1948), which thus, in fact, avoids the proper constitutional guarantee of the democratic process, for decisions are made outside the channels guaranteed by legal means. Nevertheless, however possible I may consider this system to be for a stable socialist society, I cannot ignore the present concrete, historical conditions existing in socialist states, including [Czechoslovakia], and consider this proposal as realizable in the near future. My reasons for this position, however, go beyond the limits of this paper.*

These reasons were not simply connected with the fact that I was a spokesman for the ruling Communist party. I believe they are reasons that no political scientist or politician, even non-Communist, can simply dismiss out of hand.

What were these reasons? In the first place, I felt that to raise the question of having another political party, before many other democratic changes (roughly those already mentioned) had been realized, would mean, at best, endangering the democratic reforms. For, in such a case, the CPC, with its monopoly on power and its tens of thousands of functionaries, would be dominated, not by an effort to bring about rational reform, but by the instinct for self-defense. Sensing a defeat in democratic elections, it would be driven to defend the old, dictatorial system.

In the second place, I felt that in terms of society's objective needs, the question of political parties *per se* was not important but rather how a given political party introduces certain measures when it is in power, how the elected bodies of the state, the various organs of self-administration and collective decision making in everyday life ac-

---

* The manuscript from which this passage is taken was never published in Czechoslovakia. I am quoting from my work, *The Czechoslovak Attempt at Reform, 1968* (Cologne: Index, 1975), pp. 68–69.

tually work, how the rights of citizens outside political parties, such as freedom of expression, the press, etc., are guaranteed. In socialism, I felt collective forms of decision making were an absolute priority: to ensure that the influence of the trades union and the other special-interest organizations, and the projected self-management organizations in the factories and other areas of social life, were a real force in the decision-making process at the state and party level. As I saw it, the elected organs of the socialist state ought to differ from the former bourgeois democratic parliament primarily in that they would be made up not just of representatives of the political parties but of all the other social organizations as well, in particular representatives of the organs of self-management. Parliament could even have a special chamber of self-management, in which the political parties would not be represented at all.

In my judgment, these political changes were a prerequisite to holding democratic elections. Holding democratic elections would solve nothing unless the system was first changed. And, as I have already indicated, the old dictatorial system ruled by the CPC could be nudged toward reform because it was well aware of the profound crisis it was in. The survival instinct is always strong in politics, and in Czechoslovakia at that time, reform was for the Communists a way out of the situation that would, at the same time, ensure their survival as a political force. The real consequence, however, would be a transformation of the system as a whole, and the CPC in particular, that would amount to liquidating the main buttresses of the party's dictatorship. And then, once the mechanism of a different and more democratic power was functioning in relative stability, the question of having more than one political party could be officially raised. In such circumstances, this could be the final guarantee to a pluralistic democratic system, and not the unleashing of a struggle simply to take over the existing undemocratic, dictatorial machinery of power.

I imagined it would require about ten years of reform, perhaps a little longer, to reach this stage, which is actually less time than has elapsed since the Prague Spring took place.

The main obstacles to all this, and what I was most afraid of, were having attention focused prematurely on this question by the press (which is, in fact, partly what happened) or some political groupings (particularly, a group of social democrats and some groups within KAN—the Club of Committed Non-Communists) attempting to play the role of new political parties.

I could understand why this question would be raised by those who simply had no faith in a politics of reform led by Communists and who wanted to get into the game independently, outside of the CPC. But what I could not understand was why the same question would be raised by some reform Communists who on the whole shared the general conception of gradual political reform as such. Nor could I understand how some of those people, roughly members of my own generation who had the same fundamental political experience as I did, could really believe that not only Dubček and the "progressive" wing of the party but also Bilak and the "conservatives" would start off the new politics with free, democratic elections in which the CPC would be competing with some newly-established party free from the past sins of Communists. I could not understand how, after all they had experienced in politics and in the CPC, they could still have such naive and romantic notions. I didn't think it did them credit then, and I still don't.

Concerning the second basic problem—the international context and consequences of the reform policies in Czechoslovakia—we in the research team of course knew, even in 1967, that the reforms would have to pass muster with the Kremlin. For the time being, however, we did not consider that a serious problem; it certainly made no sense to limit theoretical deliberations and discussions because of it. Internal deliberations, in themselves, would not cause Moscow to intervene, and the question of what would happen in time once the reforms had been implemented was impossible to predict, theoretically at any rate, for it quite clearly depended on the actual circumstances prevailing in Moscow (including the membership of the politburo) at the time.

I myself, however, gave some thought to the potential Soviet reaction from the moment we began our research, and in the spring of 1967 I went to Moscow. I wanted to determine what kind of reaction could be actually expected on the part of Soviet ideologists. In the Institute for State and Law of the Academy of Sciences in Moscow I gave an official lecture in which I outlined the essential concepts we had begun to work on for reforming the political system. In several official conversations, and many unofficial ones, with those from scientific, party, and state circles, I was able to test Soviet reactions to a number of concrete points in our conception of reform.

Most of the official reactions were very reserved: they found my ideas "interesting," without specifying whether this was meant in the positive or the negative sense. Some highly-placed academic ideologists attacked the conception outright. For example, the director of the Moscow Institute, Akademik Chechikvadze (who, by the way, was later stripped of his function for embezzlement and "immoral living") raised a provocative question during the question and answer part of my lecture. "In what way," he asked, "do your opinions differ from bourgeois conceptions of pluralism?" I replied that they differed in general because I was thinking of pluralism in a socialist society, and thus it related to the political organizations of the working people and the working class and not to those of the bourgeoisie at all. Concerning certain concrete problems, particularly organization and the actual mechanism of pluralism, I said that they differed in no way, and that I would welcome it if the Comrade Akademik would be specific about where, how, and why they ought to differ. Comrade Akademik, of course, said nothing: he was flabbergasted to discover that the scarecrow of "bourgeois pluralism" was not sufficient argument in itself to rule out any further discussion of the matter. Also criticized was the general notion of separating the state and political apparatus from control of the economy. But that was mostly a product of the economic reforms that were already a part of the official party line in Czechoslovakia.

My unofficial conversations were essentially different. My Soviet counterparts (some of whom were personal acquaintances and friends from my student days in Moscow) were of the opinion that although many of our reform conceptions could scarcely be considered practicable in the foreseeable future in the USSR, it would nevertheless be exceptionally important for them if something like them were in fact to take place in Czechoslovakia. They felt that reforms and democratization would become necessary in the Soviet Union as well. At that time, Brezhnev had been in power for a mere two-and-a-half years, and the general opinion (particularly in the party apparatus) seemed to be that he represented an "interim government," for none of the groupings within the party was at the time strong enough to make a direct bid for power. Most I came across hoped for the victory of a rational line based on expertise, one that would at the same time continue in the democratization process. Often these hopes were connected with the person of Shelepin. On the whole, no one missed Khrushchev; most young people in the party apparatus considered his internal policies to have been poorly thought out, lacking in conceptual strength while always experimenting with grand but short-sighted schemes of social reorganization. Only in very isolated instances did I encounter pessimism about democratization in the Soviet Union. One of my former fellow students, for example, explained himself by saying: "What you want is out of the question for us here. They'd cut our throats." "Us" here meant the Soviet bureaucracy; "they" were the Soviet people.

I returned to Prague convinced that the situation was not unpromising and that we could expect positive developments toward democratization in the Soviet Union as well. Meanwhile, however, it was clear that we had to continue our work with no immediate hope of support from the Soviet theoretical and ideological institutes, and that, on the contrary, we had to expect a certain degree of ill will from the official, leading circles of such places. Those who sympathized with our efforts were more numerous, but for the time being they had neither the power nor the position to make themselves felt. Nonetheless, I thought that by 1970 this situation might change in our favor. As it turned out, this was one of the worst appraisals of any situation I have ever made.

It was with this sum of opinions about the possibilities of political reform in Czechoslovakia and how they could be best achieved that, in January 1968, I took my place in the "working group" assigned to prepare the text of a political document that was accepted by the Central Committee on April 5, 1968, as the official political program of the Prague Spring and eventually became famous as the "Action Program of the CPC."*

---

* The Action Program was prepared and written in "working groups" composed largely of people from scientific institutes and universities. The presidium of the Central Committee did set up its own "political commission"—chaired by D. Kolder and composed of members of the presidium, secretaries of the Central Committee, and other high functionaries—to assist in preparing this program, but no one from it actually worked on the text. Kolder himself made only two appearances among those actually writing the text, and on one of those occasions it was to suggest that the text be kept short, to about ten pages, and to mention that he had already discussed the matter with the writer, Jan Procházka, who had agreed to write it if he were provided with the necessary data. Brezhnev was quite justified, therefore, to ask of B. Šimon, in the autumn of 1968 in Moscow, who the author of the Action Program was; and when he was told it had been a commission headed by Comrade Kolder, he replied: "That's not what I asked. I want to know who actually wrote it!"

The final text of the Action Program was written by the following people:

Part I. The Czechoslovak Road to Socialism: J. Fojtík, K. Kaplan, R. Richta.

Part II. Toward the Development of Socialist Democracy, a New System of Political Direction in Society: Z. Mlynář.

In this document I summarized my own opinions. It was the first time I had done so without anxiously resorting to foggy, half-formulated language to "get past" the party organs. Here I strove for clarity and practicability. Even so the conception of the Action Program deviated from my own opinions in one fundamental question: the role of the political parties and the National Front.*

Conceived as a short-term political platform, the Action Program was primarily responsible for defining the first phase of political reform. To create, at this stage, political parties in competition with the CPC for a share of the power in democratic elections had many problems, as I've already mentioned. And to write limitations on non-Communist political parties into the reform program would signify maintaining one of the pillars of the totalitarian system and, moreover, draw attention (from above as well) to these matters.

To grant a political role to the National Front, whose purpose was in fact to limit the non-Communist political parties, was asking for trouble. Besides which, we could not discuss the role of the National Front without specifying the roles of other political parties, since such groups as the trades union and other special-interest organizations, which were all represented in the National Front as well, should have been, in my opinion, as independent as possible during the course of the reforms. In my judgment, this mechanism itself was politically dead by the beginning of 1968, and I personally saw no reason to revive it.

However, there was another viewpoint in the CPC, supported in particular by a political science "working group" led by R. Rohan, who had worked on these questions in 1967 under the patronage of J.

Part III. The National Economy and the Standard of Living: B. Šimon, A. Červinka, with the assistance of several other economists, particularly O. Šik, K. Kouba, and others.

Part IV. The Development of Science, Education, and Culture: R. Richta, S. Provazník, with the assistance of various authors with reports on education, the Academy of Sciences, and the Union of Writers.

Part V. The International Position and the Foreign Policy of the ČSSR: P. Auersperg.

These people comprised the main "working group" that was directed organizationally by P. Auersperg. It worked in his office in the Prague political bureau of the magazine, *Questions of Peace and Socialism.* Their work was based on dozens of particular studies made by employees of scientific institutes, and the text also reflected the discussions in a number of smaller working groups.

* From 1945–1948, Czechoslovakia had a National Front government consisting of a coalition of all national political parties. After the Communist takeover in 1948, the National Front was continued in name only.

Hendrych. These proposals, given to me by Hendrych with the suggestion they be used as a basis for our work on the Action Program, contained the notion that the National Front could be revived and used as an instrument for CPC influence over the whole system of social organizations. At the same time, they made no attempt to solve the problem of the other political parties: these were all merely to be left as they were, as formal organizations to make the regime "look good."

In February 1968, I wrote out my position on the matter and sent it to Hendrych, who was a presidium member and a party secretary until March.* I expressed the opinion that such a conception of the National Front in the Action Program would be incorrect and not in keeping with the purpose of the reforms. And if the question of non-Communist parties were to be raised, it would create insolvable practical political problems in the first phase of reforms. Thus I recommended that the question of the National Front be mentioned only in very general terms in the Action Program, using the formulation from the constitution—which states that the "National Front of Czechs and Slovaks, in which the social organizations are associated, is the political expression of an alliance of the working cities and the countryside, led by the CPC"—and otherwise leave this moribund organization in peace, beyond the reach of the political reforms. Hendrych had nothing against this (nor did any of the other functionaries with whom I discussed the problem), and therefore the draft text of the Action Program, as complete in March 1968, contained practically nothing about the National Front and the non-Communist parties.

But at a meeting of the political commission in March, chaired by D. Kolder, there was discussion and even disagreement on this question. Several members of the commission objected to my position on the grounds that, from the practical political viewpoint, it was no longer possible simply to skirt round the problem of non-Communist parties, because it would focus undesirable political attention on the issue and create undue pressure on the CPC. Therefore, they felt it was indispensable to have the role of the National Front, and the political parties within it, clearly defined in the Action Program. The argument was pressed most energetically by Lubomír Štrougal, the

---

* The State Security forces confiscated a copy of this document, along with other personal papers, during a house search in April 1975, and therefore I do not have it at my disposal.

present prime minister of Czechoslovakia, and it was strongly supported by Josef Smrkovský. And so there was an open discussion on where we were going from here in practical politics; whether we could seriously consider eventually holding free elections in which the non-Communist parties would play an independent role. The conclusion of all the participants in the session was that this was not realistically possible. Thus, there was already unanimous agreement that during the reform process the National Front was to prohibit new political parties forming outside its framework, thus, in practical political terms, making a struggle for power in the state impossible, insofar as this struggle was to be conducted by and through political parties.

At first I took issue with this, using my general, theoretical arguments to demonstrate, for one, that it would complicate the later phases of political reform. In the course of the discussion, however, I had to admit that, from the practical point of view, those who argued that the problem could no longer simply be pushed under the rug were right. By March, the ferment in society itself, also expressed in the press, had, *de facto,* already raised the question of the role of non-Communist political parties. Having been thus persuaded, I then formulated the relevant passage in the Action Program on the National Front and non-Communist parties in the form that was ultimately ratified and published.

The Action Program represented the beginning of a whole new phase for my work. My theoretical and ideological propositions were now to be subjected to the critique of real politics. They were now about to enter into the life of society, no longer in the castrated and often ambiguous forms in which they were adopted in the corridors of the bureaucratic totalitarian system and forcefully imposed on an apathetic society. Now the proposals were to be tested at a time when the totalitarian dictatorship was collapsing, when the vast majority of society was taking an increasingly active part in developments and the various political groupings had a real opportunity to express, propagate, and defend their viewpoints.

However, an element traditional to politics entered the game: the struggle for a share of the power. And with it came the inevitable emotions, passions, and political demagogy.

I was shocked by what I saw in the world of the rulers, inside the power structure. I saw how lamentably little real understanding there was of the actual aims and significance of the reform; how the skirmishes and infighting over positions of power dominated; and how easily these skirmishes eclipsed the real problems for the whole future life of society: the people in power were even changing their political colors in order to capitalize on opportunity.

I was no longer a naive romantic in politics, nor, on the other hand, had I yet become a haggard cynic. But the romantics, the naive, and the cynics clearly had it over those who still strove for their ideals in the face of practical politics. I saw quite a few people like myself around me, but on the whole we were a minority: we were outnumbered by the romantics and the cynics.

To this day, the ousting of Antonín Novotný is described everywhere as the product of a brief but surprisingly independently-minded development in the party leadership between October and December 1967. At a Central Committee session in October, a conflict broke out between Novotný and several committee members, particularly Alexander Dubček. There were several issues involved, but the main points of contention were the party's working methods and chiefly those of Novotný himself. The conflict grew and was taken up by the presidium, where it intensified, resulting in the proposal that Novotný resign as first secretary, while remaining in his function as president. The presidium was split down the middle with five on each side—Novotný, Lenárt, Chudík, Laštovička, and Šimůnek on one side and Dubček, Hendrych, Černík, Kolder, and Dolanský on the other. Novotný sent for Brezhnev to save his position, but Brezhnev withheld his support, declaring the whole affair to be an "internal matter" of the CPC. At the end of December, then, the Central Committee began to discuss dividing the function of first secretary and president of the Republic, and in January 1968 it stripped Novotný of his party function.

It is also a known fact that before the Central Committee made its decision, preparations were being made in certain circles of the army and the security forces. Novotný, seemingly, was planning to repress the opposition by force, arresting his enemies and declaring a state of emergency. In the end, however, this did not take place. One of the generals involved fled to the West (though it was also because, as later came out, he had embezzled state property), and another one later shot himself. But Novotný himself was, on the whole, turned out of office peacefully.

The opposition to Novotný at the December and January Central

Committee sessions had been unexpectedly and uncommonly powerful. Men who until that point had been in no way connected with opposition democrats quite suddenly and energetically took up the anti-Novotný cause, men like Vasil Bilak and Alois Indra. This has been noted by historians but no attempt has been made to go further.

I think, however, that certain questions are in order here. Until Dubček took over as first secretary, it was common practice in the CPC to have Moscow approve beforehand not only the candidacy of Central Committee secretaries, but also many other important functionaries, including the leading secretaries in regional party committees. And now here was Brezhnev suddenly letting things take their own course so that an "anti-Novotný opposition" ended up forming the entire new CPC leadership. Was he sitting in the Kremlin while this was happening, anxiously waiting for the next edition of the Czech newspapers to come out? Novotný alerted his "loyal cadres" in the army and the security forces to defend him: did the Soviet ambassador in Prague, Chervonenko, know nothing about it? After all, it was common knowledge that these "loyal cadres" were loyal first of all to Moscow. And why, in the end, did the dramatic defense of Novotný not take place?

I doubt very much that everything in Moscow was left to chance and the "sovereign CPC." I tend rather to believe another version. After Brezhnev's December visit to Prague (see p. 71), Moscow decided that rather than let the thing drag on any longer, they would allow Novotný to be ousted at the next plenary session of the Central Committee. Also, it was most probably Brezhnev who put a stop to the military gambit—even though I concede that Novotný may have decided against it himself, being reluctant to use armed might "against the party." As far as the succession goes, the Kremlin almost certainly reasoned that the five presidium members opposed to Novotný would maintain their positions. Leaving aside Dolanský, who was by now too old, this meant that one of the remaining four would have to take Novotný's place, and the choice as to whether it would be Dubček, Hendrych, Černík, or Kolder was genuinely left to the "sovereign CPC." (Kolder, moreover, was hardly a likely candidate, so this in fact left three.)

On the other side, it was necessary to assume that of Novotný's five supporters in the presidium, some at least would not survive his fall and would be replaced with Novotný oppositionists. That being so, it was essential for Moscow to have its own internationally reliable cadres in on the side of these oppositionists. That is how I would explain the sudden and unusually radical anti-Novotný activity of some of the comrades. I have no concrete proof of this hypothesis, however, apart from the logic of events.

For how else are we to explain the fact that Alois Indra, the minister of transport, suddenly became involved in a political debate over fundamental issues, to an extent that astonished everyone? And how did this then "radical progressive" become, as soon as a conflict arose between Dubček and Brezhnev, one of the chief conservatives in the CPC leadership, which led ultimately to the arrest of Dubček in his name, following the arrival of Soviet tanks in Prague?

And Vasil Bilak as a "restorer of socialism"? True, his anti-Novotný stance can be explained by the fact that, among other things, Novotný clashed with Dubček, attacking the whole Slovak wing of the party, of which Bilak was a member. Yet it was common knowledge even then that Bilak represented other interests even further to the east than Eastern Slovakia. Could not these interests also have played a certain role? At the time, Bilak was a very close personal friend of Dubček's, and perhaps that too can explain his fundamental critique of Novotný. But what about subsequent developments? The very same Bilak, in quite the same way as Indra, took up Brezhnev's interests in the CPC leadership at the first sign of dissension between Brezhnev and Dubček. And, finally, he and Indra met on August 22 at the Soviet Embassy in Prague, where Bilak was prepared to take over the leadership of the party and Indra was slated to become prime minister of the "revolutionary workers' and peasants' government."

And two other men whose careers are linked with developments after the January plenary session of the Central Committee were sitting there in the Soviet embassy trying to form a new government: Miloš Jakeš, chairman of the Central Commission of Supervision and Auditing of the CPC, and Oldřich Pavlovský, a minister in Černík's government. How did Pavlovský get to be a minister? On Indra's personal recommendation, made without anyone's consultation and as an afterthought at a Central Committee session in April 1968. And who was Miloš Jakeš before Novotný was toppled? In addition to being a member of the commission whose chairman he became under Dubček, he was a deputy of the minister of the interior, Josef Kudrna, whom the "revival process" swept from his ministerial seat. He was also, like Pavlovský, an old companion of Alois Indra's from the days when they were functionaries together in Gottwaldov.

It is true, of course, that Dubček nominated both Bilak and Jakeš to their positions. In answer to the objections that Jakeš' connections with the police (and evidently not only with the Prague police) did not bode well for his new position, Dubček replied that Jakeš was a good comrade, that they had been student roommates at the party school in Moscow, and that it was perfectly all right. But if there was a stage manager's hand behind all this, it was not an inexperienced hand, for it chose actors whom Dubček would consider as his friends: and many of his friends had for years been safely controlled by the Moscow stage managers.

I don't know what Dubček discussed with Brezhnev in those final days of January when he was already first secretary of the Central Committee of the CPC, but it was this first visit to Moscow that marked the beginning of the more significant personnel changes in the leadership of the Czechoslovak party and state, and on such occasions it is a Kremlin custom to begin discussing quite concretely "questions of interest to both sides." I have no doubt that Dubček's liking for Bilak, Jakeš, and Indra found enthusiastic support there.

Consequently some things, including the ousting of Novotný, were more surprising to us in Prague than they were to Moscow. But history has strange ways, and, as things turned out, it was the hidden stage manager who became quite surprised, and, at last, he must have been beside himself with astonishment. Dubček's first great sin consisted in presenting Moscow with a proliferation of new ministers and secretaries who had not received Moscow's prior assent. Of course Dubček was later taken to task for this by Brezhnev in the Kremlin— but I'll be discussing that in the next chapter. For Brezhnev, it was the first sign of the impending "counterrevolution."

But even disregarding the conservatives in Dubček's party leadership, the debut of the reform politics in January 1968 was by no means a grandiose affair. Though the deliberations of the Central Committee plenary session fill a 1,500 page report, the conceptual discussion of reform ideas would probably occupy no more than 50 pages, and Ota Šik was the only one to deal conceptually with the social, economic, and political aspects of the potential reforms. In several other speeches we may find very open and, in the given situation, often very courageous critical ideas and comments, but no more coherent notions were offered on the research, nor on the politics that ought to have been carried out, and to what extent, after Novotný's departure. Not even the future "progressivists" at that session behaved like politicians preparing to transform a totalitarian dictatorship into a pluralistic political democracy.

Even in the communiqué released when Novotný finally did resign, there is not a hint of any more substantial changes in the offing. This, of course, did not reflect the real course of that Central Committee meeting, but it does indicate the inability of the Central Committee to understand what it had actually done by overthrowing Novotný.

It is paradoxical, but in the end Antonín Novotný himself came closest to the truth at that Central Committee meeting when he predicted that his departure would signal far-reaching changes in politics and society, although, of course, he meant this as a warning, claiming that the changes would threaten "the interests of the working class." It is also known that after his retirement, Novotný proclaimed to a circle of his most loyal followers: "Don't worry, it's all right. Dubček is a weakling, he's not up to the job, and the secretaries are spineless. Our time will come!" As far as he personally was concerned, the last part of his prediction remained unfulfilled, but on the whole it was not as ridiculous an estimate of the situation as many romantics and "progressivists" thought at the time.

Both before and after his election as first secretary of the CPC, Alexander Dubček spoke of his belief in the necessity of ruling democratically, but this was a statement of personal conviction rather than a coherent and rational political program. He spoke about the relationships between Czechs and Slovaks during the national revival of the last century, about Božena Nemcová and Ludovít Štúr, but he avoided the issue of federalization. He spoke about how, as first secretary in Slovakia, he had ruled not by fiat but by persuasion. As an example, he cited the expulsion of the historian Gosiorovský from the party by Novotný. Gosiorovský had written that a federal organization of the state would be in the interests of Slovaks, and Novotný decided to expel him from the party for saying so. Dubček, convinced that Gosiorovský was a bad Communist and a dishonest person (and I think he was absolutely right in this), was not against expelling him, but the party organization where Gosiorovský worked could not understand why it was necessary. And so Dubček spent months trying to persuade them. And he did not issue the order until the comrades themselves were convinced there was no other way. Dubček promised to run the entire party that way. There could be no doubt of his sincerity, but this was scarcely a clear indication of what his approach to the issues would be in his new position.

Dubček never wanted to be first secretary of the entire CPC in the first place. Others had to convince him, and they promised to "help" him, but he felt himself not sufficiently prepared or competent to accept such a high office. However, he was the only candidate who could muster the necessary majority in the Central Committee, and, in the end, that was the decisive factor. Immediately following his election as the most powerful man in the country, Dubček left for Bratislava to attend an important hockey game. After all, the rest could wait, everything had to be worked out with careful consideration, calmly and democratically. And the people, too, were glad to have the new top man watching the hockey game with them.

I am not mentioning all this to make Dubček out to be a politically-naive simpleton. That view was, and still is, rather widespread, but I don't agree with it, and I shall explain why later. Now I only wish to emphasize that in those first few days and weeks not even Dubček knew what his accession to power had really set in motion in society and in the CPC.

Even those old experienced party hands from the Novotný era—the Central Committee secretaries Hendrych and Koucký—were relaxed and satisfied. Sometime in February 1968, Koucký said to me, "You see, Novotný was prophesying at the January plenary session about everything that would happen if we turned him out of office, and what's happening? Nothing." I tried to set him right and mentioned the clear signs of a far-reaching groundswell in society and the party: at that point, such a movement could be observed in the press even from the isolated vantage point of the secretariat. But Koucký said I was exaggerating. About two months later he himself had to resign.

Late one evening, in the middle of February, I met Hendrych in a corridor of the secretariat building. He was literally beaming with satisfaction and immediately explained: "I've just worked it out with Eda Goldstueker—I've permitted the *Literárky* to start publishing again." He was referring to the weekly newspaper of the Union of Writers that Novotný had banned in the fall of 1967. *Literární noviny* (later called *Literární listy* and even later still, after August 1968, merely *Listy*) was a symbol of critical journalism in the Novotný era, and its reemergence meant, in practical terms, and end to all censorship. I tried to persuade Hendrych that taking such a step before the Action Program was published would result in the press becoming far more radical than before and, in turn, less disposed to accept the limitations and the political framework of the Action Program. "That won't happen," claimed Hendrych. "I've already talked it all over with Goldstuecker. They won't write against us." About a month later Hendrych was forced to resign, one reason being that public

Top left: Z.M. at age fifteen, shortly before entering the CPC.

Lower left: nineteen year old functionary of the Communist youth movement.

Below: Z.M., upper right, at Moscow University, September 1, 1953.

Right: 23 year old law
student.

Below: after return from
Moscow in 1955, employee
of the prosecutor general's
office.

Opposite: Z.M. as speaker
of the CPC.

criticism of him in the press was so harsh he would have compromised the Dubček leadership by remaining in office.

With the exception of Hendrych's departure from the ideological section, all of Novotný's former leadership—in the presidium and secretariat of the Central Committee—remained intact until the beginning of April 1968. The presidium was merely complemented by several new members who (with the exception of J. Špaček) represented no major political change. Thus of those eight months from January until the military intervention in August, there were three whole months without any clearly conceived policy declarations from the CPC leadership.

For those three whole months, the party leadership was exclusively concerned with redistributing the top party and state functions, to the detriment of the new policies. But society was not prepared to wait for the internal disputes over who would get what secretarial and ministerial appointment to be settled. Long-supressed conflicts and contradictions began to surface. And since conceptions for democratic reform had yet to be forthcoming from the CPC leadership, they began to appear beyond its reach: in the press, the radio and television, and in various public meetings and assemblies.

As long as the redistribution of leadership positions remained unsettled, it took precedence over almost everything else. Those whose positions had been owed to Novotný and who, during his rule, did more than a few things that were now compromising, were hoping to maintain their positions by declaring their support for democratic reforms. This, for example, explains why Hendrych abolished censorship. And those who were trying to usurp those positions made their democratic opinions known also as a means to achieve their ends. Thus the interests of political careers were served by yea-saying precisely as they had been in the Novotný era, the only difference being that now they required a democratic orientation. By this I don't wish to imply that the bias of leading functionaries in the CPC towards democratic reform was merely a by-product of careerism: everything I have said thus far about the development of reform communism in the CPC denies such an interpretation. But I do wish to emphasize that in the first few months after Antonín Novotný's fall, democratic "progressivism" enjoyed a boom period among party functionaries, and this for a time blurred distinctions in word and deed between those who were genuinely committed to realizing democratic reforms and those who were only interested in their political careers.

In the world of the rulers a general feeling of insecurity reigned.

Both in the presidium of the party and in the Central Committee, at least half the members sensed that their positions could not long be maintained, and it was the same in Parliament and the government. The situation in the lower, regional and district, levels of the power structure was similar. Employees in the political apparatus from the top to the bottom were understandably insecure and confused about how to handle themselves in their daily work. Hesitant about employing their traditional methods of work, they became increasingly paralyzed.

This insecurity "on top" naturally provided fertile soil for the growth of criticism from "below." The nervous power structure was hesitant to suppress critics and rebels in the usual fashion for it was quite clear to everyone that Novotný's dismissal from the highest position in the party had been a victory for critical and oppositional trends in the party. At the same time, however, this state of affairs was most certainly unfavorable for political reform. The longer it lasted, the stronger became the danger that pressure on the political system from below would intensify and thus be in a position to compete with the official reform program, which would, in turn, intensify opposition to reform in the power apparatus.

Thus from February 1968 on, I felt that the top priority for a successful reform program was to end this provisional state as rapidly as possible. In both public and nonpublic speeches and presentations, I was working to have the Action Program of the CPC issued as promptly as possible and to effect a rapid and orderly change of personnel in all segments of the political system. I still think to this day that all the necessary preconditions existed for this to happen and that both these aims were quite realistic.

The text of the Action Program was ready by the end of February in roughly its finished form. I proposed that we ratify it and release it in the early days of March. My reasoning was based on the fact that the regular CPC district conferences had already been set for March, and they would be electing new party district committees. The regional party conferences would be next, and I felt that all these conferences should be electing their new functionaries according to their attitude to the new political line. But for that they had to know what the new party line was. At the same time, these conferences could elect delegates to the extraordinary party congress, but again the Central Committee had first to convene it.

If the decision were made at the beginning of March, this party congress could sit in May and elect a new Central Committee. Also, the municipal National Committee elections, which had been scheduled for May, and the parliamentary elections due to take place in the summer could be combined and held in June. Thus by summer the entire ruling establishment in the elected state bodies would have been replaced—from the villages right up to Parliament.

I considered such a plan of action to be best in the situation. It made it possible to combine the initial necessarily powerful and explosive wave of criticism and discontent with an orderly, democratic replacement of all the old party and state functionaries. This would provide an opportunity to support rather than curtail the very harsh and radical criticism being leveled at both individuals and the system. And such criticism could have a beneficial and immediate influence in the elections: i.e., not to vote, either in the CPC or in the state bodies, for candidates against whom criticism has been focused, who had supported the system of totalitarian dictatorship in concrete ways. In such an atmosphere the newly elected party and state organs would gain the necessary authority both to execute the general conceptions of reform after the elections and to take a more effective stand against extremists, who were concerned with defeating certain elements regardless of whether this harmonized with the reforms as a whole or not.

In terms of the major problem of how to avoid having opposition parties become a real political demand in the early phases of the reforms, the approach I suggested had another great advantage: the elections would take place so rapidly that this demand could not possibly be realized. And the problem could be dealt with more conceptually before the next elections.

Also from the viewpoint of international factors—that is to say, the possible interference of Moscow—this rapid and orderly change of functionaries in the party and state organs would also give the politics of reform all the trumps. The replacement of Stalinist and Moscow-controlled personnel would have taken place according to the party statutes and state laws before Moscow could organize any effective resistance. Even with the totalitarian system erupting under continual pressure from below, expressed chiefly through the press (which roused the Kremlin into a fury), events in May had not yet reached a point where a military intervention could have been mounted. And after a party congress, Moscow would never have been able to set up a "revolutionary workers' and peasants' government" from among the CPC leadership, nor would it be conceivable that a group of "party and government leaders" might "invite in the allied troops to save socialism."

I was far from being the only one to believe that this was the best way to proceed. There were many party organizations demanding that an extraordinary party congress be convened with all possible haste, and two or three district organizations officially presented this demand to the Central Committee. Also, there was far from unanimous support for postponing the state elections.

Nevertheless, three very different political forces united against such opinions.

First of all, they were opposed by those who supported radical and consistently democratic changes in the political system. These people were spellbound by the sudden and unexpected opportunity to expound freely on their democratic thoughts and radical political recipes in public meetings and in the media. People followed what they said with interest and often with enthusiasm—and naturally they were applauded. The supporters of radical democratic changes— both from the ranks of reform Communists and non-Communists— believed that the longer this provisional state lasted and the power structure remained unsure of itself, the more democratic reforms could be pushed through and secured for the future. They considered that a rapid consolidation of the power structure—both of the party and the state—would be a threat to consistent democratization. Too many conservatives and, above all, too many "centrists" would remain in power, and they would slow down the reforms. It would all go the way of Poland under Gomulka: first the great enthusiasm and democratic euphoria, and then quietly, through the back door, the old totalitarian system would creep back. Thus, it was necessary, through pressure from below, to disrupt this system thoroughly and for as long as possible and be consistent about excluding from future political life all who supported it.

For quite different reasons, the swift replacement of people in the power structures was opposed by those who knew they would be the ones replaced—the Stalinists, genuine conservatives, Moscow agents, and careerists whose zeal in the past had discredited them. These people saw their ultimate security, or at least their last hope, in this prolonged state of uncertainty. They felt that if things developed to a point of crisis, the political power structure might be compelled by its own instinct for survival to renounce the idea of reform altogether, and that their time would come again. In those spring days of 1968, I don't think even the boldest of these people dared to hope that the Soviet army might help to bring this about. They were depending, rather, on political pressure from Moscow and on the fact that Dubček himself, when the crisis came, would have to rely on them.

The third significant political force whom the notion of rapidly changing the personnel did not suit was Moscow. Though there was clearly no unanimous attitude in Moscow towards developments in Czechoslovakia—which will be discussed in more detail in the next chapter—all political tendencies in the Kremlin were concerned not to have their influence in Prague weakened, but rather strengthened. Calling an extraordinary party congress and elections for a new Central Committee when they do not have things "firmly in hand" is something that the Soviets never welcome. They prefer to wait, strengthen their position, and then have the congress convened when they know in advance how it will turn out, who will be first, who second, and so on.

Against the paradoxical alliance of these three forces, of course, my wretched "centrism" had no chance of succeeding, and the actual development of events from February to April was not encouraging to me. And these two months anticipated many fundamental events and tendencies which were to unfold in the months to follow.

The notion that Alexander Dubček stood above all this like a saint and a naive democrat, deceived on the Left and Right by experienced wolves, is quite incorrect. Dubček was not appointed to the presidium in 1963 by an act of God: he got there after 14 years of hard work in the party apparatus. And it is political simple-mindedness to think he was ignorant of what that apparatus was like or of how to deal with it. He knew its hidden lines of force very well. And he also knew the reality of the relationship between Prague and Moscow.

As startling as some will find this, in my judgment Dubček's attitude to developments between February and April 1968 was not a consequence of his commitment to a rapid and radical democratization in society, but rather of a deliberate calculation of the balance of forces inside the power structure and the attitude of Moscow. At the time, Dubček did not perceive the genuine strength and potential political consequences of the radical democratic criticisms he had more or less set free in February and March 1968. He intended to use such criticism for his own very definite aims, which differed from the aims of those doing the criticizing.

When Dubček took over as first secretary of the party, he knew very well that as long as Novotný was president and a member of the presidium he would have no room to carry out his own policies, nor would his position be entirely secure. He knew quite well the significance of the various cliques in the power apparatus, and he knew that Novotný was backed by a definite clique that was well entrenched in positions of power. In his own interests, both personal and political, Dubček had to oust that clan from power.

At the same time, it had never been Dubček's way to assert his will through simple peremptory commands from a position of power. He genuinely tried, as he said himself, to "persuade" others "in a comradely fashion" of the necessity of his actions, which meant creating a situation in which they would appear necessary and objectively inevitable. It was in this way that he wanted definitively to remove Novotný and his camarilla in the power apparatus from their positions. And the wave of public criticism against Novotný was instrumental in achieving this aim. I consider it very probable that although Dubček was not in collusion with Brezhnev on this point, neither was he acting against his will.

Dubček himself did not conduct a campaign against Novotný. He sat on the presidium with him and even constantly let it be known that comrade Novotný, after all, was president, and that there were democratic ways of settling differences. But he did not allow Novotný to speak at the manifestation commemorating the twentieth anniversary of February 1948. And when Novotný wanted to appear on television in response to the growing wave of public criticism against him, Dubček even personally prevented it. These measures were not the actions of a political innocent devoted to the idea of unlimited democracy, but rather actions calculated to help create a situation in which Novotný would have to resign. And this in fact did happen, but not until the end of March.

However, several functionaries were unintentionally forced to resign as well by the pressure of public criticism, expressed mainly through the mass media: J. Kudrna, minister of the interior, J. Bartušek, the prosecutor general, M. Pastýřík, chairman of the trades union, and others. These particular cases happened to suit Dubček's personal aims, since they were members of Novotný's personal entourage, but Dubček was unaware that beyond that something far more momentous was taking place: i.e., that a mechanism had been introduced capable of forcing change on the system. And it was not a party or state mechanism, consisting of a democratic process within the structures of power, but rather it was a kind of public lobby backed by a free press and the free expression of opinions outside the power structure. It was, in a way, an extraparliamentary opposition, and would even have been had Parliament already been functioning democratically.

Later in the Prague Spring, when this mechanism had not only strengthened and broadened its base but in many cases ceased to serve Dubček's aims and begun pressing for changes he was against, Dubček looked on with both astonishment and sorrow. In meetings with some journalists, whom he summoned in May and June in an effort to persuade the press to be more disciplined and in concert with his aims, his eyes would fill with tears. But in terms of practical political results, his efforts were in vain. I recall several personal conversations in which Dubček said, with sincere sorrow: "Why are they doing this to me? They would have been afraid to do it under Novotný. Don't they realize how much harm they're causing me?"

On several such occasions I explained to him where I thought the problem lay. I was hoping that using this concrete instance I could awaken his interest in the conceptual problems connected with the evolution of the entire political mechanism and that ultimately he would begin to take a serious interest in wider, systemic questions and not merely in personal and power relationships. I failed. Dubček would listen, but he was evidently still preoccupied by the ingratitude of the reporters. He had little patience with abstractions, and he allowed political problems to upset him personally, almost like a patriarch wronged (similar, in a way, to Brezhnev). As soon as he got over the pain of the injustice he felt the "comrade journalists" were doing him, his thoughts would shoot off somewhere else, and suddenly he would interrupt what I was saying to ask about something quite unrelated, quite concrete.

The notion that Dubček was naive insofar as he believed so strongly in democratic ideals that they governed his practical political life and his struggle for power is incorrect. If Dubček was naive at all, it was in not knowing what political democracy really was in the life of society and therefore in the life of the rulers. He had never experienced democracy, and he did not possess the kind of abstract and systemic thinking necessary for guiding into practice the general democratic principles he himself acknowledged as proper.

Dubček believed in the greatness and the correctness of the ideas and principles of Marxism-Leninism, and he considered those who shared that belief to be good comrades and honorable people. But Dubček knew that in the practical world of politics and power, these "pure ideas" were overshadowed by entirely different and quite essential matters upon which the success or failure of Communist policies depended. He had had occasion to observe this up close throughout his life in the party apparatus. But, along with this, because his experience was chiefly from Slovakia, he tended to overrate the importance of entirely personal relationships in politics and to underrate popular pressure on government, which had been historically weaker and far less sophisticated in Slovakia than in Bohemia, even in the political democracy before the war.

When Dubček attained the highest position of power in the CPC, he almost certainly arrived with the notion that democratic political reform was necessary, that the existing system of government had to be changed, yet the measures he considered essential were precisely the kind inherent in the old system of government. As an experienced hand in the party apparatus, he knew that the main thing was to eliminate his political competition and to strengthen and regroup his own people. And he also knew he had to cover his back in Moscow. Both these things overshadowed for him the need for declaring a party program or considerations about conceptions of reform, and even holding the party congress and elections was overshadowed, for, after all, such things usually take place *after* the new first secretary has consolidated his position in the apparatus and in Moscow, not before. And ultimately, the other presidium members saw things the same way, at least most of them did. Of the new leadership members up to the end of March 1968, Josef Špaček was the only one who genuinely appreciated the conceptual approach.

The result, of course, was a historical paradox: in the early spring of 1968, freedom of the press and the consequent pressure of public opinion developed rather suddenly and out of proportion to the other forms of democratic government precisely because Dubček was proceeding in essentially the same way that leading CPC groups had traditionally done in the years of their monopoly rule.

What, then, did Dubček accomplish between January and April 1968? He created his own power base in the party leadership. It consisted of three people: Dubček, Černík, and Kolder. All three knew each other very well from years of working together in the Central Committee apparatus in the early sixties, and they trusted each other.

Together, they ousted from the presidium those they did not trust. They left only three members of Novotný's membership in the presidium: Jozef Lenárt, Antonín Kapek, and Martin Vaculík, all three of them as nonvoting candidates, not regular members. Martin Vaculík, who remained in the leadership by virtue of being the leading party secretary of Prague, was replaced in May by the new Prague secretary, Bohumil Šimon (a former colleague of the leading trio and a long-time colleague of Kolder in the Central Committee apparatus). Of the other new members in the party leadership, five had personal links to the top three men, usually directly with Dubček: Vasil Bilak (Dubček's personal friend, whom he had appointed as his replacement to lead the party in Slovakia), Jan Piller (who had long years of service in leading economic functions, where he had personal ties chiefly with Černík and Kolder), Oldřich Švestka (editor in chief of *Rude pravo,* who had already assisted Dubček behind Novotný's back), and František Barbírek and Emil Rigo (politically insignificant functionaries from Slovakia whom Dubček included among "his people").

That left only three people whose presidium membership was not a result of personal connections with the leading triumvirate—Josef Špaček, Josef Smrkovský, and František Kriegel. Špaček was elevated to this position in January of 1968 by the regional CPC organization in Brno, of which he was the leading secretary. Smrkovský, thanks to his public activity after January, became extraordinarily popular and practically the only serious contender for president of the Republic. His position as chairman of the National Assembly and member of the presidium was a kind of compensation for not having made it into the Castle. Kriegel got into the presidium as a result of various maneuvers among Central Committee factions. He was not one of Dubček's personal friends at the outset of the Prague Spring, nor did he ever become one. His main base of support was in the Prague party organization rather than in the central apparatus, and during the conflict with Novotný he joined forces with Šik, Vodsloň, and Prchlík, who later were not included among the "elect" of the new triumvirate. On the contrary, Černík, Kolder, and Dubček all opposed Šik's membership in the presidium, though for several years he had had the most integrated conceptions of economic and social reform. Černík and Kolder, I believe, were against Šik for reasons of personal rivalry.

The secretariat of the Central Committee was also a part of the new party leadership. Apart from the three members of the presidium—Dubček, Kolder, and Lenárt—the secretariat included six new people: Alois Indra (whose road to power I have already described and who, beyond that, had worked closely with both Černík and Kolder for many years), Štefan Sádovský (Dubček's personal friend), Oldřich Voleník (party secretary in Ostrava, which is one of the most powerful Communist regions and also home ground for Černík and Kolder), Čestmír Císař, Václav Slavík, and myself.

Čestmír Císař's road to glory was a winding and rather unique one. In the 1950s he had worked in the ideological section of the Central Committee apparatus and was a faithful, though relatively well-educated, Stalinist (he had gone to a French-language secondary school, and before the war he had briefly attended the university in Dijon). Among other things, he had written a review praising the collected writings of Rudolf Slánský; unfortunately, it was shortly before the latter's fall and arrest, and Císař was cast into the lowest ranks of the party apparatus, whence, after 1956, he gradually worked his way up again to become editor in chief of the party's theoretical journal, *Nová Mysl (New Mind)*. After writing a work called *We Grew With The Years*, in which he described—in a style more cultured and accomplished than was common in the party press—the development of Czechoslovakia and the CPC as a generally unbroken series of triumphs for which he gave Novotný a substantial share of the credit, Novotný, whom Císař had accompanied on some trip abroad, took a liking to him. And in 1963 Novotný raised him to secretary of the Central Committee. Given the favorable circumstances that year, Císař was able to carry out some fairly liberal policies. The few months of his rule in the Central Committee were referred to among Prague reform Communist intellectuals as "the summer of grace." Falling from favor again, he was shunted into the position of minister of education.

In 1965, during the traditional student Maytime Festival, his daughter took part in what was described as an "antiparty demonstration." As a result, Císař was removed as minister of education and appointed ambassador to Rumania, gaining, however, student popularity. This was terribly helpful to him in 1968, when the student slogan, "Císař to the Castle,"* made him a possible presidential candidate in the eyes of the public. Within the power structure, however, the idea was never taken seriously; though, along with his popu-

---

* This slogan, however, was not without some intended irony. Císař means "Caesar" in Czech.

larity among some of the intelligentsia, it did contribute to his rein-
statement as a secretary of the Central Committee.

Like many party functionaries in those years, Císař represented a
mixture of communist ideological faith and careerism. When he was
removed as minister of education and about to be sent to Rumania, I
ran into him in front of the Central Committee building. "It's terrible," he said. "I've just been to see Novotný. I bared my soul to him
and he kicked it." I replied that the moral was never to bare your soul
to anyone who couldn't care less. Císař looked at me as though I had
let my cynicism get the better of me and walked away. In October
1968, when it was clear that neither of us would be long in our positions, I had a frank talk with him. "That's all very well," said Císař,
"but what am I going to do? You can't expect me to get along on less
than ten thousand a month, can you?" I gave him a withering look,
and that was the end of the discussion.

Václav Slavík was another man not appointed to the Central
Committee secretariat because of his good relationships with the ruling trio. It is true that he was on good personal terms with Dubček,
but there were other important circumstances in his rise. Like
Smrkovský, he was one of those Central Committee members who
had helped to raise critical waves inside the party in support of reform after Novotný's departure. He had worked for years in the party
apparatus, first in *Rudé právo* (the party newspaper), then in Bucharest on the editorial staff of the Cominform (the organization of
European Communist parties) magazine, *For Lasting Peace, For a People's Democracy.* From the late 1950s on, he was head of the Central
Committee's ideological section and for a while was a party secretary
as well. Later he became deputy editor in chief of the international
Communist periodical, *Questions of Peace and Socialism,* and after 1966
he was director of the Central Committee's Institute for Political Science, which also cooperated with my research team.

During his rather checkered career, Slavík had made a number of
ideological and political somersaults, but by the late sixties I felt he
was a sincere supporter of reform. Naturally, he was also out to gain
political influence and position, but he was not a careerist, and, in
human terms, he is a rather modest and honest man. For this reason,
different factions within the political apparatus trusted him, and perhaps it was precisely his facility with these various and conflicting
people that helped elevate him to his position in Dubček's secretariat.
During the stormy developments of 1968, he arranged meetings and

compromises in many behind-the-scenes conflicts, particularly between the party headquarters and the Prague municipal party organization. He was close both to Dubček and to Kriegel, and to many people from the radical party intelligentsia and in the party apparatus.

I myself became a member of the Central Committee secretariat in April 1968 quite unexpectedly—both for myself and for others. In the first place, I was not even a Central Committee member, but merely someone from behind the scenes in the party apparatus. Being secretary of the Central Committee's legal commission did not automatically assume membership in the Central Committee itself, whereas membership in the secretariat normally did. Insofar as I was considered to belong to some faction, it was to the group around Koucký and Hendrych, whose fortunes, excluding O. Švestka's, rapidly declined in April 1968.

At that time, I was not acquainted with Dubček personally, nor was he with me, and I knew Černík only very casually. Kolder was perhaps the only one of the three I was acquainted with somewhat closely, but not on a very personal level.

I was, of course, one of the authors of the Action Program, in some ways its main author, and this strengthened my position in the corridors of power, but I had never expected any official function to follow from it. As an indication of how my services were valued by the new leadership, I was offered, at the end of March, the post of prosecutor general, which I rejected because I wanted to stay on the conceptual, theoretical side of politics. And, after this, I had even less reason to expect any high-party function.

The "working group" I was in, responsible for writing the text of the Action Program, was invited to the April session of the Central Committee, where the program was to be finally ratified. In Novotný's time, such invitations had become a form of "honorary reward" for those who worked behind the scenes. In this case, however, I was very concerned that the political commentary adequately explain the conceptual questions I considered important. Therefore, I asked to speak at the session and was given the floor. True, I was the penultimate speaker—but this turned out to be very significant, for the only person to address the Central Committee after me was Novotný himself. The unintentional but very clear contrast between Novotný's speech and mine attracted that much more attention. Among other things, I concluded with a criticism of the Dubček leadership for losing the initiative and being swept along by developments rather than themselves providing political leadership and guidance in society. I mentioned quite explicitly the danger of the "revival process" ending up as it had in Hungary in 1956. This sentence was deleted by Švestka in the printed version of my speech in *Rudé právo*, but in the Central Committee itself it roused attention. Moreover, the conservative, Stalinist part of the Central Committee were pleased to hear such words.

During the discussion on the proposed Action Program, Josef Havlín—who today, under Husák, is a Central Committee secretary, and at the time was the retiring head of the department under Koucký—moved that I be elected a secretary of the Central Committee. And during a break, Dubček sought me out and offered me a post as secretary, with the proviso that I would direct the work of the ideological section along with Císař. I told him I would have to think it over, but that I preferred to devote my time to working out further reforms of the political system in theory and practice and thus have some real influence on the activities of the state organs and the social organizations, the National Front, and so on, and that I was not really interested in purely ideological work. This did not suit Dubček very well at the moment, for that particular field had in fact been reserved for Alois Indra. We agreed that I would tell him my final decision during the next break.

I came to the conclusion that I could do the most good by continuing my work at the Academy of Sciences on general conceptions of political reform, but also have an official position on the secretariat of the Central Committee. I also felt that just as there were party economic journals dealing with questions of economic reform, there ought to be a journal of political science. Matters relating to political reform were merely discussed in the daily newspapers and cultural and political weeklies. I felt I would like to edit such a magazine. Dubček consented to my suggestion, and so on April 5, 1968, I was elected to the secretariat of the Central Committee, without a secretarial function.

However, after only two months' in the presidium and secretariat of the Central Committee I saw that making speeches at meetings of the leadership influenced nothing, and, to be in a position of power, I asked to be given a secretarial post. On June 1, 1968, I was elected secretary.

Another new man became a member of the secretariat at the same time—Evžen Erban. As a former functionary of the Social Democratic party before 1948, his new position was meant, among other things, to demonstrate that opportunities now existed in the CPC for Social Democrats and that reviving their own party was unnecessary. Erban's career, however, was not exactly eloquent in making this point, and indeed it did not. Erban was also named a secretary of the National Front, where he tended to work against rather than with its chairman, František Kriegel. For this service and others to the "normalization" politics, his sins were forgiven and he has managed to this day to hold the meaningless, though well-paid, decorative function of chairman of the Czech National Council.

This, then, is how the Dubček party leadership came into being—a product of behind-the-scenes conflicts and compromises in the power structure, influenced partly by the strengthening democratic movement both in the party and public sphere. In terms of the actual power relationships, the leadership was perhaps a rather accurate expression of the realities of that moment. In terms of the impending political problems, however, it was a self-defeating conglomeration of incongruent political forces. That in itself is proof that the trio in power—Dubček, Černík, and Kolder—had misjudged the future and underestimated the gravity of the situation.

Along with creating a new party leadership, the men in power also appointed a new president and a new government. At that time the office of president was understood almost unanimously by the party leadership to have a kind of general moral and political significance so that it genuinely represented the apex of political power. Consequently, they looked for someone who would enjoy authority both among large numbers of the population and within the party. The office was no longer to be combined with a high function in the party: the CPC leadership instinctively longed for someone who would be "above the party," someone who would subtly evoke a sense of continuity with the presidents of the first, prewar republic, though they did not want him to be a non-Communist altogether. "If only we could find some professor," is how Kolder once put it, rather tellingly. "If only Nejedlý were still alive," he went on, less tellingly this time, for the difference between Masaryk and Nejedlý in this connection quite escaped him. The effort to find "some professor" went so far as to include the president of the Academy of Sciences, František Šorm, as a candidate. In the end, everyone with any say about it agreed, on the whole without serious objections, to General Ludvík Svoboda. He genuinely seemed to be in many ways just what they were looking for, and he was elected president on March 30, 1968. After his election, Svoboda placed a wreath on the grave of T. G. Masaryk—something that had not been done since 1948.

The new government of the Prague Spring, led by Prime Minister Černík, was on the whole better qualified and more closely associated with the conceptual approach to reform politics than the party leadership itself. Certain preconditions for this went back to Novotný, whose prime minister, Jozef Lenárt, was himself a rational man and sought out more highly-qualified people than Novotný had for the various party functions. Lenárt was one of those who had been schooled in Baťa's shoe manufacturing enterprises in his youth, and it left its mark on him. In February 1967, I prepared a speech for him about the national committees, and late that evening just the two of us went over the text together. "You're a clever man," Lenárt remarked, "what are you looking for in The Shack?* Stick with the government. Over there they only shoot off their mouths. Here things get done."

At that time, it was a risky thing to say, even for him. But Lenárt did not limit himself to critical comments: the economic reforms of the 1960s had received the blessings of the party, but it was Lenárt's government, with economic ministers such as František Vlasák and Bohumil Sucharda, that had done much to realize them.

Thus, in a sense, Černík had a tradition to fall back on. Moreover, several competent people who had not received places in the party leadership had been "shunted" into the government, above all Ota Šik and Lubomír Štrougal, but also Gustav Husák. However much later developments have shown Štrougal and Husák to be equally adept at serving antireform, dictatorial politics, the fact remains that they are more able and qualified than Bilak and Kapek, for example, who are likewise pillars of "normalization" today and who in the spring of 1968 were members of Dubček's leadership—some of Černík's new ministers, like Jiří Hajek in the Ministry of Foreign Affairs, Vladimír Kadlec in the Ministry of Education, and Miroslav Galuška in the Ministry of Culture, were people with expert qualifications for their jobs as well as being convinced supporters of democratic reform. In short, the government was more suitably staffed for the needs of the reform than the party apparatus.

Beyond this question of competence, the government also proved

---

* In the party slang, "shack" (*barák* in Czech) traditionally referred to the central party apparatus.

to be more trustworthy. On August 22, after the Soviet intervention, a total of nine members of Dubček's party leadership were prepared to form a collaborationist "revolutionary workers' and peasants' government" and undoubtedly arrest and try Dubček, along with Smrkovský, Kriegel, and Černík, whereas in the whole of Černík's government only one minister (O. Pavlovský) was so inclined. Several of the highest party functionaries were preparing for the Soviet intervention, while the only conspiring government functionaries were the chairman of the Central Board for Communications, K. Hoffman, and the deputy minister of the interior, V. Šalgovič. Moreover, neither Pavlovský nor Šalgovič had been appointed to their government functions by Černík. The former was foisted upon him, as I have already mentioned, by Alois Indra, and the latter by Dubček himself.

Šalgovič's boss was Josef Pavel, whom I myself had recommended as minister of the interior. When I was summoned by V. Koucký to the Central Committee building to be offered the post of prosecutor general, Koucký mentioned in the course of our conversation that they did not yet have a new minister of the interior. Several possible candidates had refused, and he specifically mentioned Oldřich Voleník, secretary of the regional CPC committee in Ostrava. Clearly, no one was exactly lining up for the post, nor was this surprising. As I said to Koucký when he asked me for any suggestions, the minister of the interior should be someone who knows that sphere well and who at the same time would undertake to purge the entire apparatus of people responsible for the unlawful acts of the past, and who would not allow the apparatus of the State Security forces to be politically misused in the future. The problem was to find such a person, but I promised to think about it. Koucký returned to the presidium then meeting to discuss the formation of the new government, while I thought over various possibilities and came to the conclusion that Josef Pavel might be just such a person.

Pavel was a prewar Communist. During the Spanish civil war, he had been commander of the International Brigade, and in the Second World War he had served with a Czechoslovak unit in England. After the war he had been head of the Central Committee security department and later deputy minister of the interior. In 1951 he was arrested, but he was one of the few who, despite all the inhuman methods used during his interrogation, never falsely confessed to any fabricated crimes and thus escaped the stage-managed political trial. Pavel, in fact, shared in the guilt of the party's crimes between 1948 and 1951, but, in the process, he had come to know well the security apparatus, its methods and its personnel, and could take care of himself in it. From what I knew about him, I was convinced he was one of those unjustly accused Communists who had not only drawn the proper conclusions but had undergone a profound change as a result.

I had Koucký called out of the presidium session and gave him my suggestion. He agreed and said that he would present it at the meeting. What the other circumstances of Pavel's candidacy were—whether there were any countersuggestions, who supported Pavel's appointment and who opposed it and why—I have no idea. Pavel did in fact become minister of the interior. He not only remained personally independent of Dubček, Černík, and Kolder, but he was outside the Soviet espionage network as well. His life was certainly not easy. But as far as I know, he executed his charge as I believed he would: he began serious and thorough preparations for a purge of the security apparatus and he meticulously sought not to break any laws. In this he sometimes went to extreme lengths.

For example, I was present when Černík, late in the evening after the August 1 meeting of the CPC presidium with the Soviet politburo in Čierná nad Tisou, telephoned from Čierná and asked Pavel to confiscate the latest issue of *Reportér,* which was already being distributed and was to appear on the stands next morning. It contained a cartoon that had somehow enraged Brezhnev (he had already been informed about it) and went against the CPC leadership's promise in Čierná to "stop the polemics." Josef Pavel refused to obey Černík's order, saying that the prime minister had no law to cover such an instance. Černík shouted down the telephone at him, but Pavel calmly replied: "In that case you'll have to find yourself a new minister of the interior, comrade prime minister." And he hung up.

I called Pavel back and told him that in my judgment the situation was so exceptional that perhaps he ought to do what Černík had said. "Perhaps," said Pavel, "but then let him send some comrades along to do it, and not the police. If I break the law once, I'll break it again, and we're right back where we started. Back then it began as something exceptional too, and then it became common practice." I recalled how I had once refused to obey an unlawful order of the prosecutor general twenty years ago, but then I also recalled what had happened to me as a result. And I added that in his case it would be particularly regrettable, because there was more at stake now and he should not let himself be swept aside for being stubborn in such isolated cases. "It can't be helped," said Pavel. "Someone else will have to do it then."

The people Josef Pavel purged from the security apparatus on the basis of the new higher legal standards, belonged, of course, to the Soviet espionage network. It is understandable, therefore, that Dubček soon felt pressure from Moscow to put a quick end to such irregularities. In this regard, Viliam Šalgovič came to be imposed upon Pavel by the party leadership as a deputy for State Security. On the whole, it was common knowledge that Šalgovič was an old KGB agent from the war. When the presidium discussed his candidacy as deputy to the minister of the interior, someone (unfortunately I can't recall who) pointed this fact out directly. Dubček, however, supported him unreservedly and pushed through his appointment. He was probably thinking that they had to have a Soviet agent in that position anyway, and it might as well be his friend, someone upon whom—as he mistakenly hoped—he could depend at least personally.

Even with these concessions to Moscow, however, Dubček encountered growing difficulties, lack of confidence, and resistance in Moscow from the very first weeks of his rule. But this was not due to any illusions on Dubček's part concerning the receptivity in Moscow to democratic reform, nor to any ignorance about what would cause objections in Moscow, Warsaw, and Berlin, and why.

It is my feeling that in his relationship with Brezhnev, Dubček applied the same tactics as he did in domestic politics: he attempted to create a situation in which the Kremlin would ultimately be compelled to agree with his purposes and seek in them the assurance of its own policies, for it would understand that Dubček's way of dealing with things was right for the objective necessities of the situation in Czechoslovakia. In this sense too Dubček thought the wide democratic movement was something that would in the end serve his aims, for though it would arouse fears in Moscow, it would at the same time compel Brezhnev to recognize that Dubček could also guarantee his, Brezhnev's, own interests, and that he could not hope to resolve the situation favorably otherwise.

In harmony with his deepest inner convictions, Dubček never intended a break with Moscow: he would have seen that as a threat to socialism in Czechoslovakia. From the declared principles of his foreign policy to the concrete questions of personnel for key positions, he made it abundantly clear to Moscow that on fundamental questions he could be relied upon. At the same time, however, he believed that doing this would gain him more freedom of action where he felt this was necessary. He consequently took independent measures in his program and in his appointments, knowing that they would not always meet with Moscow's approval. But whenever a serious conflict seemed to be brewing, he would turn around and follow the implicit or explicit desires of Moscow. He was always hoping to thus "persuade them in a comradely fashion."

I will go into more detail in the next chapter about why he failed.

But what was going on outside the power structure while party members were jockeying for new positions? What sort of public pressure ultimately contributed to the personnel changes among the rulers?

Political extremists from both ends of the spectrum have made much of the political slogans and demands that, like the attempt to reestablish a social democratic party or to convert the Club of Committed Non-Communists (KAN) into a political party outside the National Front, were aiming directly at a power confrontation with the ruling CPC. In reality these tendencies did not represent the real wave of democratic pressure "from below" in 1968.

At the very beginning, in January 1968, after Novotný had been ousted, the public mood was merely one of curious expectation: what will "they" do now? Very few believed it might have particularly personal significance for them and even less did they think it might represent a turning point in their lives simply because those "on top" were having it out among themselves again. Perhaps it was only Communists who felt the repercussions of changes in the party leadership, but even there, among the factory, town, and city rank-and-file, the significance of these changes was far from clear. The belief that not very much had happened (something that even a Central Committee secretary, Vladimír Koucký, maintained right into March) was still shared by the people in January.

Within a few weeks, however, the situation began to change very rapidly. In the press, the radio, and on television people read and heard unbelievably free-thinking articles and speeches. At first, they merely listened curiously to see what would happen next. But the censors did not intervene, nor did the Central Committee meet to condemn the brave journalists and issue statements on what was impermissible in the "interests of the working class and the people." On the contrary, when Dubček spoke to the congress of agricultural cooperatives, he discussed not only fertilizers, productivity, corn, and live-stock but also "the self-fulfillment of man." There was pointed public criticism not only of the public works departments and their directors but also of the work methods within the CPC, the trades union, security forces, and the judiciary—resulting in the removal of leading functionaries. At public party meetings more and more people asked to speak, not to manifest the "unity of the people," but to express their sincere opinions, debate, and make proposals about where to go from there. One such mass meeting ended in a demand that Antonín Novotný resign as president. Far from being broken up by the police, or condemned later in *Rudé právo*, the meeting was carried live on radio. And what followed seemed right out of a fairy tale: eight days later Novotný actually resigned.

This happened, symbolically, on March 21, the first day of spring, 1968. What was born anew was the faith of people that they themselves meant something, that they were responsible for their own fate, that they could administer their common, public affairs.

There was a growing sense of a national resurgence, of a national destiny, that takes place only at moments of important historical change, such as in October 1918 or May 1945. There was the sudden joy at the end of a long period of despair, at the end of oppression, and the feeling of a new beginning.

While inside the power structure the democratically-inclined reform Communists were battling for power with the authoritarian-minded Communists and with the underworld of Soviet agents in the CPC, a new and powerful factor appeared on the scene of the Prague Spring: the feeling that the nation as a whole was involved in the present moment. From March to June, 1968, this factor became increasingly strong in public and private life. It was a huge public forum of hopes and desires, in which private and political hopes merged and gave rise to a kind of festive atmosphere: in the name of the better times to come the nation was generously ready to reconcile itself and forgive old wrongs.

At the same time, these hopes and longings represented the individual economic, social, and political interests of the various social strata. Workers wanted an improved standard of living, and faith that their material needs would be better satisfied was an important part of their hopes. Thus, the fact that society had entered the consumer stage of its development played a role here. Furthermore, each social stratum demanded—according to the viewpoint of its own interests—a larger share in political decision making. Under Novotný, both the workers and the intelligentsia had been dissatisfied with their degree of influence on the life of society. But they were operating not on the basis of the old class antagonisms and conflicts, but rather on the basis of the new post-1948 social conditions. In political terms, people were asking chiefly for the regime to respect their civil and social rights in the same way as legitimate states in the pluralistic political democracies respected them.

Yet how can this good will towards the Czechoslovak state be accounted for when it was still the same state people had known in the past? There were different people occupying the highest functions, but Parliament remained the unelected body everyone knew it to be, despite the past pretenses of elections. Moreover, the entire bureaucratic administrative apparatus, the State Security forces, and the discredited judiciary all survived intact except for a few personnel changes. And yet people donated to this same state their family heirlooms to help swell the state's gold reserves.

The CPC remained the same party of monopoly power and dictatorial rule that it had been for twenty years. True, it had new leaders, but all of them were people who three months before had been indistinguishable to outside observers from others in the upper ranks of the party. A new program had been declared, but how many times had this been done in the past already? Six months ago this party could not even have counted on receiving in truly free elections at least as many votes as it had registered members. And now, objectively conducted public opinion polls indicated that 70 percent of the population supported its policies, and about 25 percent of those without reservation.

Socialism for these people was no abstraction: it was the system that had been in power for the past 20 years, a period whose end was welcomed with great expectations. And yet 80 percent of the population came out in favor of socialism. It is true that people were declaring their support for their social security as well, for the state's responsibility to look after their vital necessities, and so on. But what happened to that mass discontent with the thousand-and-one problems of everyday life that those same people associated with "socialism" in practice?

I think there is only one possible answer: the people, having faith in their hopes, gave precedence to their humanistic and democratic values that had been maturing in the nation over long generations, not only as political values, but, above all, as moral values. It is a value system that fuelled the "national awakening" in the nineteenth century, a movement that developed in the struggle for national independence under the Austrian empire, and T. G. Masaryk built on it and cultivated it. It was brought up to date and developed critically in the cultural and political life of the first Czechoslovak Republic; it was violently suppressed during the Nazi occupation only to reenter public life in 1945. Again violently suppressed by the CPC after 1948 and demagogically misused, it reentered the political arena with renewed vigor in the spring of 1968.

Once fear was gone, the democratic, humanitarian national consciousness came forward as the main protagonist in the Prague Spring, and from April to June it was unquestionably the main player on the stage. In July, however, a visible and powerful antagonist appeared: the Kremlin accompanied by the Warsaw Pact as the chorus. It was then that the vulnerability of the freedom from fear was exposed, and that fear itself could make another entry. This sense of danger was shared by both the nation and the reform Communists, who were now a part of that nation: their destinies had been fused, and both became increasingly aware of it. The confidence of the nation in the reformers grew to become a kind of "*ad hoc* mandate" (an expression actually used at that time).

It had become clear, however, that even something as grand as freedom from fear is ultimately, in the world of power and violence, not enough in itself to avert a good many very serious pitfalls on the road to democracy and freedom. Several key changes in personnel were made but these only paralyzed, temporarily at that, the remainder of the dictatorial mechanism. And free expression of opinion at meetings, in the press, radio, and television was not suppressed. These things by themselves could and did bring temporary freedom from fear, but for lasting, systemic change a grasp of politics was necessary.

And how did the rulers—in the widest sense of that word, that is, the entire membership of the CPC, both reform and conservative Communists, both functionaries and rank and file—fit into this? The issue over which Communists themselves parted ways was whether they accepted or rejected the humanistic, democratic value system as a criterion for judging the correctness of developments in socialist societies. The problem is first and foremost a moral and political one, and often more moral than political. Communists became a part of their own nation, and they became quite as passionately involved in this national movement as the rest of the country. Their ideological and political past had to stand up before their own consciences. It was no longer a question of rational political thinking, and even less of any political scheming: at issue here were the values attached to human life, recognized intuitively and personally.

Thus what began as an attempt by Communists to reform the totalitarian dictatorship politically grew to become a widely based democratic social movement with a marked and often decisive moral charge. Confronted with this movement, Communists once more found themselves divided into two camps, in many cases quite different from before. A large majority joined the nationwide movement, recognized its moral strength and behaved accordingly. In many cases, however, it was an attitude that later, under the pressure of violence and a new wave of fear, would be broken once again—as it was in millions of non-Communists, simple people in whom national consciousness only spoke when they had been liberated from fear. Some of these Communists would even become active in the "normalization" process, as would some non-Communists. But during the Prague Spring, only a small minority of Communists stood outside the nationwide movement and the values it espoused. And thus, because it is impossible to be neutral in such a heightened moral and political conflict, such people not only excluded themselves from this movement they became its active and relentless enemies. This schism later became very clear during the Soviet intervention, though it had begun to take shape earlier, in the period from approximately May to July. The military intervention altered this fundamental division very little. This tiny minority in the CPC formed the Russian, Soviet fifth column in Czechoslovakia, regardless of whether its individual members were actually part of the espionage network of the Soviet embassy and the KGB or not. Frequently, however, non-Communists belonged to this group as well, some of them well-known, like Father Plojhar, others anonymous.

In this sense, those final, culminating months of the Prague Spring of 1968 were a "moment of truth" for the nation. Not because all those who submitted to the humanitarian values that lived in the "heart of the nation" would subsequently be capable of denying those values again and even actively combating them—it would have been an illusion to expect anything else—but because the "moment of truth" did show that none of those who joined the nationwide movement was able to resist it once the nation was liberated from fear.

These months were also a moment of truth in the sense that it was clear what socialism was and was not associated with in the minds of a vast majority of the nation. People accepted socialism when it was associated with humanitarian and democratic values, and they rejected it when it was associated with the values of totalitarianism. In other words, precisely the opposite of what twenty years before (and now ten years after) was officially claimed by the ruling regime and formally recognized by that same majority, whose inner convictions were and are silenced by the hegemony of fear. And it was also clear that the same was true for a great majority of the Communists of that time, as the politically-ruling stratum. Seen from Moscow, of course, it was a genuinely catastrophic situation, and military intervention was, in that sense, an entirely logical step.

As with the entire CPC, Dubček's party leadership, installed at the beginning of April, was confronted with the social activity outside the power structure. Here too individuals were distinguished on the basis of their attitude to the nationwide democratic movement, to the demands of the "revival process," as it was called at the time. And because in certain phases of this development the chief issues were not purely political but involved moral and human values as well, the top party leadership had to deal with them on this level. Suddenly the personal, human qualities of the individual leaders took on an exceptional importance and in many political situations were a decisive factor. From the viewpoint of the rational needs of political reform, however, this created a complicated and very contradictory situation.

In the course of April and May, the pressure of the new social situation began to divide the original trio, which made up the core of the new leadership—Dubček, Černík, and Kolder.

During those two months the political significance of Alexander Dubček's personality grew at a dizzying rate, something which clearly surprised both himself and those around him, not to mention the rulers in the Kremlin. And not without reason: for the first secretary of a Communist party that had ruled in a totalitarian and dictatorial way for twenty years to become the charismatic leader of a nationwide democratic and humanitarian movement was something that had never happened anywhere before in the entire history of Communism.

Nevertheless, there are several logical and scarcely exalted explanations for this extraordinary growth in Dubček's personal power. One was that quite different political tendencies among both supporters and opponents of democratic reforms considered it politically expedient to proclaim their allegiance to Dubček personally. Politically it was less binding, for example, than proclaiming allegiance to the Action Program (concerning which various groups had reservations), and its popularity, owing to the real need among the people to identify a political program with a concrete person, could be exploited. Thus representatives of differing political tendencies joined in promoting and strengthening Dubček's authority in the hope that ultimately it could be used to serve their own ends.

But this in itself does not fully explain Dubček's role during the Prague Spring, nor do his political speeches at the time. It is true that there was a personal quality about them, particularly in his delivery, but, on the whole, they did not differ essentially from other official political speeches of the time. Like all CPC potentates' speeches, they were written by aides, "working groups," or other higher functionaries (I myself frequently wrote long passages), representing all the various tendencies. Thus, as in Novotný's time, these various internal tendencies would be more or less balanced in the first draft of the speech given to Dubček. No, Dubček's political speeches alone cannot explain the role of his personality in 1968.

Is the key to his popularity, then, his being shown by the press and television in private—diving into a swimming pool, etc.? Did people succumb to his smile? Such things did play a certain role, particularly after all those years in which the rulers appeared publicly only in their official, bureaucratic guise. And yet if smiles were the decisive factor, the people's first love would have been Čestmír Císař, whose ready smile, however, might have been more suitable for advertising toothpaste, or perhaps for a United States senatorial election campaign. For the role that Dubček played in 1968, however, it was far from being enough.

I think that by far the most fundamental reason for Dubček's broad support was something quite different. Dubček believed in his ideals. He was a believing ruler at a time when the entire nation surrendered to the need for faith. People unerringly sensed that Dubček believed, and he, in his turn, felt the same belief in them. This is why he trusted people, and I think this trust was deep and sincere. And they trusted him. Oddly enough, what was fundamental here was not *what* Dubček and the nation believed in but rather the clear fact that this mutual faith existed. That, too, is understandable for a time when cynicism and formal faith had dominated things for years. And it is understandable in a nation for whom a sincere, human, humanitarian faith is a value in itself.

Everything else pertaining to Dubček's popularity was important insofar as it reflected this basic fact: that Dubček was clearly not authoritarian by nature, and his uneasiness whenever he appeared in public was precisely what increased his popularity and even his authority. He was not a good public speaker, he could not sway masses of people with his rhetoric, but in small groups of a dozen or so he commanded attention. He also knew how to listen, and it was clear that he listened with interest, that his opinions were not unalterably fixed and that he was open to ideas different from his own. He was not incapable of being influenced. And when at last he managed to impose his own will on others, which in fact happened frequently—for it was genuinely difficult to get him to change his mind once it was made up—he did it quietly and unobtrusively, without the fanfare and the force of authoritarian people. I think that of all those in the party leadership, Dubček was the least authoritarian.

All of these qualities are related to Dubček's attitude to power. He was not fascinated by power, nor was he the type of person who used power for personal gain. And, perhaps most important of all in political terms, he did not feel that power was an appropriate instrument for imposing communist ideals on the life of society. No matter how much he believed in communism and considered himself, with inner conviction, to be a Marxist-Leninist, he had a positive mistrust of the role of force and power. Dubček believed in many of the standard Marxist-Leninist precepts concerning the class war, taking place both nationally and internationally, but he recognized the role of force and power only as a means of defending Communist objectives against enemy attacks, and not at all as a means of realizing those objectives. And as long as he was not personally convinced that there was a genuine threat from a class enemy, he refused to use force to promote his ideals, communist hypotheses, and notions.

Dubček would have taken issue with being compared to Masaryk rather than to Lenin. And in part he would be quite right, for Dubček was not a Masarykian humanist. But, in certain situations, ideological labels and even the more profound tenets of a world view are less an indication of fundamental beliefs than a basic attitude toward quite concrete questions. And Dubček's practical attitude toward violent, dictatorial methods genuinely corresponded to the democratic and humanistic traditions shared by the nation: a Masarykian rejection of dictatorial violence and a longing for democratic reform.

Thus, Dubček genuinely possessed the human and political qualities to become the symbol of the Prague Spring that he was, and, in that respect, his election as first secretary of the Central Committee was an exceptionally fortunate occurrence. For the authority of the reform policies was strongly underpinned by the personal authority of Dubček, and there was hardly anyone else in the party leadership who could even have hoped to do the same.

In other respects, however, Dubček's election was less than fortunate, if not positively unfortunate, for the reforms. In the first place, Dubček himself did not fully understand his role. He did not realize how coincidental the circumstances were on which his great popularity and political authority depended. He saw them as an absolute expression of a nationwide agreement with his political conceptions and opinions. Put simply, he felt, correctly, that the nation believed in him, but he concluded that by the same token it believed as fervently as he did in Marxism-Leninism and that it supported all his concrete political measures. As his public popularity and the confidence he enjoyed grew, so did his overestimation—at least in my view—of his real political options. He felt that backed by such public sentiments, carefully-thought-out political measures were unnecessary, and he could rely merely on his good will. Also Dubček's excessive (and, as later events proved, unfounded) optimism about his ability to resist the will of the Kremlin obviously derived from his conviction that his undeniable national authority would convince Brezhnev that there was no threat of a "counter-revolution" in Czechoslovakia.

In addition to overestimating the personal factor in politics, and his faith that people well-disposed to him would act in accordance with his political expectations, etc., there was his indecisiveness, or rather his slowness to decide in situations that demanded quick decisions. This quality was the obverse of his otherwise positive attempt not to make decisions in an authoritarian manner, and always to "persuade the comrades" first. In a number of situations, when all the possible circumstances bearing on a decision were known, when everyone had repeated all the pros and cons till they were blue in the face and it was only up to him to decide, Dubček would put the decision off still further. In many cases, the decision was in fact made elsewhere, by some new circumstance, and otherwise than he himself would have liked. But in such situations, it was too late for him to do anything about it.

Thus, while Dubček symbolized policies attempting to realize the great ideals of democratic socialism, inside the actual party leadership he was often something quite different: the head of a powerful political apparatus who practiced, much as he had always done, a rather limited style of personal politics, which became bogged down both in internal petty intriguing and also in disputes with Moscow. His position with the public, however, was a crucial factor in this leadership, and not even those who were in fact against Dubček's reform policies dared to oppose him openly. On the contrary, they tried to win him over.

It was Vasil Bilak, in particular, who in presidium meetings often tried to convince Dubček he was becoming the victim of "antisocialist" forces. He explained that these forces were duping him, that their operating slogan was "With Dubček against Dubček," and that, on the contrary, he, Bilak, saw everything precisely as Dubček did. In time, Kolder too came to adopt this position. When this failed, direct criticism began to appear. Emil Rigo, as a "representative of the working people" in the presidium (he was a party functionary from Eastern Slovakia), claimed that there was talk among "the people down below" that Dubček was creating a "personality cult" for himself. Several others rather timidly added their voices to this criticism—once again mainly Kolder and Bilak. But Dubček was not naive enough to view this as sincere "comradely help," and all such attempts failed to have the desired effect.

The second man in the original trio—Oldřich Černík—unlike Dubček, was not a charismatic type of leader in the least. He was not even a "spokesman of the popular will," such as Josef Smrkovský was. Even so, he too gained a considerable degree of personal authority with the public during April and May, and thus the nationwide democratic and humanitarian "revival movement" strengthened his political position as well.

Černík was a rational, pragmatic politician, a managerial type rather than an ideologue or agitator. And it was his matter-of-factness and the cultivated way he appeared and spoke in public, rather than any particularly outstanding faith, humanity, and openness, that inspired trust in the public. In this respect, Černík would have made a good premier in a non-Communist regime as well, as long as it was not totalitarian. In a totalitarian regime, he would have maintained and supported rational and democratic forms of rule, as he in fact did under Novotný.

Černík felt that a democratic system would be more rational and effective than limited totalitarian power, and this was the main reason he supported reform. He was, of course, an intelligent and able organizer, and he understood the need capable people have to function in a system that values their abilities and grants them responsibility and position accordingly. It was from this perspective that he approached the question of democracy and civil rights.

In my opinion, therefore, it would be wrong to view Černík's association with the 1968 democratic reforms merely as the about-face of a self-seeking technocrat. Černík supported democratic development, and he also understood the moral energy that charged the nationwide democratic movement during the Prague Spring, but this moral aspect was not a point of departure for him personally. Insofar as these moral ideals were politically important in society, Černík respected them and tried to act in harmony with them. And therefore, his association with Dubček in the public mind became even stronger as Dubček's moral authority increased. Černík walked in the shadow of Dubček's charismatic personality, and some of Dubček's charisma rubbed off on him. But Černík did not support the reforms only for the political advantages: he was in agreement with the substance of the "revival process" as well.

Once, on a trip from Bratislava to Brno in June 1968, I walked with Černík through the castle park at Lednice in South Moravia. It was Sunday and the park was full of people. Many of them greeted us, and we would occasionally stop and chat with someone, and once Černík handed a ball back to a little boy. In short, it was like an idyl you'd see in a newsreel. Černík was moved, and it made him feel and look good. But he handled such situations very differently from Dubček. On such occasions, Dubček would never stop to contemplate the significance of what he was doing—he would simply talk with people. Černík, on the contrary, was always aware of what such moments meant for his position, even though he too derived a quite normal, apolitical pleasure from the fact that people liked him.

Later, when we left the crowded pathways of the park and were alone, Černík suddenly said meditatively: "Granted, all this has in fact been left over from the feudal lords, the exploiters. But to this day it has a concrete value for the people, and those lords of the castle are still somehow alive in what they left. Do you think we will leave anything of value behind us?"

In this sudden fellow-feeling for the feudal lords and keepers of the castle, Černík inadvertently and unconsciously demonstrated how he really felt on that Sunday stroll among the people: like a ruler walking among his subjects. This says much about Černík's notion of democracy. It was democratic, but, at the same time, rationalistic and somewhat aristocratic, and therefore self-glorifying and not in the least disinterested. But it was a form of belief in democracy all the same, not at all the kind of feeling and thinking connected with the values of Communist totalitarianism.

In his life and ascent through the ranks of the political apparatus, of course, Oldřich Černík learned what was required to achieve success in the world of power. And he engaged in personal politicking and appointed his supporters to various functions; more so, on the whole, than Dubček. He was also more decisive than Dubček and quicker to take an authoritative position, but, at the same time, he was often arbitrary. He was not the type of person fascinated by power in itself. He looked at power very matter-of-factly and rationally, as a means to achieving given aims. He was no ideological fanatic who wanted to create happiness for people even against their own will, but he was certainly willing to make more frequent use of power than Dubček. The truth was that he did not believe to such an extent in the power of faith, good intentions, and persuasion, and he was consequently able to see dangers in situations where Dubček was still confident in the powers of persuasion.

Dubček and Černík might thus have created a complementary political team, but unfortunately their association did not survive the stress of the Soviet intervention, something I shall discuss later. Even when they were still functioning as a team, however, Černík was unable effectively to compensate for a number of Dubček's shortcomings: he was the chief of the government, not of the party apparatus, and he could not directly help settle conflicts in the party power structure.

The third member of the original triumvirate—Drahomír Kolder—came to occupy quite a different position from Dubček and Černík in April and May 1968. The pressure of the nationwide democratic movement took the rug out from under him, and it became increasingly clear to Kolder that his future at the pinnacle of political power would be in jeopardy were things to continue in that direction.

Kolder, originally a worker from Ostrava, had been employed in the party apparatus since he was twenty-three. In 1961, he became a member of the presidium and was under the direct patronage of No-votný. In many respects, he was akin to Novotný: they were both men who "owed everything to the party." His education was very shaky, limited to party-political "schooling," and his social status resulted solely from his loyalty to the party, its official ideology and political practices. For years, Kolder worked as a high-party official in the economic sphere, but he had no qualifications for the job and gained no expertise. His position always depended more on how successfully he gauged the lines of force in the internal party conflicts.

I knew Kolder before 1968, and I think he was a sincere person, who, according to his own standards, was also honorable. Whenever he concluded that something in party policy was incorrect and bad, he followed his conscience and defended his position obstinately, like a bull terrier, and would not drop the matter until he felt he had done all he could. The practice of stage-managed political trials in the 1950s is an example of something that went against Kolder's values. Thus, as chairman of the final "rehabilitation commission" under Novotný (in 1963), he played a very positive role and went further than anyone else had done in settling a problem that was an extremely delicate one for Novotný. In the same period, there were known cases where he behaved very decently toward victims of various repressions, and he even helped those who had been wrongly prosecuted and were still in prison unlawfully in the early sixties.

Kolder, however, was neither a Masarykian humanist nor a democrat. He was a typical plebeian. His folksiness was utterly sincere, but it was primitive and boorish. He reduced all human needs to primarily material ones. The only intellectual or spiritual needs he would acknowledge were those he considered morally and mentally necessary, and that was painfully little. He had very little understanding or tolerance for anything beyond that, and he had none of the humility that simple and uneducated, but not boorish, people have.

When Novotný was still in power, Kolder once went to Paris as the head of a party delegation. What impressed him most was a huge department store, which he explored thoroughly. Later that evening, in the Czechoslovak ambassador's residence, he eased his shock with one glass of cognac after another and finally declared quite frankly, "It's awful the things we've denied our people. Don't they deserve that kind of thing too?" I believe he was being sincere, and such things did more to encourage his support for economic reform than the theoretical theses of Ota Šik. But he was also being sincere when, on that historic night, as the Soviet planes were droning over the Central Committee building where the presidium was debating how to express its stand on the Soviet intervention, he said: "Here we are shooting the breeze, trying to figure out how to condemn them, and right now our women are probably screwing with them in Ostrava!"

Kolder was genuinely unaware that on that particular night not even the most desperate Czech streetwalker would have gone with a Russian soldier, because she had more moral inhibitions than a member of Dubček's presidium. Of course, she would not have been armed with the argument of "proletarian internationalism," which in Kolder's case may have provided the moral justification. At the same time, Kolder was not a direct agent of the Soviets—like Jakeš, for example, or probably Bilak, Indra, and others—and his crossover to an explicit antireform position that served the aims of Moscow was a consequence of his genuine personal and political attitudes.

There is a widespread notion that people of Kolder's type opposed the democratic reforms because they were corrupted by privilege, high pay, and so on. This notion is not quite accurate. It is true that all highly-placed functionaries were corrupted by power after all those years, but only some of them acted against the reforms out of fear of losing those privileges.

The privileges connected with high political office have always been considerable. I had known something of them both generally and concretely for many years, yet, even so, I was shocked by the prevalence of this privileged life when I was initiated into it in the summer of 1968 as a secretary of the Central Committee.

Looking at the purely financial side of it, the position of Central Committee secretary carried with it a monthly salary of 14,000 crowns (8,000 crowns of which was the nominal pay, taxed according to regulations; leaving 6,000 crowns as a special, untaxed sum to cover personal expenses incurred on the job). At the time, it was roughly ten times the average monthly income in Czechoslovakia, and three times my income in the Academy of Sciences, where I was in the top category of independent researchers. My salary in the Academy of Sciences was equal to what my personal aides in the Central Committee earned. And my salary as a secretary of the Central Committee was one of the lower ones, for I was not a member of the presidium. The first secretary of the Central Committee, the premier, and the chairman of the National Assembly all had incomes of 25,000 crowns per month.

At first I assumed that the amount set aside for "personal expenses" incurred in the job was to be so used. I was wrong, however. Food, drink, cigarettes, and other such things consumed during the various meetings and sessions in my office were paid for from a special fund for our office, and the same was true for travelling expenses, which in any case hardly ever came up, since each secretary had a car and chauffeur, which, according to internal regulations, were available for his own strictly personal use as well.

On my first visit to a factory in my official capacity as a Central Committee secretary—I believe it was in Brno—I discovered on leaving some parcels on the back seat of the car. Naively, I thought that the chauffeur had gone shopping while I was away, and I asked him what he'd bought. Surprised, he explained that they belonged to me and were gifts from the director of the plant. There were some glasses and a carved wooden statuette of a mouflon, presented to me on the assumption that I had the same taste for socialist realism and passion for hunting that had been traditional with top functionaries. In other words, they were trifles really, purchased from a similar fund for "personal expenses incurred on the job," this time the plant director's. But it was common practice, and all one had to do was say the word, and it would not stop at trifles.

Gradually, I penetrated the mysteries of the elite's everyday life. All I had to do to get anything from a new suit to something from Paris was to indicate it in the morning to my aide or secretary, and the rest would be seen to by the director of the "House of Fashion" or the Czechoslovak ambassador anywhere in the world. It was true that by my time whatever was ordered actually had to be paid for, but even so there were several ways the already quite advantaged could increase their advantages. A factory or enterprise, that is, its director, considered it an honor to present his product to the "comrade secretary," at a nominal price and of highest quality. And it goes without saying that the same people who thus supplied "the comrades" received favors in return.

I lived in a normal tenement house and refused the offer to move into a villa, and I consequently continued to pay the same rent as before. But I could have moved into a Central Committee-run apartment building, where my rent would also be nominal, with much of the expenses being covered by the Central Committee treasury. The position also came with the use of recreational facilities—a villa in a fenced-in and well-guarded forest resort at Orlík. To stay at such a villa, one paid—as far as I can remember—290 crowns per quarter, that is, about the same as an ordinary citizen would pay for a two-week stay in some collective holiday facility, where he would sleep on a board bed, wash in the pond, and go to the toilet in a latrine somewhere in the woods.

And all these are merely the most blatant financial and material privileges. Along with the highest positions, however, there also belongs an invisible network of influence that can brush aside all the thousands of daily inconveniences and obstacles that strain the resources of the average citizen of a socialist state. Even the national health system does not apply in the upper echelons. There is a special State Sanitorium (Sanops) where a person of party secretarial status can convalesce in a special suite with a reception room and television. Top doctors are brought in from all over the country, he is prescribed otherwise unobtainable foreign medication, and so on. And his entire family has access to this facility as well.

And if these were the privileges that automatically came with high political office, think of what you could obtain if you only put your mind to it. These privileges were continued by the most democratic leadership the CPC had ever had since it seized power. The salaries themselves were somewhat lower than they had been in Novotný's time, and Dubček discontinued Novotný's practice, known as "passing out the envelope," by which Novotný would regularly reward Politburo members and Central Committee secretaries with five-figure amounts in sealed envelopes, for "upgrading their salaries," naturally according to his own choosing.

From what I could deposit in a bank account of my salary as a Central Committee secretary during the six months I held the office, I was able to supplement my income over the next three years, when, from January 1969 on, I worked in the National Museum with a net monthly salary of 2,050 crowns. But what about those who drew their salaries, not for six months, but six years? I am still not entirely sure what these people do with their money. In Czechoslovakia, after all, one cannot speculate, invest, or convert money into capital. Of the few cases I know first hand, after they had bought a car, a villa, and various luxury items, they spent vast amounts of money to provide their children (and in some cases their relatives and inlaws as well) with a luxurious and essentially parasitic life style, which means they bought more cars and more villas. A strange aim in life for the top functionaries of a Communist party.

Naturally enough, those who live for years like this become habituated, and the desire to maintain their status can affect their political behavior. To a certain extent it affects everyone. I know from my own experience that even after six months I became used to some of those privileges to the point where I no longer questioned them. It did not go so far that I would have altered my political opinions simply to preserve my privileges, but, on the other hand, I would certainly not have proposed disbanding the State Sanitorium, even though I considered it to be a corrupt institution. In short, privileges always spoil people, particularly when they are associated with power. But the extent of the corruption is determined by the human, moral foundation in every person, a foundation that is laid long before they take their place among the powerful and the privileged.

I met two types of people among the party functionaries who had been so corrupted that their entire behavior was affected. The first type were rational people who had originally felt moral compunctions and therefore were well aware they had transgressed, which caused them to lose their faith and become cynical. The second category consisted of people of a quite different type—plebeians. Their behavior was also determined by a limitless corruption, but they had never known moral compunctions, not even before entering the world of power and its privileges. Their moral scale of values was so primitive that they embraced corruption uncynically, quite sincerely and naturally. These people often did not feel that they were corrupted, for by their own crude standards they were honest and upright. In the CPC as a whole, the plebeians dominated the older generation, but they were outnumbered by the cynics in the generation most active in 1968. Drahomír Kolder belonged inwardly to the generation of plebeians.

Although the material advantages connected with high office also played a role in his case, I suspect Kolder felt that power and high office were a measure of his own worth and significance. Like many others, he was no more than what political power made him; without it, he would have sunk into uncertainty and obscurity. He had no identity independent of his official role. Thus, when Kolder increasingly became the target of attacks and public criticism that he was helpless to stop, he reverted to the only sure things in his life, the values of total political power, justified by "the interests of the working class." This was not simply out of fear for his own fate, but because existence itself was inconceivable to Kolder outside the traditional forms of political power. (Another presidium member, Oldřich

Švestka, was a similar case.) Nonetheless, Kolder did, up until the attacks, support the reforms to the extent that his personality would allow. And in this he differed from Vasil Bilak, for example.

Kolder even felt a need to reaffirm the old political values at a time when it wasn't best for his position. Thus, when the CPC refused to participate in the Warsaw meeting of July 1968, called by Brezhnev and the five Soviet bloc parties, Kolder was the only Central Committee member to declare openly that personally he did not agree with it and thought that Brezhnev was right, though he would bow to the will of the majority.

After all I have just written about Kolder, however, one might well ask whether such a person can really do anything for democratic reforms? And, even if he could, is it really worth having such an ally?

Both these questions are important in politics, and I would reply in the affirmative to both. If I thought otherwise, I would not have gone into politics in Czechoslovakia, either in 1968 or 1958. Politics always involves morality, which can even be essential. But, at the same time, the actual roles of people in politics are important regardless of what the people are as individuals and even what their intentions are. In lumping together the actual roles of people with their human, moral qualities, you create an impossible situation in regard to political aims, the balance of political forces, and essential political tactics.

Naturally, it would have been ideal if, instead of such men as Kolder and Švestka, all the important political roles could have been filled by people who were also morally prepared for public office in a democracy. But in terms of realizing the reform, this was unnecessary, not did the reforms make such demands. These men could have contributed by keeping to the roles they were assigned and capable of performing and not opposing reform. Besides which, is this ideal realistic? In particular, was it possible in a political system that had been a totalitarian dictatorship for twenty years? Clearly, only those who had previously stood on the upper rungs of the ladder would be likely to attain high office in the first, and even subsequent, phases. And though, oddly enough, as the Prague Spring showed, these were very diverse people, some of whom showed an almost surprising ability to work for change, it was too much to expect them to be exclusively, or even largely, men possessing the optimal political, human, and moral qualities.

However, even in a working democracy that has not recently emerged from a totalitarian past, conditions in this sense are never ideal. Were the top leaders of the political parties of Masaryk's time—from the Agrarians to the National Socialists—all an ideal amalgam of democratic and humanitarian values? Were there not careerists then too, people who were cowardly, and politics that were corrupt? Undoubtedly so, but in their roles they were all subject to a democratic system of government and administration. It was this system—and not the moral purity of the individuals in power—that guaranteed democracy and, to the extent that politics has any influence here at all, the relative legal force of humanitarian ideals in everyday life.

Personally, I felt, and still feel, that even for the deeper human and moral significance of the "revival process" of 1968, it was more important to secure at least the outlines of a more democratic system of government than it was to purge the ranks, through witch hunts, of the morally suspect. Those radical reform Communists who took the second course remained more bolshevik than they themselves would be willing to admit, for they suffered from the same revolutionary-radical illusion that, if one is guided by revolutionary purity, political power alone can bring about a viable moral order on this earth. And yet how many times had this already been tried in Czechoslovakia!

Ultimately, the moral judgments that were passed on various leaders in 1968 are telling proof of the wrongness of that notion. For example, those who considered Kolder and Švestka's presence on the presidium antithetical to reform saw Gustav Husák as their replacement. And what did Husák do when he finally made it to the presidium? Or another example: at a municipal conference of the CPC in Prague in July 1968, Alois Indra was accused, in absentia, of having belonged to the so-called "security five" when he was a CPC secretary in Gottwaldov. This was a regional organ that, in the 1950s, held kangaroo courts and unlawfully sent people to jail. In some exceptional cases, they even passed death sentences. I knew that the accusation was false because when Indra had held office in Gottwaldov these security fives were no longer in existence. Consequently, I stood up and pointed this out. At the same time, I had no illusions whatsoever about Indra's political position, for he was by now quite unequivocally against the reforms and supported the Moscow line. That evening, Radovan Richta sent me a private message requesting me to think seriously about whether I could remain in my position given my attitude toward Indra; the "progressive wing" of the party, he said, would not support me under such circumstances.

And, at the time, Richta enjoyed some authority among the "progressivists." He was the ideologist of relegating communism to the distant future and of the scientific and technological revolution, and, as a matter of fact, he was also author of the slogan, "Socialism with a human face." It was he who put those words into Dubček's mouth and into the Action Program. I know quite certainly that many radical reform Communists were eager to appoint Richta not only in Švestka's or Indra's place but in mine as well, for he was truly not a "centrist." But what was Richta after 1969? He became the epitome of cowardice, and close friends who had looked after him like a brother when he lay gravely ill in a tuberculosis sanatorium and held no office and had no political influence were among his victims.

There is a minor but nevertheless telling story about him from the early seventies. Richta once picked up a girl hitchhiker in his private car. While they were passing a convoy of trucks full of Soviet soldiers, she spat through the window at them. The poor girl was under the impression that the person who had given her a lift was a normal Czech. When Richta had passed the convoy, he pulled over and threw the girl out of his car, knowing, or course, that the soldiers she had spat at would arrive at any second. Kolder would not have done a thing like that. Perhaps he would never have picked up an unknown hitchhiker in the first place, but if he had, and the same thing had happened, he would have tried to persuade the hitchhiker of the importance of internationalism. He was capable of "inviting" the Soviet soldiers into Czechoslovakia in August 1968, but he was incapable of that very concrete act. Unlike the author of the popular slogan about the human face of socialism, Kolder was not personally a coward.

But I don't want to go into any further detail about the individual members of that leadership, for the general circumstances in which they ruled are important as well.

Jiří Hájek, who was minister of foreign affairs in Černík's government, was once invited to a joint meeting of the presidium and secretariat of the Central Committee because they were discussing questions of international significance—the upcoming meeting with the Soviet politburo at Čierna nad Tisou. During the first break, after about two hours of discussion, he drew me aside and asked in a whisper: "If this is the party leadership, I ask you, how can I be minister of foreign affairs?" I replied, "Don't worry, it's all right; after all, I'm a secretary here too."

Clearly, meetings of the party leadership more resembled a debating society or, in contrast, the editorial board meeting of some magazine than an important state function. They either dealt with quite general political and ideological themes, in which people would expound on their worldviews or perhaps on events leading from the October Revolution through the Second World War right up to the Twentieth Congress of the CPSU and the CPC Action Program, or, conversely, they discussed quite concrete and ordinary daily occurrences or statements made or printed somewhere, not unlike a local party organization trying to evaluate politically what people were saying at the barber's. An outside observer might well wonder when they would finally begin discussing what was on the agenda. Jiří Hájek, for example, was expecting a discussion to begin on preparations for the meeting with the Soviet politburo: what questions they wanted to focus the meeting on and why, what the Czechoslovak arguments would be and what arguments, on the contrary, we could expect from the Soviet side, how far we could retreat on individual questions and where we would stand firm, what alternative proposals we might expect on certain points and how we would react to them.

But Jiří Hájek never did find out what he wanted to know. He learned only that Antonín Kapek was behind the Soviet Union heart and soul and no one could ever change that. He learned that Vasil Bilak was satisfied with the socialism we had constructed and that the question now was how to beautify it, so to speak, where to plant the flowers and hang the pictures, but that some people wanted to tear the whole thing down and start building something strange and new. Jan Piller, for his part, informed the meeting that he had heard of a certain speaker at a meeting of K-231 (a club that offered membership to those who had been imprisoned under the law for the defense of the Republic, No. 231) wanting to hang all Communists, and if that wasn't real anti-Communism, nothing was. On the other hand, he was convinced that the revival process was healthy and correct and that we ought to explain both the pros and cons to the Soviet comrades. Čestmír Císař spoke on the theme of freedom of the press, which, he said, was essential and healthy for socialism. It was necessary to prevent criticism of individual faults from becoming dogmatic generalizations. Emil Rigo warned that the functionaries in his factory were concerned about how things would turn out, and he quoted them as illustration. Meanwhile, Alois Indra was taking detailed notes in a large, paginated notebook bound with ribbons in the national colors, which in Czechoslovakia indicates a notebook for state secrets, and for the time being he said nothing. In any case, there was no hurry, for party leadership meetings usually went on for eight, ten, twelve hours, sometimes even longer.

I did not take notes (which I later regretted), but, regardless of whether or not the above-mentioned statements were made at that particular meeting and in that particular order, I feel they accurately capture the method and spirit of party meetings under Dubček.

Sitting at the head of the large table, Alexander Dubček more or less attentively followed the ever-thickening goulash of opinion that such debates always created. He let things democratically take their course until even he felt the comrades had completely unburdened themselves, and then he would recite his credo: what we must do above all is concentrate our forces on the positive tasks, develop positive work and, in so doing, overcome the negative phenomena. Our policies enjoy the great support of the working people and with such a force on our side we can't lose.

I do not wish to imply, however, that the party leadership during the Prague Spring did not make some politically pertinent and also important decisions. But the actual decision-making process was quite different from what normally takes place in a democracy. The means by which the party leadership arrived at its decisions also explains how it could accept a whole series of undeniably reform-minded resolutions while almost half its members were aligning themselves increasingly against reform, and some of them were even secretly supporting the idea of a Soviet military intervention.

The decision-making process was essentially the same under Dubček as it had been under Novotný: all high-level documents were prepared by working groups. And because there was at least a kilogram of paper to go through at every meeting—I have deliberately singled out the weight because that and the volume were the first things the leadership members looked at when the bundle of documents was dropped on their desk a day or so before the meeting—this bundle was then given to aides, who made summaries of the individual documents. No one individual could have read through it all even if they had wanted to. Of course, sometimes the very same people who made the summaries were those who originally manufactured the documents.

As a rule only about a quarter of the questions the leadership dealt with had any genuinely significant and general political importance. And even then the working documents were prepared by the various "working groups," employees of the apparatus and aides of members of the party leadership. And in that particular sphere, the reform Communists were in an even stronger position in the spring of 1968 than they had been under Novotný. They certainly had more power there than in the party leadership itself. Moreover, they had people who were capable of conceptual thought, and who could combine their conceptions with organizational and practical proposals. Thus, many of the proposals approved by the party leadership had genuine political significance, and, on the whole, they were well formulated, unlike how they were debated by the party leadership.

In the event of an unforeseen occurrence requiring spontaneous action by the party leadership, they always appointed two or three people, from among the hidden army of aides, who were capable of formulating a position. And while the rest of them went on debating in the usual way, the selected individuals would write a draft resolution. When this was presented to the entire leadership, it became the catalyst for fresh debating, which continued for several more hours, drifting again from the topic until, at last, under the influence of general weariness and stupefaction, the leadership finally accepted the resolution in essentially its original form.

Čestmír Císař and I were the ones most frequently entrusted with drafting resolutions in such situations. For example, we wrote the texts of two well-known resolutions of that period: the "Position of the Presidium of the Central Committee of the CPC on the Manifesto entitled 'Two Thousand Words,'" and the "Position of the Presidium of the Central Committee of the CPC on the Letter of the Five Communist and Workers' Parties," which preceded our negotiations with the Soviet politburo in Čierná nad Tisou.

In many ways, the case of the "Two Thousand Words" appeal is a characteristic demonstration of conditions in the party leadership at that time, and therefore we shall take a closer look at it. The text was written by the author Ludvík Vaculík, which was enough in itself to guarantee that the words would be effective and well chosen, and it came out on 27 June 1968, on the eve of the district party conferences that were to elect delegates to the party congress. It appeared simultaneously in *Literární listy* and about three other dailies. And it was signed by many people, mostly intellectuals but also athletes, popular actors, and professional people, both reform Communists and non-Communists, including some who had been radical since the spring, and some about whom this could not really be said.

The actual contents of "Two Thousand Words" was nothing exceptional at the time: it had all—except for a few ideas, such as Vaculík's notion of democratizing the political system with the help of "citizens' committees and commissions"—been said before in various ways in many articles in the press and in radio and television. There could be no doubt that the author's main aim was to express the fear, common among the radical Communist intelligentsia, that the entire "revival process" could be impeded and jeopardized by the continued prevalence of many conservatives, representatives of the old totalitarian system, inside the CPC. Moreover, the letter explicitly stated that these people derived their support from abroad, and it clearly expressed the fear of a Soviet intervention. Throughout the entire letter, however, political problems were inextricably and hopelessly entangled with human and moral problems. Such "linkage" was characteristic of that time, but it was impossible to provide political answers to questions formulated in this way. And this was clear from the inner conflict in the text, where the basic human and moral problems the author wanted to highlight were impossible to resolve with the political means he himself very hazily proposed.

Had Vaculík published this text as his own article and only in *Literární listy*, it would have been taken as a highly eccentric, but genuinely personal, viewpoint on the problems of the day, and there would probably not have been the political controversy there was. The problem was that the letter was in fact an appeal, a manifesto. It had been signed by many supporters, and they were soliciting others to do the same. It had been published simultaneously in several newspapers and was intended to stimulate a public debate on the problems of the present situation, and thereby influence important deliberations inside the CPC and preparations for the coming party congress. What this meant in practical terms was that the conception of reform in "Two Thousand Words" and not the CPC Action Program was to become the focus for political discussions both in public and inside the CPC.

Now, in a democracy, there would be nothing criminal nor even unusual in this. Pluralist political systems are founded on the principle of freedom for concerned citizens to organize themselves and influence public opinion as well as pressure the government. Such systems are therefore undisturbed by such things, much less politically threatened. The population takes such activity for granted and knows that no one is necessarily trying thereby to overthrow the state, or unseat the government. And those who govern in a democratic system know it as well. In Czechoslovakia, at the end of June 1968, however, things were different. The regime was still a totalitarian political system that had yet to be democratized. The proposed changes in the political system were still only on paper, with one serious exception: freedom of expression really existed. Both the governed and the governors were accustomed to forms of political conduct quite different from in a democracy, and therefore an appeal like "Two Thousand Words" had a far greater impact than it would have had in a democracy or than its contents actually warranted.

In June 1968, the main issue inside the power structure was whether the necessary number of key people could be united on the basis of official reform, that is, within the framework of the Action Program. To publish what amounted to an alternative program at this stage meant, practically speaking, to threaten this whole process. And what was more, of course, Moscow was looking on. "Two Thousand Words" was published roughly two weeks before the famous Warsaw Letter, in which the five Soviet bloc countries meeting in Warsaw sent an ultimatum to the Czechoslovak party. The threat of such collective action was already in the air, and, in fact, "Two Thousand Words" spoke very openly about it. It was clear, therefore, that those who stood behind the appeal considered it proper to support, despite the circumstances, what amounted to a more radical program than the official party leadership was willing to condone.

This was undeniably a move on the part of the more radical wing of the reform Communists—particularly the radical Communist intellectuals—and an attempt to pressure the party leadership to radicalize. But in what direction? To oust people from office who had begun to oppose reforms precisely because they feared for their positions. And in a situation where most of these people would have been retired in two months anyway, at the CPC congress. Why the appeal then? Because the radical wing of the reform Communists were afraid that not enough conservatives would be removed from office, and this concern blinded them to other circumstances far more serious and dangerous for the reforms as a whole.

This is why I myself considered the publication of "Two Thousand Words" a very serious political act and, in the given situation, one that threatened the success of the reforms. I did not believe that people would immediately begin setting up their own "citizens' committees and commissions," as Ludvík Vaculík's had suggested. But I was afraid it meant that certain influential reform Communist intellectuals had decided to enter the fray with all their powers of persuasion—which, at that time, had in some ways more sway over public opinion than the official leadership's—and in a manner that would lead to conflicts among those in power strong enough to threaten the stabilization of reform and bring even more pressure to bear on the party leadership from the Kremlin. I don't think that, politically, there was anything more at stake at the time, but in the situation it was not insignificant.

But how was the party leadership as a whole to respond to "Two Thousand Words"? Sometime after lunch on the day it appeared, June 27, a special meeting of the presidium and the secretariat was suddenly called. As far as I can recollect, the members from outside Prague could not come at such short notice and were absent, and a number of members who were there did not know what it was all about. It was not the custom to read newspapers—there was no time for that. A special news digest was prepared daily for the leadership, but "Two Thousand Words" had not yet appeared there. As a result, the discussion got off to a somewhat slow start while many of us were trying inconspicuously to read the incriminating text, like schoolchildren with cribbed notes under their desks.

First to speak were those who saw "Two Thousand Words" as something like a declaration of war against the Soviet Union. They talked about anti-Soviet provocation, about Budapest in 1956, about civil war, about the liberation of Czechoslovakia in 1945, and similar themes, all of which could have been inspired by "Two Thousand Words" only with a great stretch of the imagination. Quite surprisingly, given his viewpoint at all other times, Josef Smrkovský energetically added his voice to the discussion. He had just returned from Moscow, and, possibly under the influence of that trip, he too felt the issue of civil war and tanks was relevant: "And I refuse to be responsible for having to have tanks settle the situation," were his very words.

Obviously it made no sense to propose anything at that juncture. Time would do its work as it had done in other similar situations. When the first round of discussion exhausted itself after about an hour, the discussion turned to speculating on what the personal intentions of the authors and many signatories of "Two Thousand Words" were: what the various people really thought; what they were after and why; who knew what about whose past; what mischief or, on the contrary, what good they had ever done; and so on. Because

"Two Thousand Words" had been signed not only by rank-and-file Communists but also by some Central Committee members, there was cause to debate as well the party regulations and Leninist principles of democratic centralism. All of this consumed at least another hour.

At this point it was usual to take a break. The breaks allowed the atmosphere to change, and often, but not always, new subjects would be taken up at the resumed discussion. Smrkovský, who in the meantime had gone to a session of Parliament, was back now and reported on what was discussed there. As there was nothing new, it gave cause for a good deal of repetition. Then someone, perhaps Smrkovský himself, proposed that the government take a stand on the issue. And since the government could not make a stand unless the presidium made its position clear first, it was in Černík's interest to get the ball rolling. This was the turning point in the discussion, for it now became necessary to think about what to put in the resolution. And thus the other trend of opinion was introduced, the one concerned about the fate of reform politics as a whole. But here too the discussion remained inconsequential and abstract: the Action Program, positive work, the benefits of the democratic movement, freedom of the press, and so on.

And then at last a concrete problem appeared: someone actually had to draft a resolution. Mlynář and Císař were appointed. Because I had seen this coming long before, I already had something prepared, and I took part in the debate in such a way as to provoke discussion of the ideas I thought were important to include in the resolution. Then Císař and I went to our offices, and each of us wrote out a draft, knowing roughly what the other would say. We then combined them into a common text, providing alternative passages in places, particularly where we thought the presidium would lean toward the alternative. So the two of us, at least, had a matter-of-fact debate among ourselves about what we wanted the resolution to contain and why. Meanwhile the presidium meeting was partly recessing and partly still going through the vicious circle of discussion in which everyone knew in advance roughly what everyone else would say and why.

Night had long since fallen and normal people were watching television. The party leadership would not know what had actually been on television until they read their special bulletins next day. Perhaps it would be necessary to hold another session. In the blackness outside the Central Committee building stood the black Tatra 603 limousines, the windows of the committee room glowed in the darkness, and passers-by would, perhaps with a certain respect, given the nationwide political and democratic fever, think that the Dubček leadership was there, guiding the "revival process" even at night. Several other windows were glowing in the night as well—the offices of presidium members—and in each office sat a typist, an aide, and a chauffeur, in case comrade so-and-so needed dictation, assistance, or a ride somewhere. In the meanwhile, these employees-in-waiting would talk, read, knit sweaters, and drink black coffee.

The meeting continued, and Císař and I brought in our draft resolution. Naturally this provided an opportunity not only for amendments but also to repeat yet again what had already been said. Černík left because he had to convene his government that night. And Piller arrived, clearly aglow from more than a single glass of alcohol, and just when the leadership was debating over whether to include the phrase "we have no reason to doubt the good intentions of the authors of 'Two Thousand Words' " (for, after all, as someone said, we don't even know who the authors are), Piller reassured the party leadership that the militia commanders in his region stood behind Dubček and were ready to move against anyone he pointed out. The meeting went on almost devoid of new suggestions, nothing in the sense or substance of the draft was amended, and thus was slowly born another resolution of the highest organ of political power in the land.

The room was full of smoke, and Josef Lenárt opened a window. It was daylight outside. "For God's sake, people, don't be crazy. The birds are singing," said Lenárt. Everyone fell silent for a moment. And, sure enough, from the Letenská park across the river came the full-throated, joyful, and utterly unpolitical song of blackbirds and thrushes. For some reason no one—conservatives, progressives, or centrists—said a word. Alexander Dubček thanked everyone and adjourned the meeting. And the historic resolution of the Central Committee of the CPC on the manifesto "Two Thousand Words" came into being.

Given these working methods, the resolution was passed despite the fact that it was far from being acceptable to the individual members of the party leadership. Those who saw the specter of civil war and tanks behind "Two Thousand Words" did not insist that their particular fears be expressed in the resolution, but they continued to feel that way (with the exception of Smrkovský, who soon afterwards changed his mind). Those who, on the contrary, would have liked to reach some understanding with the radical forces did not write those feelings into the resolution either; though they, too, still felt that way. Thus, although everyone approved the resolution, which stated that the main problem was to unite all Communists behind the Action Program, the existing groups in the party leadership continued to act according to the same opinions they had held before the resolution was passed.

Thus Alois Indra issued an internal memo to the regional party committees that practically interpreted the situation as the beginning of a counter-revolution, and he ordered what amounted to a state of alert. At various meetings and rallies, men like Bilak, Kolder, Švestka, Jakeš, and others spoke as they pleased, which meant roughly as they had before the resolution was passed. Kriegel and Smrkovský made public statements emphasizing appeasement, more in the sense that nothing serious had happened and the most important thing was the good will of everyone involved. This same spirit emerged from a meeting with the signatories of "Two Thousand Words," which Dubček, Černík, Smrkovský, Slavík, and perhaps others as well attended.*

As I have already said at the beginning of this chapter, I am still not certain today whether the reforms could have been safeguarded even if everything had gone as I had intended it to in the spring and summer of 1968. Perhaps the Soviets would have intervened anyway. In this case, of course, it is better that "Two Thousand Words" was published. For if we disregard the question of political tactics, it must be acknowledged that this manifesto played a very positive role. It showed citizens that they themselves can act as free people with their own political interests. As an act of protest against despotism, "Two Thousand Words" was a kind of model in both form and content for the future. Nine years after Vaculík's appeal, there was another quite different yet in some ways similar manifesto in Prague: Charter 77. Ludvík Vaculík and several other signatories of "Two Thousand Words" also signed the Charter. But this time I too was among the signatories, along with several others who in 1968 sat in the party leadership and supported the resolution against "Two Thousand Words": František Kriegel, Bohumil Šimon, Václav Slavík.

However, the situation was different from 1968. Present-day

---

* See Josef Skvorecký's book, *Miracle* (*Mirákl*), for a description of how people outside the party saw the meeting.

Czechoslovakia is once more ruled by a totalitarian dictatorship, but it is not preparing for democratic reform; on the contrary, it is entrenching itself as a despotism. And, therefore, those who want to walk upright like free people can do nothing else in the absence of freedom but behave as though they really were free, utterly disregarding the problem this might create for the despotism. Because making allowances for Husák's leadership will not bring democracy any closer, whereas free, upright citizens are enormously important for that future time when the road to democracy is opened again. But learning from the experience of 1968, including the experience of "Two Thousand Words," will be equally important for such a period. Towards this end, I think it is proper for me to repeat my opinions here openly, and I hope that no one genuinely concerned about democracy in Czechoslovakia will see this merely as a stubborn attempt to vindicate myself. As I said before, I wish to emphasize that I am not even certain any more that my way was right.

Back then, in the summer of 1968, however, I was convinced that there was no other hope for democracy than a gradual, and in many ways politically cautious, reform of the entire political system and that any other approach would jeopardize the real chances for democratization.

Put briefly, I saw the potential development of the political and social institutions after the Fourteenth Congress of the CPC, which was in preparation, as follows.* The following two years were to have been a period of transition and evaluation, in which a new state constitution would have been drafted and, consequently, the election of a new Parliament facilitated. At the end of those two years, it would then be necessary, on the basis of the experience gained, to establish a new and more democratic electoral system and the notion of self-management in factories and other work places. We would then also have experience in how more democratic trade unions would function, as well as other organizations, including the CPC itself, which—in the spirit of its new party statutes, already-published in proposal form—would have been transformed into an essentially more democratic organism. I felt it was necessary, however, to preserve the hegemony of this altered CPC for the time being. The prob-

---

* For a more detailed and documentary version, see my *Tanks Against the Congress: The Extraordinary Fourteenth Congress of the CPC* (Vienna: Europa-Verlag, 1970), pp. 214–19, "An Analysis of Party Activity and Social Development after the Thirteenth Congress and the Main Tasks of the Party in the Near Future."

lem of a plurality of political parties and their independent participation in democratic elections could be solved over the next ten-year period. According to my estimates, in other words, the democratization of Czechoslovakia, both conceptually and practically, should have been completed by 1978.

In terms of practical politics, such a plan seemed realistic to me in the summer of 1968. The party conferences in June and July, which elected delegates to the party congress, showed clearly that it was precisely the "centrist" current that predominated inside the party. About 80 percent of the delegates elected to the new congress supported the centrist position, and the remainder was more or less equally divided between the radical reform Communists and the Stalinists. And a similar division of powers could be reasonably expected in the new Central Committee and its presidium.

Outside the CPC, in the rest of Czechoslovak society, I expected that the wave of almost festive enthusiasm would give way, after the Fourteenth Congress, to conflicts and popular discontent. But there was also reason to assume that a good majority of the population would continue to support the rational politics of gradual reform. Certainly, the triumph of my political viewpoint in the new party leadership elected by the congress would have meant a conflict with the radical reform Communists. But I saw nothing exceptional in that, not even for a democratic system. In a democracy there are always unavoidable conflicts with the political extremes on both the Left and Right, but of course they can be resolved by democratic means.

However, the fate of not only my political notions but the development of the entire nation was ultimately decided, not democratically and internally through disputation, but by authoritarian means, in the Kremlin.

CHAPTER 3

FACING THE KREMLIN TRIBUNAL

Just before midnight on August 20, 1968, at a presidium meeting, Černík was called to the telephone. When he returned, he asked to speak. He reported that the minister of national defense, Martin Dzúr, had just called him and told him that Soviet troops, along with units from four other Warsaw Pact countries, had crossed the borders into Czechoslovakia. My first instinctive reaction was most like the shock I had once experienced years before in an automobile crash.

Into my mind came images from the end of the war—barricades, tanks, wounded and dead in the streets—mingled with the faces of those nearest to me and vivid recollections of the South Bohemian countryside and the monstrous structure of Moscow University, and all with the clear feeling that this was the ultimate debacle of my life as a Communist. Then followed a brief sensation of the meaninglessness of it all—particularly thoughts and actions. And only then did the unreal but tangible reality return: the very same committee room with the very same people as a few seconds ago; yet it was an entirely different world, one that had nothing in common with the world of a few moments before.

I saw what was beind said and done around me as if in a movie: Černík explaining how Dzúr had been *de facto* placed under arrest in his own office by two Soviet officers, that he had only been allowed the one phone call—to the prime minister—and otherwise was without recourse and that other top army personnel were probably in the same position. Then Dubček said, "So they did it after all—and to *me!*" A confusion of voices, and someone—perhaps Kriegel—said something about betraying the nation, and someone else suggested immediately inviting President Svoboda to the meeting. Vasil Bilak stood up, paced nervously back and forth behind the row of chairs and shouted, "Alright lynch me! Why don't you kill me?" No one reacted to this, perhaps most did not even hear him, just as the other voices, declarations, gestures, and movements went largely unnoticed. For a brief time, most people were utterly absorbed in their own thoughts. I think that for those, like Bilak, who had foreknowledge of the intervention, it was an equally fateful moment. Their shock did not come from an unexpected catastrophe, but as sudden release from hidden inner tension, and they too succumbed briefly to involuntary behavior.

I became increasingly aware that this was the irrevocable ruin of everything I had devoted my life to over the past years, and, in particular, of reform communism. Suddenly, any hope for political reform now, after a military invasion, seemed complete nonsense.

When I spoke, therefore, I announced my resignation: given the situation, I could no longer strive with conviction for my goals. Dubček spoke in the same terms and also said that he was resigning. I think that he too, for many reasons, felt the situation as a personal defeat. "If they have something against me, why don't they deal with me directly? I don't care if they string me up by the ribs, I would, in any event, answer for everything." And, judging from this statement at the time, he must have felt like the Slovak folk hero, Janošík.

Dubček's resignation gradually brought everyone back to reality. Talk now began about no one resigning and how all the legally-constituted organs had to remain intact; no new organs must be set up, nor could there be any personnel changes under pressure from the intervention. This part of the meeting was also attended by Ludvík Svoboda. He was pale, externally calm but inwardly upset. He did not say much during the entire meeting but, as far as I can remember, he did expressly support the view that no one should resign.

Even in this situation, the old routines were still enacted, though tragicomically. A resolution had to be prepared, and Mlynář was appointed to draft it (I think that was Dubček's idea). A plenum of the Central Committee, the government, and Parliament had to be convened. The impossibility of defending ourselves militarily against the intervention was discussed, but it was hardly a debate, more a unanimous affirmation of the fact. No one even suggested fighting back: only various arguments for the impossibility and impropriety of such a step were presented.

However, this decision was not then, nor is it today, considered indisputable by many people who were outside the party leadership. Why then did this leadership unanimously rule out defensive military action? I shall present the arguments on which the decision was based.

In the first place, the Czechoslovak army, like the armies of all other Soviet bloc countries, is not independent. Soviet officers occupy key positions in it; its arms and its technology (military communications systems, codes, and so on) are not only familiar to the Soviet army but ultimately under its control.

The army's disposition throughout the country makes any effective defense against attack from the Warsaw Pact "allies" impossible. And there is no guarantee that many of the commanding officers will not go over to the Soviet side in the event of such a conflict. So that even ignoring the enormously superior strength of the potential aggressor, it would have been impossible effectively to defend the country militarily. All the clearly outnumbered Czechoslovak army might have done would have been to offer temporary local resistance to the advancing troops.

As a sidelight, we should add that Dubček's personnel changes in the army command on the basis of personal sympathies didn't help matters. This meant that the minister of national defense and the army chief of staff, for example, may have been "Dubček men," but their loyalty to him was not exclusive. Back in May 1968, for example, Defense Minister Dzúr had described the situation in the Czechoslovak army to Marshal Jakubovsky, commander in chief of the Warsaw Pact forces, as being inadequate for battle-readiness. In so doing, Martin Dzúr in fact provided an excuse for the presence of the Soviet army on Czechoslovak soil: to ensure the "defensive capability of the Socialist community" against a possible "attack by imperialism." Jakubovsky gave Dzúr a friendly embrace and said, "A friend has understood a friend!"

At the same time, there was General Bedřich, chief of staff of the Czechoslovak army. He was incompetent and a Stalinist but a childhood pal of Dubček's: they had grown up together in Soviet Central Asia. General Prchlík, on the other hand, while obeying the letter of the Warsaw Pact, had attempted to strengthen the relative independence of the Czechoslovak army. As a result, under Soviet pressure he was ousted as chief of the Defense and Security Department of the Central Committee. From July on, Dubček ran the department himself, or, to put it more precisely, the department ceased to play any role whatsoever.

Politically, it was clear that armed resistance—of necessity limited to local skirmishes—would only have aided the interveners. It would have created a situation identical to the Hungarian model of 1956: shooting, armed conflict, and loss of life would have provided convincing evidence that "counter-revolutionary forces" bent on civil war actually existed. On the contrary, one-sided armed violence on the part of the interveners against a pacific country would remain for the entire world the most convincing proof of who the aggressor was.

Besides these arguments, however, there were also arguments of an ideological and psychological nature. The entire political conception of the Dubček leadership, the reform Communists, and the Action Program all derived unequivocally from the ideological thesis that democratic reform was not in conflict with Czechoslovakia's basic commitments to the other Warsaw Pact states. The party leadership did not reckon on a falling out with the Soviet Union like that of Yugoslavia in 1948, nor did it desire this. On the contrary, it considered it important to demonstrate the possibility of having an independent political line while within the Soviet bloc alliance.

Naturally, it is difficult to speak for others in this, but personally I could not in good conscience have accepted responsibility for risking a single human life in calling for armed resistance, given what we could have expected in the way of political gains. That night, and later during the Kremlin negotiations, I was aware for the first time that my political positions had direct implications for the lives and deaths of perhaps many thousands of people. And such a situation is quite different from one where a person can think about what the proper, principled, and moral thing to do is in the abstract. I sympathized with President Svoboda, who repeatedly raised the issue of the potential loss of human life. I am not one who can simply brush such an argument aside with a supercilious sneer, as publicists often do.

At that meeting on the night of August 20th, however, only the political reasons and the responsibility for human lives were actually discussed. The other arguments were implicit.

And then, suddenly, Dubček announced that he had received a letter from Brezhnev three days before, which he now felt he should read to the presidium. He was extremely upset and stammered more than usual as he read it. The letter was full of the standard Moscow ranting against the anti-Soviet and antisocialist material in *Literární listy* or *Reportér* and how this violated agreements made in Čierná and Bratislava. It was like absurd theater. Here were people anxiously wondering what would happen in the next hour, both to the nation and to themselves personally, who, without ever admitting it aloud, were worried about possible arrest and deportation; and beside them, people who would have much preferred to be in the Soviet embassy by now forming a new government. And here these two camps were, sitting silently together, each preoccupied with their own thoughts while the words of the man who had set the whole calamity in motion were droning on in stammered phrases.

Many people left to make telephone calls, chiefly, I think, to their families, something I too wanted to do but couldn't because I was roughing out a draft resolution on the situation. Dubček finished reading the letter, and one of the conspirators tried to open a discussion on Dubček's fatal error in keeping Brezhnev's letter a secret for three days, but by this time no one was interested in polemics. Someone suggested that Dubček telephone Brezhnev, but he rejected the idea with the bravura of a Janošík, and added politely: "I expect they will be getting in touch themselves." I presented my draft of the resolution, or, more precisely, the appeal, "To All the People of the Czechoslovak Socialist Republic."

A sentence explaining why we could not defend ourselves militarily was struck out. The party leadership felt that any reference to armed resistance, even a negative one, was dangerous. The following sentence, however, remained intact: "For this reason, our army . . . [was] not given the order to defend the country." All that was missing was the reason why. But this bothered no one, and, oddly enough, to this day not a single work on the Prague Spring quoting this text has taken note of the omission. Perhaps it is because party resolutions often contain far greater illogicalities.

And then began the well-known controversy over whether the presidium would at least support an unarmed, political, and moral resistance to the intervention. The following sentence was at issue: "The Presidium of the Central Committee of the CPC considers this act not only contrary to all the fundamental principles governing relationships between socialist states, but also as a denial of the basic norms of international law." Of those who had voting privileges in the presidium, Bilak, Kolder, Švestka, and Rigo came out against this sentence. And they were supported by Indra, Kapek, and Jakeš, who did not have a vote. What was odd was that not even these people tried to defend the intervention as in harmony with international law. They merely insisted that the formulation complicated the situation, that the conflict was essentially one between Communist parties and should not be carried outside their "common household." But they made no attempt to justify the intervention itself, and merely repeated that we shared the blame for it because we underestimated the threat. Not one phrase such as "fraternal international assistance," "the necessary rescue of socialism in Czechoslovakia," and so on, which were to become so frequent later on, passed their lips that particular night.

In the heated discussion that erupted when Kriegel and Smrkovský referred expressly to those who identified with the intervention as traitors of the nation, the other members of the presidium all stood behind the proposed resolution. Of those who had voting privileges, they were Smrkovský, Kriegel, Špaček, Černík, Piller, and Barbírek; and of those who did not, Šimon, Císař, Slavík, Sádovský, and myself. I no longer remember what position Lenárt took, but I don't recall he supported Bilak's group. Dubček balked only at the words "denial of the basic norms of international law." But when the vote was finally called and Dubček's turn came, he said, "What am I hesitating for—it's true!" And he voted for. Ludvík Svoboda was only at the meeting by invitation, and he had no voting privileges; I don't recall that he took part in this particular controversy.

By this time it was almost half-past one in the morning. When Dubček ended the meeting by sending each member "back to his post," which expressed the extent of what could be done under the circumstances, the entire pro-Moscow group disappeared with relief, except for Jakeš, who may have been assigned the task of keeping an eye on the rest of us. Černík left to join the cabinet, and Císař as well left the Central Committee building. All the rest of us stayed behind.

Many articles, studies, and books have already been written on the gradual deterioration of relations between the Dubček leadership and the Soviet politburo before that night. I did not personally take part in any of the meetings—which also included other Soviet bloc parties, particularly Poland and the GDR—during which relationships worsened: March 23–24 in Dresden, May 3–4 in Moscow, and July 29–August 1 in Čierná nad Tisou. But at the Bratislava meeting between representatives of six Soviet bloc parties, I was not only present but took part in the working session on the "Declaration of the Communist and Workers' Parties of the Socialist Countries," in which the first secretary and prime minister of each party could, if they wished, have advisors and translators present.

Brezhnev, in the name of the Soviet delegation, was the one who presented the draft of the declaration, and it was then gone over sentence by sentence by the other representatives. Given the complexion of the meeting, most of the initiative in the discussion came from the CPC delegation.

The meeting in Bratislava took place within 48 hours of the Čierná nad Tisou encounter between the Soviet politburo and Czechoslovak presidium, which ended in a rupture on the evening of July 31. Dubček and other members of the CPC delegation had walked out of the meeting after P. Shelest had made shameless statements about the Czechoslovaks' alleged attempts to wrest the Carpatho-Ukraine from the Soviet Union and about Kriegel not being a fit negotiating partner because he was a "Jew from Halič." The Soviet politburo apologized, but the negotiations continued only in small groups. On the morning of August 1, Dubček met alone with Brezhnev and the idea of holding a six-party meeting in Bratislava was born.*

As far as I know, the impression Dubček gained from this private meeting was that Brezhnev was in conflict with the "hawks" in his own politburo (represented by Shelest, though the people really behind them were the marshals of the older generation), and was genuinely looking for a way out of the predicament that would vindicate his moderation and enable him to stand up to pressure from Ulbricht and Gomulka, who were united with the Soviet "hawks" in pushing the situation toward open conflict and a military intervention in Czechoslovakia. The real arguments behind the scenes had little to do with the public attacks against *Literární listy,* which were only the propagandistic, ideological guise, but rather were based on the claim that the security of the entire Soviet bloc was threatened, and that the conditions in Czechoslovakia were impairing the defensive capability of the bloc and weakening its political unity under the hegemony of Moscow.

---

* Nothing official was ever published on the Čierná nad Tisou negotiations except a brief communiqué. There is, however, an official transcript, deposited with the CPC Central Committee as a secret document. It is about 500 pages long and was read by members of the party leadership who weren't at the meeting, including myself. I also discussed many details of the meeting with direct participants, specifically with Dubček, Smrkovský, Špaček, and Šimon. Some facts were revealed in an interview with Smrkovský published after his death abroad (see *Listy,* No. 2, 1975).

In the meeting between Brezhnev and Dubček, a certain point of common interest did emerge after all. If Brezhnev was concerned to demonstrate the impregnable solidarity of the bloc, this was acceptable to Dubček because it meant that Czechoslovakia's internal political problems need not be part of the negotiations. An agreement could be reached strictly on the basis of Czechoslovakia's commitments to the bloc that would have been impossible if internal political matters were included in the discussion. Given those conditions, Dubček agreed to take part in a meeting with the five bloc parties that had met earlier in Warsaw, and Brezhnev agreed that the internal political situation in Czechoslovakia would not be subject to discussion. At that price, Dubček was willing to sign anything affirming the hegemony of Moscow and the membership of Czechoslovakia in the Soviet bloc, thinking that in doing so he would avert the pressure of the "hawks" and thus the danger of a military intervention. And, in any case, it was consistent with his thinking. As I have already said, he genuinely had no intention of pulling Czechoslovakia out of the Soviet bloc. He was convinced that Brezhnev did not want to intervene militarily and that therefore he would gain his support by making concessions to bloc solidarity. Brezhnev also promised Dubček to see to it that no one (by which he meant in particular Gomulka and Ulbricht) would make the internal political situation in Czechoslovakia the target of criticism at the Bratislava meeting.

In fact, of course, the Soviet draft declaration did contain a number of formulations relating to the internal problems of Czechoslovakia. Concealed in the hackneyed, seemingly innocent, propagandistic style were political criticisms reminiscent of the Warsaw Letter. Hence the long debate that followed.

In retrospect, however, all those verbal and formulaic victories that our delegation won were merely illusory and, in any case, were in a text that no longer made any difference. After much effort, for example, we managed to change a sentence that stated that the international situation had become more acute and the danger of conflict with imperialism had increased. The final version ran: "As a result of the aggressive policies of imperialism, the international situation remains complicated and dangerous." While the proposal claimed that there were only two "forces for peace" standing against the revanchist government of the German Federal Republic—the German Democratic Republic and the West German Communist party—the final version speaks only of "the activation of the powers of revanchism, militarism, and neo-nazism in West Germany," and it expressly states that beside supporting Walter Ulbricht and the Communist party of Germany it was also necessary to support "those forces struggling against revanchism, militarism, and neo-nazism and for democratic progress." In the paragraph where the draft declaration mentioned the binding commitment to "common precepts relating to the building of socialist society," our delegation managed to insert the sentence: "At the same time, each fraternal party will seek creative solutions to questions related to further socialist development, taking into consideration national particularities and conditions."

There is also a sentence in the Bratislava Declaration that supporters of the post-August 1968 "normalization" course have interpreted as a justification for the intervention, and as that which committed Dubček to acquiescence. The same sentence, only slightly altered, was included in the Czechoslovak-Soviet treaty of 1970, and it is in general used as an ideological justification for the so-called Brezhnev doctrine of limited sovereignty for the Soviet bloc countries. The sentence runs: "It is the common international duty of all socialist countries to support, defend, and consolidate these achievements, which have been made through the heroic efforts and dedicated labor of each country's people."

This became the subject of a lengthy discussion. While none of the CPC delegation suspected it might be interpreted as a preliminary endorsement of military intervention, I think it did evoke certain fears, especially since it was immediately followed by, "This is the unanimous opinion of all participants in the meeting. . . ." My suspicions were aroused that there may have been some interest in being able to point directly to this in an agreement with the CPC. Therefore I suggested adding to it the clause, "While respecting the sovereignty and national independence of each country," joining this clause to the original sentence with a dash and ending the whole complex sentence with a period.

Brezhnev himself immediately entered the discussion at this point with an unbelievable objection: "The dash in this instance," he said, "would go against the spirit of the Russian language!" Gradually it came out that neither a comma nor a colon—nothing, in fact, that would make the clause an inseparable part of the sentence—was acceptable in terms of the Russian language. After all, there was an explicit mention of sovereignty and national independence two paragraphs further on, just as there was about equality, territorial integrity, and fraternal cooperation. Why, therefore, should it be mentioned in every sentence? Other principles equally sacred are not repeated, the declaration has to be brief, etc.

This reaction of Brezhnev's naturally only increased our suspicions about the unsavory intent behind that sentence. Nevertheless, the text was a mutual one, and Ulbricht, Gomulka, and Zhivkov did not mind; they all supported Brezhnev's effort to maintain the linguistic purity of a declaration that from beginning to end was the product of party jargon, regardless of whether it was Russian or Hungarian. Kadar, by the way, as far as I remember, quite explicitly did *not* support Brezhnev in this and several times in the course of the discussions even sided with the CPC delegation in proposing text amendments.

Was Brezhnev, even then, thinking in terms of the future military intervention? Perhaps, but I think rather that at this stage he was only covering his options and that no concrete decision to intervene, which occurred seventeen days later, had yet been made.

Dubček tried to win an improvement in the balance of power by bringing in representatives of Rumania, Yugoslavia, and perhaps even Albania as cosigners. He indicated that the declaration would have, as a result, far greater international significance, and he volunteered to act as mediator during his upcoming meetings with Tito and Ceauşescu, suggesting that the signing of the "Declaration" might be delayed until that time. The general reaction, however, was like a nest of hornets poked with a stick, and nothing came of this attempt, nor could it have been otherwise.

And thus the Bratislava meeting ended with dinner in the late afternoon hours, ceremonial signatures, and hugs and kisses at the station. It was my first experience of "top level negotiations" in the Soviet bloc, and it was a devastating one.

Walter Ulbricht and Wladyslaw Gomulka were hostile, vain, and senile old men. It was quite clear that they had no interest in understanding the developmental problems of their own countries, let alone of their neighbors. Both of them fairly radiated a self-satisfied intoxication with their own power.

I overheard a conversation between Ulbricht and Dubček, in which Ulbricht declared: "I was under the impression that I was coming here on an official visit, but at the airport all I could hear was 'Dubček, Dubček.' Is it because I don't understand Czech?" He, of course, perceived this as proof that Czechoslovakia had abandoned internationalism. And he saw nothing unusual about expecting public glorification of himself as a token of Czechoslovakia's friendship "toward the people of the GDR."

Gomulka and Ulbricht both continually made acid comments on the situation in Czechoslovakia in the course of casual conversation. It was not merely political hostility; their remarks were full of personal ill will and malevolence toward something that was causing personal difficulties for them at home, something they feared and, at the same time, for all their dictatorial powers, felt utterly helpless to do anything about.

The Bulgarian leader, Todor Zhivkov, was still relatively young at the time (he was not yet 55), but he was outstanding for his quite exceptional dullness. My years of close contact with many high functionaries had taught me not to have high standards, but observing a living Zhivkov from up close was shocking all the same. When trying to follow what someone else was saying, he did so with the tense concentration of someone who knows that if he doesn't pay absolute attention he won't understand a thing. During the working sessions he sometimes intervened unwittingly to oppose objections with which Brezhnev was getting ready to comply, thus complicating Brezhnev's role. I noticed that two or three times in such a situation Brezhnev ignored Zhivkov when he wanted to speak, and then gestured to him to stay out of the debate.

In such company, János Kádár stood out far above the others, both in the political and the human sense. From various sources, I knew that Kádár's position on the Prague Spring was very different from the other Soviet bloc leaders. Meeting him personally in Bratislava not only convinced me of this but it also gave me a sense of his human dimension and how his experience of 1956 remained something that affected his conscience as well as his politics.

After dinner, Kádár stayed behind with Dubček and myself and talked with us for about half-an-hour. Politically, he felt that we in Czechoslovakia were faced with two alternatives: either we ourselves must intervene forcefully to stop some of the developments, or there was danger someone else would. He never put things in a way that would leave him open to accusations of broaching a Soviet intervention, but by drawing analogies to Budapest in 1956 he made it very clear what he had in mind. He said that successful reforms in Czechoslovakia would mean hope for similar developments in Hungary. And then he spoke of his personal problems and feelings on taking over the government in Hungary after the Soviet intervention. He urged Dubček to realize how incomparably more difficult it was in such circumstances than anything he might encounter while he was still master of the situation. Kádár had the qualities of a politician who was capable of stubbornly and effectively defending an apparently hopeless minimum of national interests, a person who was uncorrupted by his own power because he had never lost sight of his real aims. Certainly, he was a politician perfectly suited to maintaining just such a minimum, but developments in domestic Hungarian politics in the ten years since our encounter confirms, I think, that Kádár was able gradually and inconspicuously to enlarge that minimum as well. What he will do, or will be able to do, if those tiny steps forward reach the point where a more conceptual and fundamental democratic reform becomes the order of the day is, of course, another question.

It is known that on the 17th of August, Kádár initiated a meeting with Dubček in the small town of Komárno on the Czechoslovak-Hungarian border. Judging from my own personal impression of Kádár and what I heard about that meeting afterwards from Dubček, I believe Kádár was trying to warn Dubček at a time when he, Kádár, already knew that the decision to intervene militarily had been made in Moscow. After the intervention, Dubček himself admitted that some of Kádár's statements could have been so interpreted. He also said that when they parted on the station platform, Kádár asked him almost desperately: "Do you *really* not know the kind of people you're dealing with?"

The very same day, Brezhnev, in the name of his politburo, sent the letter that Dubček subsequently read to the presidium on that fateful night. From all this, Dubček, too, must have concluded that there had been a new, adverse turn of events in Moscow and that military intervention was once more a distinct possibility. I don't believe, however, that Dubček felt anything effective could be done quickly, and therefore he chose, as he so often did in such cases, to put the matter off until the situation became clear. When it did become clear three days later, he was no longer in a position to decide anything.

After the 20th of August 1968, it was often questioned whether there was anything Dubček and his leadership could have done to prevent Moscow from resorting to military intervention to protect its hegemony. Those Moscow agents in the CPC leadership in August 1968 who tried to exploit the intervention to strengthen their positions claim, along with later proponents of "normalization," that it could have been avoided. They blamed Dubček for not informing the leadership about the Dresden and Moscow meetings, of "concealing" Brezhnev's final letter, and so on. Such accusations are absurd, and they only serve the personal interests of the "normalizers." But to find a serious answer to this question, we must try to discover the reasons that led the Soviet leadership to decide on military intervention in the first place.

The reasons for the intervention stem from two separate but related types of interest: on the one hand, the foreign policy interests of the USSR as a superpower and, on the other hand, the competing interests of a power struggle in the Soviet leadership. It was interests of both kinds that led to the ousting of Khrushchev in October 1964 and culminated in the invasion of Czechoslovakia in 1968.

In terms of foreign policy, Khrushchev's era meant the end of the cold war. It reduced the danger of a military confrontation with the West, it opened the door to beneficial economic cooperation between the USSR and the world, and it enabled the Soviet Union to penetrate into various areas of the world, particularly in the developing countries, using diplomatic, economic, and even military means. In these respects, Khrushchev undeniably strengthened the position of the USSR as a superpower in the new conditions of the postwar world. At the same time, however, he lost China and Albania, without really retrieving Yugoslavia, and the Soviet army withdrew from Austria. His anti-Stalinist policies caused domestic political unrest in Poland, Hungary, and ultimately even in Czechoslovakia, and Rumania began to ease itself out of the disciplined strait jacket of the Soviet bloc. The Communist movement outside the bloc began visibly to disengage itself as an instrument of Moscow's foreign policy interests. In these respects, Khrushchev had noticeably weakened the position of the USSR as a superpower.

But the question is which was more important: that he lessened tensions with the US or that China became an anti-Soviet power?— that Soviet influence was strengthened in some African and Latin American countries, far beyond the borders of its own empire, or that inside that empire, in Eastern and Central Europe, Moscow's hegemony had become more problematic? It all depends on the political and military perspective. And here is where the Soviet Union's foreign policy interests relate directly to the struggle for power in the Soviet hierarchy among the various groups, each with its own perspective.

After the Second World War, the Soviet army replaced diplomacy and the Communist International as the most dominant force in Soviet foreign policy. And the war-generation marshals still had considerable influence in the Soviet army at the end of the Khrushchev era. Put very simply, their general strategy was based on the slogan, "You can only count on what you have at home," which epitomizes the theories of the victory of socialism in one country and of capitalist encirclement that were at the heart of Stalin's outlook. For Stalin, "socialism in one country" was delimited by what was within his immediate—i.e., military and police—control, and how many formally independent states were included in this "one country" was irrelevant. Stalin's greatest concern was to create the strongest possible military-industrial power. In relation to the rest of the world, which represented that "capitalist encirclement," "socialism in one country" was isolationist. It depended for its position in that world on a network of ideological and political agents through which Stalin successfully controlled the Communist movement.

From the view of such strategic and foreign policy interests, the Khrushchev period appears as a series of setbacks. "Socialism in one country," practically speaking, disintegrated. Moreover, developments in China began to give rise to an enemy before which all Russian empires have traditionally trembled in fear—the enemy from the East, from Asia, which revived the specter of Genghis Khan and the ancient slavery of Russia. For the old Soviet marshals, who were still thinking, after all, in terms of conventional weaponry and wars, it must necessarily have been a far more terrifying prospect than the sum total of "American imperialism" across the ocean, equipped with the most modern technology for unconventional wars of the future.

These Soviet marshals were directly in league with powerful forces in the civilian wing of the Soviet power structure—the party, political, and police apparatus—who were children of the same Stalinist era and were concerned at the collapse of Stalinist discipline throughout the empire and in Russia itself precipitated by Khrushchev's policies. And I believe these marshals were one of the main forces behind both Khrushchev's fall and the invasion of Czechoslovakia.

Khrushchev's policies, however, also had powerful and influential supporters inside the Soviet power structure. Some of them were military groups (in command of missile units, etc.) and others interested in the development of a modern arms industry. There were also pro-Khrushchev groups active in diplomacy and foreign trade. Such people have an indisputably wider and more modern view of the super-power interests of the USSR than old Second-World-War marshals and their bureaucratic associates. They see the foreign interests of the USSR chiefly in its ability to compete with, above all, the United States, employing modern arms production and the economic, political, and military penetration into distant but strategically important areas, including diplomatic offensives that would create for the USSR room for advantageous political maneuvering in the world constellation of powers.

For such groups, the Khrushchev era was not unsuccessful. On the contrary, it meant an offensive in directions that tended to promote such a superpower strategy. However, Khrushchev was too impulsive: he made a good many ill-considered decisions that led to serious and undesirable consequences and provoked growing opposition inside the Soviet bureaucracy, thus becoming more a liability than an asset for those groups who shared his strategic interests.

It was in the context of the conflict, at all party levels, between the old Stalinist marshals, who advocated a strict economic and political control of society, and non-Stalinist groups who advocated rational, mostly technological and also, by Soviet standards, democratic approaches that Khrushchev fell from power and was replaced by Brezhnev in October 1964. During the next three years—until the toppling of Novotný in Prague—these conflicts in Moscow remained unresolved. Leonid Brezhnev had in fact become czar out of necessity and the benevolence of others, in a situation where no one group was powerful enough to assert absolute control, and he still did not have "his" politburo. Practically none of the members owed their position to him; on the contrary, he owed his to them. It was not until 1970 that Brezhnev gradually managed to replace most of the politburo members he had inherited with people who were beholden to him.

How was the Prague Spring affected by what was going on in the Kremlin?

In the first place, the actual unseating of Novotný was related to those conflicts. As I have previously mentioned, Novotný had been attached to the Khrushchev era and, as a result, was on very bad terms with Brezhnev. He had also, ever since the summer of 1967, fraternized with the Stalinist marshals in Moscow. It has been said that he did so in order to counterbalance pressure from Moscow, since 1966, to station Soviet troops on Czechoslovak soil, something which Novotný resisted. He did agree to the deployment of strategic weapons and specialized units to man them (about 8,000 men altogether), but he refused to accept a garrison with conventional weapons and large numbers of troops. To Novotný's way of thinking, the combination of a harder line at home with his concession to the presence of strategic weapons would gain him the confidence of the Moscow "hawks," and his poor personal relationship with Brezhnev would not necessarily get in the way. Novotný himself probably considered Brezhnev a temporary and unstable figure to whom it was not wise to commit himself.

Thus when Novotný was replaced, Brezhnev expected, among other things, a strengthening of his personal influence in Czechoslovakia and a corresponding weakening of the marshals' influence. This was likewise perceived by the "hawks" in Moscow, who consequently began to implicate Brezhnev in the rapid growth of the democratic movement that soon followed. At the same time, Ulbricht and Gomulka, who also had compelling, domestic political reasons for opposing reforms in Czechoslovakia, were in close contact with the Moscow "hawks." Their own regimes, both based on their personal power, were in a state of crisis equally as profound as that of the Novotný regime, and here was an infectious democratic plague raging right next door. And the network of Soviet agents in Czechoslovakia (in the CPC, security forces, army, and other state organs) was also, in essence, connected with the Moscow "hawks." This included the Soviet embassy in Prague (run by Ambassador Chervonenko and Ministor-Counselor Udaltsov). All the intelligence sent to the Kremlin through these channels was slanted to favor the "hawks'" position.

The struggle for influence in Czechoslovakia—and thus the struggle over which interpretation of developments there would become official—was, from the outset, not a product of ideological orthodoxy, but a direct and important aspect of the internal struggle in the Moscow power structure.

During the Kremlin negotiations on August 26, 1968, Brezhnev said, more or less in passing, that the military option had been approved in May 1968. In other words, it was not the Action Program or the personnel changes on April 5, 1968 that triggered this decision, neither was it the Central Committee resolution on convening an extraordinary congress nor the publication of "Two Thousand Words," which both occurred after the decision. The military option was accepted before the May plenum of the CPC Central Committee, which took place from May 29–June 1, 1968, because right after his reference to the May decision, Brezhnev added: "Then it seemed that it wouldn't be necessary." The May plenum was the first indication of a change in course. And despite the heightened criticism of developments in Czechoslovakia at the May 4 meeting in Moscow with Dubček, Černík, Smrkovský, and Bilak, it was clear from the course of the meeting, and the press and ideological campaign surrounding it, that the Kremlin had not made the decision yet and still felt that economic and political pressure would suffice. Nevertheless, the decision was made very soon after—sometime between May 5 and 29.

It seems most likely that the decision to include military intervention as an option was reached on the return from Czechoslovakia of Marshal Grechko (who was there with a military delegation on May 17-22) and Alexei Kosygin (who was in Karlový Vary [Carlsbad] on a "cure" from May 17-25). The issue was first raised in the secret meeting prior to this on May 8 in Moscow between the leaders of the five parties that later became the interveners—the CPC was not even invited, neither was the Rumanian party—evidently as a result of pressure from Gomulka and Ulbricht. But before the actual decision was made by the Soviet politburo, "inspection trips" were made by representatives of both groups, the marshals and the technocrats, that is, the politicians. The result was a compromise: intervention yes, but only if extreme circumstances warranted it. In practice, they were to try to influence developments in other ways.

What prevented those of the more rational, and in fact Khrushchevian, bent from seeing eye to eye with the "hawks" on the question of military intervention? Certainly it was not a belief that "socialism with a human face" represented the hope of socialism and the Soviet Union. They saw developments in Czechoslovakia in terms of the interests of the Soviet bureaucracy and its rule inside Soviet society and in the whole Soviet bloc, and in this they were akin to the "hawks." But they opposed the intervention for fear that such a step would do grave harm to what they saw as the achievements of Khrushchev's policies in the world: the relaxation of tensions with the West, new perspectives for the development of economic and political ties with the rest of the world. They were afraid intervention would weaken their position at home as well, in the Soviet Union, and ultimately strengthen the position of the more orthodox Stalinist forces.

These forces in the Soviet politburo that were in a certain sense favorable to the reforms in Czechoslovakia therefore did not arise as a result of the reforms themselves. They existed independent of the developments in Czechoslovakia and were the product of Soviet international and domestic concerns. The same is true of the Kremlin "hawks."

The reforms of 1968 could have taken place at all only if there had been an extended stalemate between the main rival forces and they had not been able to agree on the necessity of military intervention. Only in this way could the CPC leadership have influenced events.

In November 1968, in a personal and, considering the time, genuinely friendly conversation, Brezhnev said to Bohumil Šimon, who led the Czechoslovak delegation to Moscow to celebrate the October Revolution, "You thought that when you were in power you could do what you wanted. But that's a basic mistake. Not even I can do what I'd like; I can achieve only about a third of what I would like to do. If I hadn't voted in the politburo for military intervention, what would have happened? You almost certainly would not be sitting here. And I probably wouldn't be sitting here either."

Brezhnev was being perfectly sincere here, and he confirms my view of the situation in 1968. The Kremlin "hawks" were able to use the problem of democratization in Czechoslovakia as a key issue in resolving the power conflicts inside Moscow at that time. They were consciously exploiting what they felt was an extremely opportune issue for them. Given the lines of force then inside the Soviet power structure, they were absolutely right.

When Marshal Grechko returned to Moscow from Prague at the end of May, he was almost certainly armed with arguments in support of the marshals' hawkish position. But what did Kosygin return with? I think he could only have had one truly serious insight: that it would be very risky, perhaps even dangerous, to gamble the fate of the group that wanted a more rational continuation of Khrushchevian policies on an unequivocal defense of Dubček and his policies. It might have cost this group their position in power. Had they not "raised their hands" for the arguments of the "hawks"—though not necessarily setting a time for troop action—perhaps they really would be in the politburo no longer.

Why? Because socialism was "threatened" in Czechoslovakia or civil war was on the horizon? Because the CPC leadership wanted to pull Czechoslovakia out of the Soviet bloc? Not at all. Kosygin knew that all of these arguments were just so much ideological and propagandistic bombast, necessary to conceal the internal Communist conflicts.

Kosygin may not have viewed events in the Prague Spring from the vantage point of the old Soviet marshals and their allies, but he certainly saw them in terms of the interests of Soviet hegemony. And from the information at his disposal in Moscow, and from his trip to Czechoslovakia, where he spoke with several members of the Dubček leadership—including some who were unknown in Moscow, like Čestmír Císař—and where for several days he lived and breathed the atmosphere of the Prague Spring, even though it was in the rather exclusive setting of the colonnades of Karlový Vary, he must have drawn conclusions that brought him, willy-nilly, closer to the "hawks' " way of thinking.

He saw that the totalitarian system in Czechoslovakia was not only in a state of profound crisis but that it was being transformed both from the top down and from the bottom up. He saw that the mechanisms which, in his eyes and in those of the entire Soviet bureaucracy, were indispensable guarantees of Communist rule, no longer functioned in Czechoslovakia. Power must necessarily and rightly have appeared unstable to him. Nor can he have shared Dubček's faith in some nonviolent form of Marxism-Leninism or in the democratic and humanistic sentiments of the Czechoslovak population, and he was certainly incapable of imagining that Moscow's interests could be guaranteed by a communist party that ruled in this manner. He did not share the notion on which the entire conception of reform, including the Action Program version, was based, that such a democratic experiment would provide in Czechoslovakia the necessary security for Moscow's hegemony. After all, the Soviet bureaucracy as a whole had ousted Khrushchev for experiments that were far less daring and far less dangerous for the empire.

Some of Kosygin's personal experiences in Czechoslovakia must have given him pause to wonder as well. He was the second most powerful man in the empire after the czar himself, and yet the Czechoslovak rulers could not protect him from prying journalists. While walking through the colonnades of the spa, a little jug of mineral water in his hands, he was set upon by an impertinent lady reporter, filmed and then televised as he tried to squirm out of unpleasant questions. His conversation with a Central Committee secretary, Čestmír Císař, could only have strengthened Kosygin's doubts. In response to Kosygin taking him to task for employing some unacceptable formulation on Leninism and its general importance for the world in some recent ceremony in honor of Marx, Císař defended his ideological convictions, though he ought to have realized that he was being tested by the chief government inspector to see whether he was worthy to administer an important province. Císař must have therefore struck Kosygin as an utter novice. Císař did not understand this until later, and, in a conversation with me, he attributed his blunder to his imperfect knowledge of Russian. Later, Císař did everything he could to correct the unfortunate impression he made on Kosygin, and he was especially agile in his efforts after August 1968, but to no avail. This was perhaps less due to his imperfect knowledge of Russian than to his imperfect knowledge of Russian literature: in the Chekov short story, "The Death of a Clerk," an official inappropriately sneezes in the presence of some potentate, and, terrified that it might ruin his career, he tries grovellingly in every way he can think of to make amends, making a complete nuisance of himself to his superiors. He thereby definitively destroys his career.

During his May visit to Czechoslovakia, Kosygin personally confirmed the disunity of the Dubček leadership and the presence in it of agents of the Moscow "hawks." This later also must have been an important consideration, for it could not be ruled out that the "hawks" might achieve their ends in Czechoslovakia without the help of the moderates in the Kremlin, and consequently outflank them and gain supremacy.

All these factors together, in my opinion, resulted in the decision by the Soviet leadership sometime around the end of May to include military intervention as an option for dealing with Czechoslovakia. To forestall such an event, something would have had to happen to strengthen the more moderate and rational Kremlin group in such a way that they could weather a conflict with the "hawks" over Czechoslovakia.

Nothing of the sort, however, happened, particularly inside Czechoslovakia itself. On the contrary, in every respect things developed in a direction that ultimately facilitated military intervention. This may be observed very clearly after the May resolution of the CPC Central Committee, which set the date, September 9, 1968, for the extraordinary Fourteenth Congress. The opponents of reform had everything to fear from this congress, and it must have spurred them on to the offensive, which clearly began in earnest from about the middle of June.

To this day, analyses of the Prague Spring generally hold that the May resolution was a victory for the conservative forces, that it marked the beginning of open moves against the reforms. It is generally claimed that the "rightwing forces" (i.e., the radical reformists) were singled out as the main source of danger. But this is simply not true if you consider the text of the resolution itself. I wrote it, and I know how careful I was to formulate the necessary warning against both the left and right extremes so it would not lend itself to some one-sided simplification. The May resolution states: "The party considers it fundamental in this situation to prevent the socialist character of power in the state and the social system from being challenged either by right-wing, anti-Communist tendencies or by conservative forces in favor of returning to pre-January 1968 conditions, which were incapable of ensuring the development of socialism." All the rest of the May resolution was consistent with the Action Program, and it in no way limited it. In fact, it went further than the Action Program in spelling out the system of self-management as a current practical task, the relationships within the National Front, and also the activity of the mass media. These last two questions raised hackles among the radical reform Communists, but it was because their demands had gone beyond the bounds of the Action Program and not because the May resolution represented a one-sided victory for the conservatives. Rather, this document was simply characteristic of what the radicals called "centrism": it insisted on maintaining the framework of the Action Program against both radical and conservative tendencies.

It is true that the conservative forces, including Soviet agents in the CPC, used this resolution, or those parts that suited their purposes, as a critique of the radicals. The radicals, however, rather than defend themselves on the basis of the Action Program, counterattacked the conservatives roughly from the position in the "Two Thousand Words" manifesto. The consequence by June was a heightened struggle between the radicals and conservatives and not the unification of political forces that was the basis of the May Resolution.

Because the radical reform Communists, practically speaking, controlled the media, they appeared to be the dominant trend. Inside the CPC itself, however, the "centrist" orientation was then dominant: about 80 percent of the congress delegates elected in late June and early July were centrists. But for the antireform forces, including the Soviet "hawks," both the public ascent of the radicals and the massive victory of the "centrists" in the CPC were seen as clear setbacks, and they responded accordingly. Of course, the public activity of the radicals suited their strategy best, but in fact their attack was directed against the reformists in general, including the CPC "centrists." The Warsaw Letter may attack the signatories of "Two Thousand Words" as supporters of a "counter-revolutionary platform," but on the 21st of August, 1968, it was not Ludvík Vaculík or any other signatory whom the Soviet soldiers and Šalgovič's State Security forces went looking for but rather Dubček, Černík, Smrkovský, Kriegel, Špaček and Šimon, whom they arrested in the Central Committee building.

From the moment the Moscow "hawks"—that is, the marshals in collusion with part of the Soviet political bureaucracy and, beyond that, chiefly with Ulbricht and Gomulka—won the politburo's consent to the military option at the end of May, they took the offensive. They were temporarily frustrated by the May resolution, which Brezhnev and the other Soviet politburo moderates endorsed, but the respite was a brief one, and in two or three weeks the hawks were in the ascendancy again. With the war between the radicals and the conservatives in Prague as ammunition, the "hawks" argued that the very existence of party power in Czechoslovakia, and thus Soviet interests as well, was threatened, and they began to press for an intervention. They had notable success in the Warsaw meeting, to which they "invited" the CPC in such a way as to make it extremely difficult, if not impossible, for them to attend at all, thus making the schism appear active even at the highest level.

Could the Dubček leadership have accepted the "invitation" to the so-called discussion? Not without provoking such domestic political conflicts that the intervention partisans would only have been provided with another source of endless arguments. For, in fact, it was no longer a question of discussion and possible appeasement: the Warsaw meeting was a tribunal in which the verdict had been passed in advance, the text of which was then issued as the Warsaw Letter. To accept the Warsaw evaluation of the political situation in Czechoslovakia would have meant not only rejecting the course of reform but, more than that, evoking a massive wave of nonconfidence, discontent, and resistance on the part of the population towards the CPC leadership. To go to Warsaw and reject the verdict would have meant creating an obvious and irreparable rift with Moscow and the four other neighboring states, which, again, would only have furthered the interests of the intervention partisans.

Not attending the meeting while inviting the participants to bilateral discussions was clearly the only possible political solution. But it brought no more than a brief pause in the "hawks'" offensive. With the Warsaw meeting, the "hawks" had reached the point of no return, and there was no longer anything Dubček or anyone else could do. If the "hawks" did not take their Warsaw position to its logical conclusion in military intervention, it would mean political defeat and their ouster from power. After the illusory peripeteia in Čierná nad Tisou and Bratislava, I believe the "hawks" launched the new and final round in their offensive, around August 10, 1968.

It was at this time that the Soviet politburo went on vacation. The physical absence of the leadership from the Kremlin is traditionally a ripe moment to attempt a palace revolution. While I have no factual evidence, I believe that sometime around August 10 a new alliance of sorts was forged between the "hawks" and some of those previously undecided, welded together, most likely, by the offer of the secretary-general position to someone. Candidates for such a post are always to be found, and there was no dearth of aspirants particularly at that time. I don't know who it was—perhaps Shelepin—but I assume the stakes were no less. To identify the probable participants in such an attempted putsch one need only refer to whom Brezhnev later removed from politburo and party leadership positions.

The marshals made their move, and General Shchemenko, who was certainly a representative of the Stalinist clique, was suddenly named commander in chief of the Warsaw Pact forces. And the highest-ranking marshals began shuttling between the Ukraine, Poland, and the GDR, and movements of large military units were observed. Then, about August 15, the politburo members interrupted their vacation and rushed back to Moscow. Soon afterwards, two meetings took place, perhaps including non-politburo people as well, at which time the intervention was decided upon. That would have been around August 17 or 18.

I consider it highly probable that Brezhnev and the politburo moderates forestalled a putsch in the Kremlin by rapidly taking the initiative and uniting with the "hawks" over the military intervention in Czechoslovakia, thus defusing the main arguments of the anti-Brezhnev forces. In such a situation, nothing Dubček might have done in Prague could have averted the invasion itself.

The only thing that might still have caused the Soviet politburo to reconsider their decision in August was the threat of a wider military conflict. As I have already discussed, the Czechoslovak army was in no position to pose such a threat. It would have to come from the West—and no such danger existed. Developments in Czechoslovakia in 1968 did nothing to alter the interest that the West in general had in maintaining the established spheres of influence in Europe. As far as the US was concerned, Brezhnev was reassured by them of this on August 18. I shall say more about why later.

But even given this fact, and the fact that the Soviet Union is incapable of defending its essentially violent and hegemonistic interests inside a multinational empire other than by force, was military intervention utterly unavoidable? Was it at all possible to influence the course of events in such a way that the Kremlin masters would have been unable to agree on it, or would have been afraid to take such a step, from the viewpoint of their own interests? There is no simple, straightforward answer to this question, and, moreover, every such answer has only a hypothetical value. Nevertheless, fully aware of the limited significance of such speculations, I still think that Czechoslovak reform Communists could have done—and in fact were obliged to do—far more than they did to maintain disunity among the Soviet leadership on the question of military intervention, and further, to give them more cause to fear taking such a step.

The period from January to May was crucial in this regard, and it was then that the "hawks" won their first victory in Moscow. If conditions had been stabilized in that period, if the extraordinary congress had already taken place in May, the leadership in Moscow would have been more likely to remain divided over the issue of military intervention. Of course, in such circumstances the Prague Spring, rather than snowballing as it did into that nationwide democratic and humanitarian movement, would probably have remained a gradual institutional reform movement directed largely from above, only very slowly dismantling the system of totalitarian dictatorship. As a consequence, there would have been neither so much hope and enthusiasm, nor so much disappointment, apathy, and despair. It is also possible that regardless of what was done, strong antireform pressure would have come from Moscow anyway, and in this case probably not even the conceptions of the Action Program could have been completely and rapidly implemented.

From June to August, the question of military intervention superseded internal developments in Czechoslovakia. By this time, the factors behind this decision were beyond the control of the reform Communists in Czechoslovakia. Domestic political developments continued to provide the partisans of intervention with official ideological and propagandistic arguments, but it is scarcely credible to suggest, for example, that had "Two Thousand Words" never been written the forces for intervention would have found no other arguments to justify their plans.

In the same period, the Soviet espionage network in Czechoslovakia, in cooperation with East German agents, increasingly manufactured its own arguments. Several proven acts of provocation are known to have occurred: the discovery of "American arms" near a road in the Sokolov district in Western Bohemia; the distribution of leaflets; etc. The petition demanding the disbanding of the People's Militia was also a provocation. When I met personally with Pavel, the minister of the interior, we both agreed that the crowds involved in this agitation, on Příkopy Street in the center of Prague, should be investigated. Pavel's security men discovered that there were more than fifty agents of the State Security police among those actively agitating for the disbanding of the militia. It was almost certainly a provocation organized by Soviet agents inside the State Security forces. Also the infamous "Letter from 99 Pragovka Workers" protesting the reform movement was clearly orchestrated by Soviet agents. All such incidents in Czechoslovakia were always very promptly reported in the Soviet press in an exaggerated and demagogic manner.

After the Warsaw meeting, the entire pro-Moscow group in the CPC leadership stopped supporting any proposed measures that should in principle have been welcome in Moscow. Prior to the meeting in Čierná nad Tisou, I presented the presidium with two proposals: one to give the government extraordinary powers to ban, for a period of three months, any publication that issued material damaging to Czechoslovakia's foreign relations; and the other to make the National Front the only legal platform for any organization with the aims and purposes of a political party. My assumption was that the CPC delegates would have to accept similar conditions in Čierná anyway, and that therefore it was in the best interests of the reforms to take the initiative ourselves. And finally, neither proposal went substantially beyond the bounds of the Action Program framework.

The presidium rejected both my proposals. Under pressure from the radical reform Communists, neither Smrkovský nor Černík, with whom I had a prior understanding about these proposals—as I had with Dubček—kept to the original understanding, and in the end they withdrew their support. Even Dubček did the same. Interestingly enough, however, no one in the pro-Moscow group supported them either. Although in the preceding three months they had never missed an opportunity at leadership meetings to point out articles in the press and political organizations outside the National Front as the chief threats to socialism, not one of them came forward to support my proposals. This would almost certainly not have happened before the Warsaw meeting. And there is only one possible explanation for such a change in attitude: the pro-Moscow group in the CPC leadership was by this time consciously and single-mindedly preparing for a Soviet military intervention, which would favor the hawks, and thus they had not the slightest interest in lessening the threat of conflict in the Čierna nad Tisou negotiations.

If, therefore, I was critical of the radical reform Communists for short-sightedly and at times irresponsibly contributing to a situation unfavorable to reform, this does not mean that I was unaware of the antireform role played by the militant CPC conservatives and the network of Soviet agents in Czechoslovakia. From July onwards these forces worked on the domestic political front expressly to help prepare the military intervention. However, I can hardly censure them for taking action against what they disagreed with. Given their intentions, what they did was logical and correct, which cannot be said of the radical Communists.

There is, however, one outstanding thing to be said in favor of the radical Communists: they saw the danger of military intervention far move clearly than Dubček's own leadership did. The radical reform Communists suffered from no illusions in this regard, and from approximately May onwards they frequently and openly warned of the danger of Moscow extinguishing the democratic process with military force. For this same reason, they also gave more thought than others to precautions, and they sought allies among Communists and leftist forces outside the Soviet bloc and entertained the idea that Czechoslovakia might have to openly oppose the bloc, as Tito did in Yugoslavia in 1948.

Because the radical reform wing was most strongly entrenched among the intellectuals, the press, and the other media, these opinions found a certain currency among the public as well. Naturally, this created a very unpleasant situation for the Dubček leadership, because Moscow was able to point to such opinions as proof of "anti-Sovietism" and of efforts to "disrupt the unity of the socialist states," thus posing a threat to the interests of the entire Soviet bloc. Therefore the CPC leadership mounted several sharp attacks on the radical reform Communists in this regard. For example, the May resolution states: "It is inadmissible for Communists to forget that distorting and exaggerating certain differences of opinion and even propagating mendacious reports of the 'danger of a military intervention' (e.g., in connection with the maneuvers of Warsaw Pact units, etc.) have an extremely harmful effect on the whole course of the present policies and play into the hands of certain circles in the capitalist countries and their efforts to disrupt the unity of the socialist countries.

"The Central Committee of the CPC declares that all negotiations past and present with representatives of the USSR on a party and government level have issued in positive conclusions and that the way has been opened to deeper cooperation and assistance, which is extraordinarily important in resolving some of our present economic difficulties, and that the Soviet comrades have expressed the will to provide us with such aid."

Thus Dubček's leadership deliberately concealed the true state of affairs and lied in the interests of Moscow, because they thought that in doing so they were lying in their own interests as well. But, as later events proved, such calculations were based on an illusion.

I think it was simply not politically realistic to expect the CPC leadership to accept a position knowing it might lead to a break with Moscow and the whole Soviet bloc. The only point on which they could unite and which would avoid creating ungovernable domestic political conflicts (both in society and inside the CPC) was the one on which they actually did unite: that the reform was achievable even while maintaining all the relationships and commitments between Czechoslovakia and the USSR and the Warsaw Pact bloc. To tell the truth, however, I also think that in this question the Dubček leadership was far from only being guided by such a rational grasp of political necessity, but that the ideological illusions of the reform Communists in the leadership played a large, if not a crucial, role.

Because it is difficult to speak for others in such delicate matters, I will speak only for myself. During the Prague Spring, I had no illusions that the party leadership in Moscow might see our reforms as some kind of desirable model. I genuinely did not feel that the proper conditions for such reform existed in the USSR, and I knew that the process of democratizing Soviet social life would be a long and complex one. Nor did I suffer under any illusions that the Soviet Union might have anything but a standard great-power foreign policy, and that the publicly declared principles of independence and sovereignty for the Soviet bloc would take precedence over Soviet interests. Furthermore, I did not think that the Moscow leaders spent most of their time wondering about the best way to develop socialism along the humanitarian and democratic lines of the European socialist tradition and, ultimately, according to the original hypotheses of Marx. And yet I still had many illusions, and it took the military intervention of August 1968 to dispel them.

Before the intervention, I believed that the Moscow politburo's overriding concern was still, after all, the development of socialism, vulgar though its theoretical notions of socialism may have been. I believed it still paid homage to the idea of socialism, at least to the extent that the CPC presidium under Novotný had done. But that was an illusion. For the Moscow politburo, as a whole, socialism had already become identical with its own power, with the social order it had created in the Soviet Union. The Brezhnev politburo did not even have a rudimentary, minimal notion of some kind of improved, freer, and more democratic order than the "realistic" minimum that already existed. For me, such changes were what communist ideology was all about.

For the Moscow politburo, nothing could take precedence over their own purely power-hungry interests.

Before August 1968, I had felt that the USSR had begun to learn from its own mistakes and that, at least in the most basic sense, it was learning to implement its bloc policies more in accordance with the distinctiveness of each nation. I felt that after what happened with Yugoslavia and China, and also with Poland and Hungary in 1956, the Kremlin would choose more flexible and thus more productive methods of economic, military, and political control. Though, it is true, some politburo members (those who were more moderate and cautious on the question of intervention) thought this way, the politburo as a whole demonstrated in the end that, where possible, the USSR would continue to use the most primitive methods of maintaining its hegemony, even against its own allies, and that in fact it cared little for alliances with relatively independent states if it could safely, without risking another world war, impose total subjugation.

Thus ideological illusions prevented me from seeing the reactionary political role of the Soviet Union in its empire. Nor did I correctly understand the nature of the changes that took place after the ousting of Khrushchev. The period from 1964–67 in the CPC was one of successive victories for the forces of reform, and I simply did not see (nor did many other Czechoslovak Communists) that precisely the opposite was going on in the Soviet Union at that time. Though Khrushchev himself could only be considered a reform Communist with many reservations, his policies were, after all, directed consistently at the destruction of many Stalinist mechanisms of government. After his overthrow, some of these mechanisms were gradually restored.

It is certainly true that the military intervention in Hungary in 1956 took place during Khrushchev's rule; however, I subscribed to the communist rationalization that the intervention had been provoked by armed assaults on some units of Rakosi's totalitarian dictatorship. Furthermore, I felt that the uncertainty of the Khrushchev leadership after the Twentieth Congress had also been a factor. Since neither of these conditions existed in 1968, military intervention was surely ruled out. This was an illusion, for the shooting in the streets of Budapest had obviously been provoked by the Soviets to justify the military intervention. And it was also an illusion to think that any efforts toward democratic reforms and national independence in the Soviet empire would not make any Soviet politburo feel uncomfortable. As long as the Soviet Union is ruled by a totalitarian political regime, the "invincible alliance of free nations" will only be an empty phrase in the Soviet national anthem and any national democratic movement in the empire will simply be too contagious and dangerous for the Soviet Union to tolerate.

It was as a result of such ideological illusions that the Dubček leadership, rather than secure the backing of foreign allies as a safeguard against Soviet intervention, chose from the outset to declare the reforms an exclusively internal Czechoslovak affair. Even at the end of March, when it was clear that a counteroffensive by the Kremlin (and also by Ulbricht and Gomulka) was beginning, the CPC leadership did not alter its position. It continued to emphasize that the reforms were an internal matter, that Czechoslovakia did not interfere in the internal affairs of the others and therefore neither should they. They chose the tactic of placation with oft-repeated assurances of Czechoslovakia's everlasting loyalty to Moscow's interests in the Soviet bloc, and merely requested that they be allowed to work out alternate solutions to their own internal problems.

Thus when the Soviet Union finally did attack Czechoslovakia on the night of August 20, 1968, it could be certain not only of encountering no effective native military resistance but also of no international action. Naturally Czechoslovakia had the sympathy of the democratic world public and the support of several Communist parties, but what was missing was a system of well-conceived political relations with foreign powers of such a nature that military retaliation by them would pose a real political threat to the Kremlin. The case of Rumania has shown that a system of such relations can be constructed. The question is whether it can be done in half a year. The Dubček leadership, however, did not even try, even though there were opportunities at the beginning of the reforms.

If there was any chance of developments in Prague influencing Moscow's decision to intervene, I think they can be reduced to: 1. executing rapid personnel changes in the entire party and state system by holding elections and an extraordinary party congress by June 1968, thus stabilizing the entire political system, and, of course, substantially limiting the free development of the nationwide democratic movement that made the Prague Spring famous; and 2. undertaking at the same time a foreign policy offensive (both within the Communist movement, with countries such as Yugoslavia, Rumania, and China, and outside it, with important countries in the Third World and also with western democratic political forces and states), a policy that would have corresponded to the general spirit of the Czechoslovak reforms.

It is true that I worked hard during the Prague Spring to realize the former possibility, but I did nothing about the latter. Under illusions concerning the nature of power politics in Moscow, my evaluation of the international context of the Prague Spring was just as wrong as that of the other reform Communists in the party leadership. That is another reason why I am no longer convinced that intervention would have been avoided had my conceptions at the time prevailed.

The Dubček leadership must therefore bear the political responsibility for not having arranged international backing for its reform efforts, but to infer from this that they are to blame for the intervention itself is like saying that a person who doesn't arm himself and isn't careful is to blame for being attacked by robbers. Perhaps he should in fact have been more circumspect and less naive—he should have known that those he took for friends were really just robbers—but this does not mean that anyone but the robbers is to blame for the crime.

The retrospective criticism of the Dubček leadership by the pro-Moscow proponents of "normalization" is something quite different. According to their line, if the Dubček leadership had implemented the politics of "normalization" from the outset, there would have been no intervention. That may well be true, but there would have been no political reforms either, not even in the modest form suggested by the Action Program. This kind of criticism rejects the notion of reform altogether. If the CPC leadership in January 1968 had admitted no reform Communists at all, but only Bilak, Indra, Jakeš, Kapek, and others like them, it is true that there would have been no Soviet military intervention. Such a situation, of course, would have had only one thing to be said in its favor: it would not have been necessary to appoint Gustav Husák head of the party and the state.

When Alexander Dubček formally adjourned the presidium meeting in the early morning of August 21, 1968, the corridors around the chambers were a hive of activity. Dozens of party functionaries and journalists were running about or standing in little groups waiting for instructions. But there were no instructions. Nevertheless, several important decisions were improvised.

When the first sentence of the presidium resolution was read out over the air, the radio transmitters went dead and only an ominous silence wafted from radio sets all over the country. This had been prearranged by the minister of communications and Soviet agent, Karel Hoffman—in cooperation with the Soviet network in the State Security forces (led by Šalgovič) and in the Czechoslovak Press Agency (led by Šulek)—as part of a plan to stop all radio and television broadcasts. Likewise, Oldrich Švestka, the editor in chief of *Rudé právo,* prohibited the printing of the resolution and replaced it with a text of his own. However, thanks to decisive action by Smrkovský and the alertness of the radio station operators, who immediately arranged for auxilliary transmission, the Dubček leadership's resolution was finally broadcast and was printed on the presses of *Rudé právo* sometime after two o'clock in the morning.

The second serious decision made spontaneously was the convening of the extraordinary Fourteenth Congress. The initiative came from the municipal party committee in Prague, whose first secretary was B. Šimon. On that night of August 20, he and Dubček discussed whether to convene the congress immediately or not. Dubček, as far as I know, was undecided. Personally, I believe he was afraid that the assembled delegates might simply be massacred by the soldiers, and he could not imagine how the congress could practically take place just then. In the end, however, he did not oppose the committee's plan to convene as many delegates as they could get. And so the organizational preparations for a party congress got under way that very night, and on the morning of August 22, 1968 the delegates convened in the works canteen of one of the ČKD plants in Prague-Vysočany.

Military aircraft bringing tanks and troops to the Prague airport in Ruzyne were roaring over the Central Committee building at increasingly frequent intervals on the night of the twentieth, and the building itself began to empty as regional and factory functionaries, and journalists as well, returned to their places of work. Some members of the party leadership and their aides and assistants remained in the building, along with some Central Committee employees who had managed to reach the building after hearing the news on the radio. Towards four a.m. I was sitting in Dubček's office along with Dubček himself, Smrkovský, Kriegel, Špaček, Šimon, Sádovský, Slavík, Jakeš, and Kapek. I am absolutely positive that all these people were present; Barbírek and Rigo may also have been there, but of this I'm not sure. Piller, as far as I can recall, did not stay there with us, but I could be wrong about that. And Bilak, Kolder, Švestka, Indra, Voleník, and Erban were almost certainly *not* present in Dubček's office. Erban may well not even have been at the afternoon session of August 20th; at least I cannot remember that he spoke there before midnight.

Sometime after four a.m. a black Volga from the Soviet embassy pulled up in front of the Central Committee building, followed immediately by armored cars and tanks. Soldiers in Soviet paratrooper uniforms—wine-colored berets and sailors' jerseys under their shirts—jumped out of the armored cars carrying automatic weapons. The tanks and soldiers surrounded the building, and tight cordons of troops blocked off all the entrances. Several officers and a platoon of paratroopers ran inside.

I was watching this with all the others from the window of Dubček's office, and I felt the same sensation of unreality that one has watching a film. Yet I remember saying to myself very clearly: yes, those are the same soldiers you welcomed and embraced joyfully on May 9, 1945, with whom you drank vodka and were friends for five years in Moscow; they are not shadows on the silver screen, and very soon their automatic rifles will be pointed, not at the czarist cadets in the Winter Palace, nor at the surviving Reichstag guards, but at you, personally. At the same time, something inside me kept insisting that it was all a kind of misunderstanding: I knew their language and their way of thinking, their military ranks and commands; I could imagine what they talked about off duty and how they regarded their own commanding officers, and even what they thought of Brezhnev himself. It was quite unthinkable that they'd shoot me just like that.

No? And why not? Had I already forgotten the stories my roommates had told me at Moscow University, all of them veterans of the front? Had they never before on similar occasions shot perfect strangers who were not the least bit dangerous because they were unarmed? And yet what I felt in that moment was different from what I had felt one night during the war, after Heydrich (the *Reichsprotektor* in Czechoslovakia) had been assassinated by Czechoslovak paratroopers sent from London. The Nazi military and police patrols, armed with very similar-looking machine guns, were searching at random for Heydrich's assassins in the different quarters of Prague. They walked through the street where we lived too, and I saw them from the window, gray specters disappearing into houses and flats. I knew that my father, who had been an army officer before the war, had his old uniform concealed in the closet, and somewhere else in the flat was a hidden weapon. I was very simply and deeply afraid because they were the enemy, and I knew that if they entered our flat, that would be the end. They didn't, as it turned out.

These soldiers now entering the Central Committee building did not evoke in me that simple, animal fear. Of course, I was no longer a little boy who would be unimportant to those who would soon be here. But I knew they had their orders, and those orders could hardly have been to kick in the door to Dubček's office and open fire with their automatic weapons. It was far more probable that we would be arrested, taken away somewhere and perhaps even put on trial: things were far from over at this point, and there were several possible outcomes. But it was not my conscious thoughts that were important here, it was my spontaneous feelings and a kind of instinctive sense of security. Where did they come from? Probably from my communist faith and from the many years I had been a member of the privileged ruling caste.

My feelings were of the same order as those of the functionaries arrested in connection with Rudolf Slanský's trial. In many cases they knew the secret policemen who arrested them intimately, and in some cases had even given them orders to arrest others. When their turn came their first reaction was this instinctive certainty that there was some kind of misunderstanding: it was simply unthinkable that the police could suddenly be used against them. It was the false security of faithful Communists and people with the privilege of power. It may well be a feeling far older than communist faith and government: the church authorities who found themselves before the Inquisition must have had this feeling at first, before it was dispelled by torture and ultimately when they were burned at the stake as heretics.

It is again difficult to speak for others in such matters, but I don't think I was the only one with this secret, unconscious feeling. At least not if the behavior of all those subsequently held captive for hours under Soviet machine guns is any indication. In his posthumously published memoirs, Josef Smrkovský recalled how after witnessing from the window of Dubček's office a Soviet paratrooper accidently shoot a young man marching at the head of a peaceful parade of people carrying the Czechoslovak flag and singing the national anthem he immediately called Ambassador Chervonenko to declare him responsible for the young man's death. Could Smrkovský have reacted this way had he not felt—despite the guns aimed at his head—that he was still a partner of the very power occupying his country, that he was one of the rulers, just like Chervonenko and Brezhnev?

Suddenly the doors of Dubček's office flew open and about eight soldiers and low-ranking officers with machine guns rushed in, surrounded us from behind around a large table and aimed their weapons at the backs of our heads. Then two officers came into the room. One was a colonel, who was shorter than the other, almost dwarfish in stature, but to compensate he wore a whole row of medals, perhaps including the golden star signifying a "Hero of the Soviet Union." He also had the arrogant authoritarian bearing of a sergeant major. He announced that he was "taking us into custody" and began to issue various commands. Then someone—perhaps it was Dubček—said something, and the colonel roared out: "No talking! Sit quietly! No talking Czech!" If he hadn't added that last condescending phrase I might have tried to ignore him. But it suddenly and quite spontaneously provoked in me such feelings of anger, humiliation, fear, and that strange sensation of immunity that comes to ex-rulers, that I lost my temper and shouted imperiously at him in Russian: "Behave as you were told! Where do you think you are, anyway? You are in the office of the First Secretary of the Communist Party. Do you have orders to silence us? Of course you don't! So obey your orders!" The colonel was flabbergasted and started to say something but then thought better of it. Without a word he looked around the room and then left. A while later he returned with an escort and continued to behave arrogantly, but not a word was mentioned about not talking. He began making a list of those who were present, which suggested to me that his superiors had no idea who was where. Perhaps they did not even know where the members of the pomised "revolutionary government" and the "revolutionary tribunal" were either.

The soldiers cut all the telephone lines in the room and closed the windows so that the crowd, which had gathered outside beyond the cordon of paratroopers, could not be heard singing the national anthem and shouting slogans and chanting Dubček's name. But even with the windows closed, the sound of the crowd and occasional shouting somewhere in the distance filtered through. We were sitting around the table, silent now, each of us with a paratrooper behind us pointing his gun at our heads. Bohumil Šimon reached into the bookshelf behind him and pulled out a book at random. It was a history of ancient Greece.

"Well now, let's see what we're in for," said Šimon, and, as in the well-known parlor game, he let the book fall open and pointed his finger haphazardly at a sentence, which he then read to us. It was someone's—perhaps Plato's—comment that democracy is not the best form of social organization because it leads to a general decline in discipline to the point where even animals are allowed to walk freely in the streets. "There, now you know why they're here, comrades," said Šimon, and he closed the book. This lightened the mood, and we began to talk with each other.

František Kriegel glanced at his watch. It was shortly after five A.M. on August 21, 1968. "I don't think much will happen before eight," said Kriegel, "until they get everything together. We're all tired, and I'd advise you all to get some sleep. We're going to need clear heads." With these words, he stood up, walked over to an empty space behind the chair Dubček sat in when he chaired the meetings, lay down on the carpet, put his briefcase under his head and prepared to go to sleep.

Besides Smrkovský, Kriegel was the only representative of the old, prewar generation of Communists in the Dubček leadership. He had come to Czechoslovakia sometime in the 1920s as a refugee from the frontier territory between Poland and the Ukraine, where the various armies shooting it out in the civil war had only one thing in common:

a tendency to anti-Semitic pogroms; hence Shelest's remark that Kriegel was a "Jew from Halič." Kriegel was a Communist who had been through the civil wars in Spain and China as a medical doctor, which he had studied to become after emigrating to Prague. Those in the know say that Kriegel is a good doctor, and not one of those whose medical reputation depended on politics.

I have known Kriegel since 1947, when he was a Novotný representative in the secretariat of the regional party committee in Prague. He was always one of the most intelligent in party functionary circles. He was an educated and cultured man, with an independent streak, excellent organizational abilities, and a profound experience of life and politics, with a vision that went far beyond the provincial horizons of the vast majority of functionaries. Of course it was precisely this, coupled with his being Jewish and a veteran of the Spanish civil war, that caused his political downfall in the fifties. He survived those years in political disfavor, first as a functionary in the health service and later as a regular doctor. In the sixties, Novotný chose him—as he did Smrkovský—to demonstrate his willingness to rehabilitate purge victims of the fifties, and thus Kriegel became a member of the Central Committee, a member of parliament, and generally an active public figure once more.

In the sixties, Kriegel was not a man of the party apparatus: he belonged to none of the factions, nor was he ever especially liked in the apparatus. As I have already mentioned, he was not appointed to the party leadership either as a man of the apparatus or as a personal friend of Dubček's, Černík's or even less of Kolder's. In this leadership he usually assumed a position very close to that of the radical wing of reform Communists. At the same time, however, his thinking was always politically rational. In fact, I think that of all the people in Dubček's leadership, Kriegel was the least susceptible to ideological illusions, including those concerning the nature of Soviet superpower politics. In some questions, he very probably had no such illusions whatsoever.

For a long time, however—in fact until the mid-seventies, when we both lived in the ghetto of party outcasts—my personal relationship with Kriegel was not one of friendship and trust. I think that apart from our political differences in 1968 concerning the possibilities, tempo, and methods of reform, there were several personal factors. To my mind, Kriegel is rational in politics but also extremely self-assured and not above imposing his opinions and conceptions on others. He tends not to trust people with a different viewpoint, though this does not at all mean he is unfriendly or aloof towards them. I was not unlike him in this regard, and this obviously colored our mutual relations, as long as we were both in the world of politics and power.

František Kriegel was one of those party functionaries who did not reduce politics to the internal struggles for power. He saw politics as movement and activity in society itself, both in Czechoslovakia and the world. It was therefore natural that he ascribed greater significance to the nationwide democratic movement than he did to currents inside the power structure. This does not mean, however, that Kriegel was lost in the jungle of behind-the-scenes infighting, or that he avoided such conflicts. On the contrary, he was quite capable of asserting his own interests there as well. But he was more concerned with social developments, and as a result he became the main target for the Stalinists' attacks. The fact that he also happened to be a "Jew from Halič" and that his life history was very suspect and irregular to the KGB, simply complicated matters.

Outside of politics, František Kriegel is a good man. I have perhaps never known anyone else who could, with such ease and spontaneity, reassure people in situations of extreme pressure, danger, and stress. He is a physician not only by profession but by his very nature. But even physicians have their faults, and Kriegel is sometimes stubborn, prone to suspicion, and perhaps even prejudiced against those whom he does not have ample reason to trust.

On the carpet of Dubček's office towards the morning of August 21, 1968, Kriegel really did fall asleep. About ten minutes later, a powerful snoring arose from where he lay, and it was so sudden and so loud that all eight paratroopers stiffened and instinctively pointed their automatic weapons at the reposing Kriegel. At first I though he was doing it deliberately, but he went on snoring so contentedly and naturally that all of us, including our guards, soon realized that he was genuinely asleep. The guns returned to point once more at the back of our heads.

As Kriegel had correctly forseen, nothing happened at all for about three hours. We sat there for the most part immersed in our own thoughts; occasionally two people next to each other would discuss something, and someone else would read. Dubček's office had a washroom of its own, and everyone who went there was accompanied by a paratrooper, who stood by the door. When we were finished, he would go in and make a thorough check, inevitably emerging with his right arm wet to the elbow. He had obviously reached into the water-tank, and perhaps even into the toilet bowl itself.

About nine o'clock, shortly after Kriegel woke up genuinely refreshed and took his place among us at the table, the dwarflike colonel entered the room again, this time accompanied by two more Soviet officers and three men in civilian clothes whom we suspected—even before they opened their mouths—of being members of our own Czechoslovak State Security forces. I almost certainly knew one of them from somewhere, a light-haired, slightly obese man of about forty. Perhaps I had once lectured to him about socialist democracy, or at one time he may have worked somewhere in the political apparatus, where I might have run into him. But he just stood there silently while a taller black-haired man did the talking. He asked Dubček, Smrkovský, Kriegel, and Špaček to follow him.

One of the four, I think it was Dubček, asked him why. In reply the black-haired secret policeman uttered another formulaic sentence, which I cannot recall precisely, but was something like, "In the name of the revolutionary tribunal led by comrade Alois Indra." Smrkovský asked what kind of organ that was, adding that as chairman of the National Assembly he had never heard of such a body and it wasn't mentioned in the Constitution either. Dubček, however, cut short the dispute saying, "Josef, forget it. It's not worth arguing over." Then the secret policeman ordered all four to hand over their weapons. Smrkovský laughed and mockingly searched himself, turning his pockets inside out and placing a jackknife on the table saying, "We don't need weapons against our own people." The perplexed secret policemen, who in the meantime had moved closer to Dubček, stopped. Dubček stretched his arms out and, with his disarming smile, said to the one closest to him: "Go on, search me, search me!" Although the Soviet colonel did not understand the conversation, he did grasp the inappropriateness of the whole scene and ordered them all to leave the room. Smrkovský put a couple of lumps of sugar that were lying on the table in his pocket and turned to the rest of us with the words, "I advise you to take some too, it'll come in handy, I know from my experience in the Ruzyně prison," and he was led out of the room.*

It was now clear to everyone where the situation was headed.

---

*In an interview published posthumously (in *Listy*, No. 2/1975) Smrkovský describes these details somewhat imprecisely.

"Things are getting warmer," someone remarked. A long period of tense silence followed. Those whom it might have concerned occupied their thoughts wondering how this "revolutionary tribunal" might work. It was a far more realistic preoccupation than considering the arrival of the paratroopers with automatic rifles as the beginning of the end.

For long periods of time nothing much happened, and I cannot vouch for the precise timing, or even the order, of the individual incidents that followed. The Soviet officers returned once more—this time without their Czech escort—and called for Šimon, Jakeš, and Kapek, whom they led out of the room. It was an odd combination, and we discussed every possible explanation we could think of for putting those three together. Šimon, after all, did not belong with the other two, and the three of them together could certainly not have been put before a "revolutionary tribunal." As it happened, Šimon was put along with the first four arrested, and the other two were probably taken away for meetings with the Soviet authorities.

New orders were then, evidently, issued to the guards, and they relaxed and sat down in the chairs with their guns no longer aimed at us but resting on their laps or in front of them on the table. At noon the sirens of the Prague factories suddenly began to wail. At first the soldiers leapt up with their guns at the ready again, but then they relaxed.

"What's that?" I was asked by the lieutenant who had been assigned to look after me. He was not wearing a paratrooper's uniform but one belonging to the normal infantry, and he had treated me politely from the beginning. A documentary film from those days shows this same lieutenant looking out of a window of Dubček's office. Smrkovský said he was looking out of the window with him when the soldiers down below shot a young Czech man, and added: "He was a decent sort of fellow." I recall that when there was shooting down below, this Soviet lieutenant became extremely upset and at one point was clearly holding back tears.

"What does it sound like?—factory sirens," I replied.

"But why?" he asked.

"I don't know. Let me go and find out. I'm curious too."

"I'm not allowed to do that," said the lieutenant. I added that the workers were probably going on strike and were declaring their intentions with the siren.

"The workers turned on the sirens?" he asked incredulously.

"Why not?" I replied.

"You don't mean to tell me," the lieutenant went on, "that workers have access to the sirens? The management must have given the orders, and so the sirens are blowing."

And that is how my discussion with the lieutenant guarding me began. I discussed how things were different in Czechoslovakia and how even he must be able to see for himself that the situation was exceptional and people were reacting accordingly. He did not seem convinced. Then I asked him why he thought he had been sent to Prague. His reply was on the whole very coherent and on approximately the same level as Brezhnev's letters: he explained the "counter-revolutionary situation" in Czechoslovakia, quoting from *Literární listy* and *Reportér,* both of which he knew by name. He spoke in a rather cultivated Russian with a certain ideological conviction. I asked him why he felt personally threatened by articles in our literary newspapers, and his answer took me utterly by surprise: he said he was a graduate of the Moscow institute for literature. He had not been able to find work in his field, however, and so he had joined the army instead.

Other discussions developed between the detained and their custodians, insofar as the detainees' knowledge of Russian would allow. The paratrooper assigned to Václav Slavík finally began talking French with him, and it turned out that he too was a university graduate who was now using his education in this rather odd fashion.

The Central Committee building had been entrusted to the famous Taman division, which also traditionally takes part in the various palace revolutions in the Kremlin. It is a highly élite, select unit. One has to admit that, by quite unexpected standards, the selection was truly of high quality.

That afternoon Dubček's personal chauffeur, Jožko Brizník, brought us food from the kitchen of the party hotel. Not only that, he had telephoned all our families to inform them of our situation and slipped messages from those family members he had managed to contact under the serviette on the coffee tray. Brizník had known Dubček ever since the resistance battles of the Slovak national uprising (August 1944), and it was there that he became familiar with the mentality of the Soviet soldiers and officers. He could also speak Russian. As I learned later, he was able to get in and out of the completely surrounded Central Committee building very simply: in a self-assured tone he just told the guards: "I am not subordinated to you; I have my own orders and my own commanders." Thanks to the tremendous confusion of military, political, and police units, something which no guard could ever be expected to keep straight, the trick never failed.

When we had finished eating, we noticed our guards looking longingly at the leftovers of meat, salami, bread, and beer, and someone asked them if they were hungry too. With that, they betrayed a military secret to us: they hadn't had anything to eat or drink since the night before. They eagerly set about finishing the food, and with this the last remnants of their caution disappeared. "My" lieutenant willingly dismantled his automatic rifle on the table when I compared his model to my own as a second lieutenant in the Soviet army during my military service in Moscow. He explained the difference between the old and new models and praised the qualities of his weapon: it was reliable in the heat of Soviet Central Asia and north of the Arctic circle. It was not until I said that they should all take their marvelous weapons and go north of the Arctic circle that he realized how inept his behavior was in the situation, and he hastily reassembled his weapon and went off by himself.

I became convinced that if this lieutenant and I were to go off somewhere for a week to live and drink together, he might well recognize the absurdity of the whole military intervention. There may well have been many like him among the Warsaw Pact troops. For discussions between the Soviet soldiers and Czech citizens were taking place not only in the exclusive milieu of the Central Committee building and with elite guards, but on the streets of Prague and other towns and cities, between simple Czech citizens and the soldiers on their tanks. Those were no elite troops, and they had no idea why they were in Czechoslovakia, and often didn't even know that that was where they were. There are known cases of ordinary soldiers who thought they were in West Germany or even Israel. But in the end, does it really matter what such soldiers think? Their personal opinion does not in any way change the fact that their commanders and government can treat them like a mindless herd, nor the fact that they will shoot and kill whomever their commanders point to.

Five days later, in the Kremlin, I was talking to Marshal Grechko and told him I thought his army in Czechoslovakia was ideologically disintegrating. "Perhaps," replied Grechko, "but it doesn't matter. If they fall apart, we'll replace them. I can replace them ten times over." He said it so smugly that I felt compelled to retort, "Is that all?"

Grechko looked at me with marshal-like fury, but he said nothing and walked away.

Back in the Central Committee building, at about ten o'clock in the evening, the stunted colonel returned but now his face was completely transformed. He smiled and announced that a meeting was being convened at the highest level, and that Dubček and the other comrades would be representing our party. He said that we were quite free to go where we wished, and that next morning we could return to the Central Committee building for work as usual. He even added that he personally was very glad things had been sorted out. He dismissed the guards, shook hands with those present, and then sat down to talk with someone—I believe it was Sádovský. I got up and left.

I lived close to the Central Committee building, and so I proceeded to walk home. Many people were standing outside the building, beyond the cordon of paratroopers, waiting to see what would happen next. Naturally, they were suspicious of anyone who came out unescorted and was deferentially let through the cordon by the soldiers. Then someone recognized me and called me by name. At once a small crowd formed around me, and people asked what had become of Dubček. I told them, truthfully, that there was no one from the party leadership left in the building, and that apparently some meetings were being arranged that Dubček was to take part in. At the time, it never crossed my mind that the dwarfish colonel might have lied to us. It was something I could hardly have dreamed up myself, and therefore I was certain that he must have been told as much by his superiors. But whether this meant that one of the top Soviet statesmen had in fact concluded that they would have to negotiate with Dubček, it was almost impossible to say. The question was not cleared up for another 24 hours—at the Soviet embassy and the Castle—and approximately 48 hours after that Dubček was in the Kremlin. During the whole of the following day—August 22, 1968—there was no indication that the Soviets would talk to Dubček. On the contrary, a "revolutionary peasants' and workers' government" was supposed to be formed that day at the Soviet embassy, under the chairmanship of Alois Indra.

On the morning of August 22, I had to decide whether to join the delegates assembling in Vysočany for the Fourteenth Congress or go to the Central Committee building to find out what was going on there. When Dubček and others were arrested the day before in the name of the "revolutionary tribunal" and Alois Indra, it seemed entirely possible that the pro-Moscow group in the party leadership was attempting to set up some new, collaborationist bodies to head the party and the state. My suspicions had been confirmed that night, when I had been informed that the pro-Moscow group, represented mainly by Bilak, Indra, Jakeš, and Kolder, had in fact gone to a meeting of about 50 Central Committee members at the Praha, the party hotel. I also found out that speeches were made there indicating a certain faction in the Central Committee was willing to begin collaborating with the Soviet army, and that a deputation headed by Bilak was elected and authorized to negotiate with the commander of the occupying armies, and so on. All this contradicted what the Soviet colonel had said about negotiations involving Dubček. I felt that the most important thing now was to find out more about it, and therefore I arranged to keep in touch with people at the Fourteenth Congress in Vysočany and then went to the Central Committee building. Tanks were still surrounding the Central Committee building when I arrived, and it was cordoned off by soldiers, but people with Central Committee passes were allowed through. Inside, it was no longer occupied by soldiers, at least not visibly, and our offices were empty. Bilak, Indra, Kolder, Jakeš, Lenárt, Švestka, Piller, Barbírek, Rigo, Sádovský, and myself—in other words, eleven out of a 22-member party leadership—assembled there. Dubček, Černík, Smrkovský, Kriegel, Špaček, and Šimon—all of whom had been arrested the day before—were missing. Three secretariat members— Císař, Slavík, and Erban—were also absent. I cannot recall whether Oldřich Voleník, another secretariat member, was present or not. I also can't recall noticing A. Kapek, but I believe he was absent that day. In addition, however, two people who were Central Committee members but not members of the leadership appeared at this meeting: General Rytíř, the former chief of staff under Novotný, and O. Pavlovský, the minister of domestic trade and commerce in Černík's government.

Bilak chaired the meeting. He explained the presence of Rytíř and Pavlovský by saying that at a special meeting of the Central Committee the day before, they had been elected along with himself and others to form a special deputation that met with the Soviet army. Summarizing the conclusions of the meeting, Bilak stated that the precondition for any settlement of the situation was to negotiate with the Soviet army command and the Soviet embassy. And the rump of the party leadership must issue instructions to that effect to the regional and state organs, and it must declare itself competent to enter into negotiations "at the highest level."

Sádovský and I raised the question of what had become of Dubček and the others. Bilak could give no concrete answer and merely said that he had received assurances that the comrades were safely in Soviet custody. It was then proposed, from several different quarters— by Piller, Barbírek, Rigo, and perhaps even Švestka and Lenárt—that any negotiations must first aim at establishing contact with the arrested party leaders and that, rather than form another deputation, what was left of the party leadership, with no exceptions, should conduct negotiations, and not with the army leadership, but with the Soviet ambassador. The first request to Ambassador Chervonenko would be to contact Brezhnev with the demand that all six arrested members of the leadership be released and that any further negotiations be carried out by the party leadership as a whole, collectively. These proposals were not openly opposed by Bilak, Indra, Kolder, and Jakeš. On the contrary, they accepted them all, and Bilak then left to telephone Chervonenko.

At about noon, a meeting with Chervonenko was arranged. All eleven members of the party leadership were to go to the Soviet embassy, where telephone contact with the Kremlin was promised (the direct telephone line from the Central Committee building to the Kremlin had been disconnected by soldiers the day before). Bilak also announced that the Soviet army would arrange transportation to the Soviet embassy in its own vehicles. Oddly enough, all those present, with the exception of Bilak and Indra, rejected this mode of transportation. So Bilak and Indra went to the Soviet embassy in Soviet armored cars, and the rest of us drove in several Central Committee automobiles.

The embassy, naturally, was surrounded by several defensive lines of tanks, armored cars, and cordons of soldiers. Inside, on the staircases and along the corridors, it looked like a state of siege: soldiers and uniformed and plainclothed KGB men, all fully armed, were lying or sitting on the stairs and standing at every doorway and window. They took us to a room next to Chervonenko's office, and there was a table spread with vodka, cognac, wine, sandwiches, and caviar, but there was no one there to negotiate with us. The comrade ambassador had apologized, we were told, and asked us to wait.

So we waited, and nothing happened. After about half an hour, someone in civilian clothes, probably a KGB officer, came in and asked to talk to me. We went outside the room, and he passed on greetings from one of my former fellow students in Moscow—who, as I knew, was now a lieutenant-colonel in the KGB—and he, a total stranger to me, offered me assistance. In reply to my suggestion that he arrange for Chervonenko to let us talk to Brezhnev, he laughed and said that was beyond his competence. Then I remembered I had to contact my liaison with the extraordinary party congress. It would probably be difficult to do so from the embassy building, so I told the man I had a far simpler request: I had to make a telephone call, if possible from one of those special telephone lines that they must have here somewhere. And he really did help. He took me to a room with a special phone, which I used during the next few hours to issue reports of our negotiations. These reports were then transmitted (though in a somewhat distorted form) to the congress delegates.

This gave rise, by the way, to a rather comic situation. In the room where we were waiting for Chervonenko, there was a radio broadcasting detailed reports of the Vysočany congress, among other news, and it was reported that a pro-Moscow faction of the presidium was at the Soviet embassy discussing the establishment of a quisling government, and that the members were divided for and against. This report caused panic among those present. Drahomír Kolder kept shouting: "Goddammit, how can they know that?" It never occurred to anyone that I might have telephoned the news out on Chervonenko's own special telephone.

Waiting for Chervonenko lasted several hours. In the meantime, Bilak and Indra arrived an hour late, owing to their means of transport. Their Soviet armored car, shortly after leaving the Central Committee building, crossed a bridge over the Vltava and was blocked by an accident in which a tram had collided with some Soviet military vehicles. The armored car could not even back up, so the commander of the vehicle suggested that Bilak and Indra change cars. Meanwhile, however, a crowd of curious onlookers gathered, and both men were afraid to be publicly seen getting out of a Soviet armored car. So they sat inside the steel-plated monster for almost an hour under the hot August sun. They arrived at the embassy in a pitiful condition and in a miserable frame of mind.

Chervonenko finally showed up in the afternoon. He listened to our request to contact Brezhnev and then left the room. It was another hour at least before he reappeared and said that unfortunately their telephone link with Moscow was not working. I suggested he try to reach Moscow through the communication lines of the Soviet commander in chief, General Pavlovský. "Their connections don't work either," Chervonenko replied shamelessly. I told him the situation must be very grave indeed if communication between the entire army and Marshal Grechko was cut off, and Chervonenko, utterly unruffled, replied that yes, the situation was extremely unpleasant. Then he came straight to the point: any further delay would simply be a waste of precious time; the connection with Moscow would be reestablished in time, and then they could decide on what was to be done about Dubček, Černík, and the other members of the Czechoslovak presidium. But, in the meantime, he advised us to think very concretely about how, in this exceptional situation, to constitute an exceptional organ of authority. Such an organ ought to combine party and state leadership functions, and it should be a revolutionary workers' and peasants' government. He personally felt that the comrades present should form the core of such a government, for they all held legal functions and enjoyed the confidence of the Soviet comrades. He suggested that we consider the proposal seriously, and then he left.

The situation was therefore clear, and the discussion began. By this time, all the eleven members of the party leadership, whom I have already named, were present, as well as the minister of domestic trade and commerce, O. Pavlovský, and Šalgovič, who was already at the embassy when we arrived. On the other hand, General Rytíř, as far as I can recall, was not present at these talks in the embassy.

The discussion got off to a slow start, for no one would propose anything concrete. Then Vasil Bilak set the framework, saying that it was nothing more than what we had already agreed upon that morning. But until we got a connection with Moscow, we could prepare the proposal suggested by comrade Chervonenko. He, Bilak, personally thought that it was the proper course, but it would not be definitely decided until the entire party leadership were present.

Then Jan Piller—in an effort to avoid what had become for him a much too acute situation, and perhaps also because he was part of a plan to help get rid of Sádovský and me at this delicate juncture, for it was clear that neither of us would cooperate in this new venture—suggested that he, Sádovský, and I go to Vysočany as a presidium delegation and help to direct the course of the deliberations there. We had learned from the radio that the delegates had already declared themselves the official party congress and were electing a new Central

Committee. I refused on the grounds that the leadership, which was supposed to be discussing a proposal to form some kind of revolutionary government, could have nothing to do with the Vysočany congress. Besides that, we had already declared that morning that Chervonenko was supposed to negotiate with the entire leadership, and therefore I was not about to leave the talks now. Sádovský also refused. This, however, created a dilemma: no one else would have dared to show up in Vysočany with Piller, and Piller alone could hardly have presented himself as a "delegation," so the proposal was dropped.

Then a two-hour discussion began about the composition of a revolutionary workers' and peasants' government. Some of the discussants claimed that with this organization we would in fact be proceeding in harmony with the presidium declaration of the night before last, which had stated that everyone was to remain in their legal functions. But given the fact that a new leadership had to be installed, it was clear that new bosses had to be appointed. It was suggested that party affairs and the party apparatus be directed by Vasil Bilak, and government affairs by Alois Indra.

If I say "it was suggested," this is because these proposals really did surface in the course of the discussion, in which the group consisting of Bilak, Indra, Kolder, Jakeš, Lenárt, Švestka, and Pavlovský had evidently come to some prior agreement. Perhaps Piller was in on it as well, but sometimes his conduct—perhaps deliberately—indicated indecision. I don't think that Barbírek and Rigo had been apprised of things beforehand, and they frequently disrupted the whole scenario. Šalgovič, as far as I can remember, was mostly absent during discussions about the composition of the revolutionary government. Sádovský and I had no part in the game at all.

Vasil Bilak accepted the function of new party boss with sham reluctance, saying that since it was the will of the other comrades, he would do the best he could and with the utmost integrity, to guide the party through this difficult time, etc., etc. With Indra, however, there were complications. When he began to express formal reluctance, someone, I think it was Sádovský, took him at his word and said that if that was how he felt he shouldn't take on such a position. I added my agreement and suggested that Lenárt ought to have a say in this: after all, he had been prime minister under Novotný; why could he not be so again? This suggestion was supported by someone else, perhaps Barbírek. Lenárt, however, rejected the proposal, saying that according to the presidium resolution he was to remain in his present position. As if the same did not apply to Indra and Bilak.

This, however, introduced a serious hitch into the historic deliberations, and Vasil Bilak was forced to demean himself and come over to whisper in my ear that "Indra will take the job; it's just that he's tired now and apathetic." That may well have been, for Indra made no effort to resolve the deadlock in the discussion. Thus, without settling the question of who would be the boss of a government representing the revolutionary might of the workers and peasants, the discussion shifted to responsibility for the individual administrative departments.

Oldřich Pavlovský nominated me for the job of party/state chief of culture and the press. If I had taken it seriously, I could only have been annoyed, for it would be hard to imagine a more thankless function in the present situation. Nevertheless, I had to say something, and at this point I did not want to admit openly that I would have nothing whatsoever to do with this bogus government: it would have been short-sighted of me to be excluded from any further negotiations, especially when we were still in the Soviet embassy. So I merely replied that there were more important functions that should perhaps be discussed first, such as who would be the minister of the interior. Oddly enough, however, no one present wanted the job, and I recall that Jakeš energetically resisted any suggestion that he be appointed.

Then Emil Rigo quite unexpectedly remarked that he did not want to be a minister in any government whatsoever because he could not, at the same time, continue in the party leadership. And then Barbírek insisted that he was a functionary of the Slovak National Council and didn't want to be a minister in Prague and have to leave Bratislava. These interjections by the two least likely members of the leadership to become ministers were almost certainly unplanned, and they threw the scenario considerably off course. Bilak, Kolder, Lenárt, and others launched into long-winded arguments for why Rigo could be a minister while remaining in the party leadership.

Emil Rigo was the first, and possibly the last, Gypsy in the history of the Communist movement to occupy a presidium position. At certain moments, he had the irrepressible and stubborn temperament of his race, and his distaste for a ministerial chair was quite simply unshakable. It was Chervonenko, when he reappeared, who was able to settle Rigo's problem with ease. "Of course you needn't be a minister, comrade Rigo. You can remain in your East Slovakian Iron Works factory, but you'll be a member of the workers' and peasants' government just as you have been a member of the presidium till now." Since Chervonenko put it that way, Rigo admitted that yes, he supposed it was possible. Why not?

The discussion continued, time passed, and there were no concrete results, so that when Chervonenko appeared again, he discovered to his displeasure that he still did not have a revolutionary government. In fact, he did not even have a prime minister. By now it was evening, and quite clearly, according to the scenario, everything should have been settled long ago, so Chervonenko had no other choice but to put his own shoulder to the wheel. He announced that he had just talked with President Svoboda and told him that the party leadership at this meeting would soon inform him of their proposal for what should be done next, and that therefore we had to arrive at some conclusions.

It was clear that some kind of resolution of the situation could no longer be put off. Consulting each other in whispers, Sádovský and I agreed that we would both announce our rejection of the entire conception of the present talks and any further discussions along those lines, and we insisted on returning to the original demand: that we meet first with Dubček and the others and only then begin to negotiate. At the same time, we had to get out of the embassy in one piece, we said to ourselves, and not end up with Dubček, wherever he was. We did not know his whereabouts, and Chervonenko told a bold-faced lie when he said that Dubček and the others were on Czechoslovak territory. It would have been true only had the Soviet Union acknowledged its prewar borders with Czechoslovakia, for that night all those arrested were in the Transcarpathian Ukraine, kept in pairs in KGB barracks.

Chervonenko's reference to negotiations with President Svoboda gave me an idea for a resolution that might be acceptable to all sides. I asked to speak and said that according to the Czechoslovak constitution it was possible for the president to head the government if the prime minister were unable to carry out his function. While we were sitting here, the government of the Republic still existed, even though it lacked a prime minister. Moreover, comrade Indra had expressed doubts about playing a leading role in government affairs, and we had not been able to decide on how to allocate the ministerial responsibilities, something which, in any case, was superfluous, because a full complement of ministers already existed. Therefore I suggested that all of us present should go to the Castle and continue our discussion with the president. I said that as far as I personally was concerned, I refused to accept any function at all in the body here referred to as the "revolutionary workers' and peasants' government." That, I said, would represent an attempt to change the existing constitutional organs in direct contradiction of the presidium resolution and, as far as I knew, of the position of the president himself, who had taken part in that meeting two nights ago. The situation was insoluble as long as the fact of the military intervention and the withdrawal of the troops were not first negotiated.

Sádovský spoke in roughly the same spirit. Chervonenko remained calm on the outside, but he must have been aware that his plan to set up a revolutionary government was not working out. And his meeting with Svoboda would only reinforce this awareness.

First, Chervonenko turned to me and began trying to persuade me that I was making a mistake to refuse participation in the new leadership. I was a capable man, he said, and there was no reason for me to refuse. He understood very well that the situation might at the moment seem hopeless, as if everything were collapsing, but you had to take the long-range view. In five years, just as in Hungary, things would look differently and wounds that now seemed irreparable would eventually heal. He told me I ought to think about the future of the people, the party, and of myself, and not succumb to ephemeral emotions. How could I possibly think that the soldiers would turn around and leave after only just coming? What would become of the country in that event?

I didn't think for a minute, I replied, that once having decided to intervene they would leave today or tomorrow. But the mistake was coming here in the first place. This would have such long-term consequences that it will take far longer than five years for the situation to sort itself out. It had yet, in fact, to sort itself out in Hungary. But, in any case, I insisted that any further negotiations take place at the highest level, and I proposed, once more, that we go to the Castle and there demand what we had demanded in the first place: that we be put in contact with Dubček and the others.

A brief debate ensued, and, oddly enough, no one objected to my proposal that the negotiations continue at the Castle. Chervonenko himself asked some detailed questions about the possibility of a constitutional solution with the president's participation, and then he too accepted the proposal.

It was late in the evening, around eleven o'clock, when we arrived at the Castle escorted by Soviet officers and armored cars. Chervonenko was already with Svoboda and was obviously proposing that he assume the premiership. Meanwhile, we discussed who, in the name of what was left of the party leadership, should convey to Svoboda the substance of our negotiations at the Soviet embassy. In the end Piller was appointed: Bilak and Indra did not feel up to it.

Then the door to the next room, Svoboda's office, opened and a very angry Chervonenko stormed out, strode through our hall, and left. In a few moments, Ludvík Svoboda appeared. He was upset, but he controlled his temper well and held himself erect like a soldier, more so than usual. He greeted us and suggested that representatives of the government be present at our talks. He went next door where they were meeting and then, as far as I can recall, he returned with three members: Štrougal, Machačová, and Kučera.

Štrougal sat down opposite me at the table and asked in a whisper: "What's it all about?" On a piece of paper I wrote: "About whether you're willing to join the revolutionary workers' and peasants' government." I passed the paper back to him, he looked at it for a moment in bewilderment, then wrote something on the paper and passed it back to me. "What's that?" it said. Before I could reply, however, Piller began to present the proposals from the Soviet embassy meeting.*

As soon as Piller was finished, I asked to speak, and Sádovský and I both repeated our decision not to join the proposed government, offering the same reasons we had given Chervonenko. Then Svoboda asked whether all the rest agreed. Štrougal, speaking for the government, very resolutely and categorically rejected Piller's proposals. And with that Ludvík Svoboda declared: "What you are proposing to me here is something I cannot, and will never, do. If I were to do anything of the sort, the nation would have to drive me out of this Castle like a mangy dog."

Then he outlined a proposal of his own: he would go to Moscow himself and negotiate the return of Dubček, Černík, Smrkovský, and the others. He had already told Chervonenko that this was the only course of action he would consider, and now the matter had been de-

---

*This piece of paper with Štrougal's question somehow ended up in my pocket, and I had it in my possession until April 1975, when it was confiscated by the State Security forces during a house search. Perhaps when they read this book they'll realize what it is they have.

cided and he would fly the next morning, accompanied by three members of the government: the deputy premier, Gustav Husák, the minister of defense, Martin Dzúr, and the minister of justice, B. Kučera, who was not a Communist and would thus represent the other groups in the National Front. He suggested that the remainder of the presidium select three of its members to accompany him to Moscow as well. He went on to say that he knew comrade Brezhnev and was personally acquainted with Soviet marshals, and it was therefore quite impossible that there was not some explanation to this tragic misunderstanding. He said he believed that his direct intervention in Moscow would straighten everything out. And finally he declared: "And when the Soviet soldiers finally do leave here, you'll see, the people will throw flowers at them again just as they did in 1945."

The contradiction between Svoboda's opening and closing sentences astounded me. But this was not the last time Ludvík Svoboda was to surprise me. That night of August 22, 1968, however, the crucial thing was that Ludvík Svoboda definitely foiled Moscow's plan to set up a quisling government. Looked at politically, of course, the nationwide passive resistance to the occupation, which had persevered for two days, and also the deliberations of the Fourteenth Congress in Vysočany, both played important roles. But the fact remains that the personal role of President Svoboda was decisive, and this should not be forgotten when we examine subsequent events and his unfortunate political role in them.

Svoboda's words affected the rump of the party leadership, not like a cold shower, but rather like a good, sound thrashing. Vasil Bilak suddenly appeared for what he really was, no more than a failed tailor, full of ambition, lust for power, and malice. He sat hunched over in his chair, looking no one in the eye and rubbing something between his hands with nervous, jerky movements. Anyone catching his glance could see in his eyes a boundless, almost animal fear of the impending and fateful debacle. The shattered remnants of the presidium still had to select people to accompany Svoboda from among their midst, and Bilak, Indra, and Piller were chosen.

The same night I talked with Ludvík Svoboda alone for about half an hour. He told me how a woman had telephoned him and recommended that he shoot himself to protest the occupation, and how he explained to her that he felt it was his duty to sort the situation out. And the woman had apparently replied, "Ah, Mr. President, but how beautiful it would be if you were to shoot yourself."

I have no idea how an unknown woman managed to get a telephone connection with the president, although in those days anything was possible. But it may well have just been one of Svoboda's delusions.

I was later told by several other people that they had heard Svoboda recount a rather different version of the same story. But other things that Svoboda said that night testify to the strange paths his thoughts took. He said that the main purpose of his journey to Moscow was to arrange for the return of Dubček, Černík, and Smrkovský. He was convinced he could persuade Brezhnev and the marshals to agree to this. "And then comrade Dubček can submit his resignation," he said in the same breath, "and everything will sort itself out." Before we parted, Svoboda assured me that he would never, as long as he lived, forget anyone who stood beside him in this difficult time. No matter what happens, he said, everyone who stood by him now could count on that.

I went home with the feeling that I might well have been hallucinating all day. This was my third night without sleep and the nervous tension had gone on unabated for more than 48 hours. I took some sleeping pills, but no sooner had I fallen asleep than the telephone rang. It was Věněk Šilhán, who had been elected to the presidium by the new Central Committee in Vysočany and authorized to direct its work until Dubček's return. He told me that the presidium had appointed me to come to Vysočany and work in my capacity as a secretary of the Central Committee. We agreed that I would go there in the morning, and worked out how I would get there.

On my way to Vysočany on the morning of Friday August 23, I saw the people of occupied Prague in daylight for the first time. The brief ride to the Soviet embassy the day before had taken us through streets teeming with Soviet soldiers and the elegant Bubeneč quarter, where, to the naked eye, all was calm. Now, however, the route took me through the main working-class districts of Prague—Karlín, Libeň, and on to Vysočany. There were fewer tanks and soldiers here than in the city center, but these districts gave a better picture of the nationwide resistance to the occupation.

Everywhere, building walls were covered with slogans and handpainted posters. People were reading the newspapers and leaflets that were being turned out by printing presses everywhere, despite the efforts of the occupying forces to stop it. It was the picture of a city whose inhabitants were absolutely united in unarmed, passive resistance against alien interlopers. Flags and the Czechoslovak coat-of-arms in various forms decorated the streets and shopwindows, and people were wearing them in their lapels as well. Wherever anyone had fallen a victim to Soviet bullets, there were improvised memorials with masses of flowers and state flags. Street signs had either been pulled down or altered (most often being renamed "Dubček Street"), and sometimes the signs were simply switched with others. Direction indicators at major intersections had been destroyed or turned in the wrong direction, and they were frequently painted over with various signs like, "Moscow—2000 km." In places, buildings were pockmarked by gunfire, and many shop windows were shattered, providing an opportunity in many cases for exhibitions of popular creativity that made very inventive propaganda against the occupation.

Most of the slogans reflected the theme of national sovereignty, but very frequently this was expressed in connection with the slogans and demands of democratic socialism. Quotations from Lenin appeared, or slogans like "Lenin, awake! Brezhnev has gone mad!" The names of Dubček and Svoboda were emblazoned in huge letters across the walls of houses and along the fences and hoardings on the outskirts of the city, and slogans expressing confidence in them, along with Smrkovský and Černik were a main feature of the street decorations. Signs like "Go home" were scattered among others that reflected the residue left by years of anti-American propaganda in Czechoslovakia. Thus the old international slogan against US imperialism, "Yankee go home," became "Ivan go home," and signs like "USA in Vietnam, USSR in Czechoslovakia" appeared. The initials USSR were often written with the two Ss in the form of the Nazi SS lightning bolts. There were also hammer and sickles equated with swastikas. Typical too on the walls were anecdotes and cartoons ridiculing the occupation soldiers as misguided dolts. There were also signs in Russian, often unintentionally slipping back into Czech, written in the cyrillic script.

These signs and slogans, and the groups of people engaged in discussion with the soldiers on their tanks, testified to the people's efforts to sway the occupation troops. It was something that could not have taken place with the Nazi armies when they arrived in March 1939. People were convinced that these Soviet "Ivans" were merely exploited simpletons who had no idea what they were doing; and people wanted to explain the situation to them. The nation too, then, felt something of what I have already described, that feeling which for me came from years as a Communist among the ruling elite: a belief that perhaps it was, after all, just some kind of misunderstanding, that all this could simply not be true.

The new party presidium elected at the extraordinary congress had its headquarters inside the huge factory complex of the ČKD works in Vysočany. The approaches to its administrative offices were guarded by armed members of the People's Militia. The documents from the Fourteenth Congress itself, as well as the main political measures passed by the Vysočany leadership, are generally well-known and have been published abroad. Therefore, I shall limit myself to some impressions gleaned from my two days of work at the congress.

I think the Fourteenth Congress on August 22, 1968 had exceptionally important and positive influences on the course of events. It was largely due to this congress that the party maintained its decisive political authority in the minds of a majority of the population. The congress took an unflinching stand that was appropriate to the situation. It reified the very vague and generalized condemnation of the aggression issued by the Dubček leadership on the morning of August 21 in several simple political demands. Chief among these were the departure of the troops, the return of all public functionaries to their proper, constitutional positions, and the observance of all international legal norms, including the statutes of the Warsaw Pact itself. At the same time, the Fourteenth Congress—clearly mindful of the 1956 Hungarian events—did not support demands for withdrawing Czechoslovakia from the Warsaw Pact or a declaration of neutrality. But this did not stop it from turning to the international Communist movement with an appeal for help and from very explicitly excluding the pro-Moscow and conservative party faction from participation in any of the bodies elected by the congress.

Thanks to the stands also taken by the National Front and the government, both of which publicly recognized the Vysočany Congress, the general impression in the nation was that the party was continuing to function as the ruling political force in the land, and was doing so in the spirit of the Prague Spring. For several days, the congress made it appear that the forces of reform communism had won an unequivocal political victory in a situation which, taken as a whole, meant their utter defeat.

All of this was exceptionally important not only in domestic political terms but also in terms of the options open to Moscow. The Fourteenth Congress created an entirely unexpected and extremely difficult situation for the Moscow politburo. For although the entire military operation against Czechoslovakia was conceived and planned very haphazardly, Moscow did make a definite attempt to have the whole action appear politically legitimate. From what appeared in the Soviet press during the early days of the invasion, from what went on in the CPC leadership between August 20 and 22, and from other information that I subsequently had access to, I have concluded that the political plan for the intervention looked something like the following.

A group in the CPC leadership, chiefly consisting of Bilak, Indra, Kolder, and Jakeš, but to which Švestka, Piller, Lenárt, and Kapek also belonged (and which counted on the support of Rigo, Barbírek, and perhaps even Voleník), promised the Kremlin that they would engineer a domestic political justification for legalizing the intervention. This group had its final preparatory meeting on the morning of August 20 in Alois Indra's office in the Central Committee building. At the presidium meeting scheduled at two o'clock that afternoon, the first item on the agenda was to have been a discussion of a position paper by Indra and Kolder based on a situation report submitted a week before by the information bureau of the Central Committee (headed by J. Kašpar), which contained both objective and biased appraisals of the economic and political state of the country. The Indra and Kolder position was a tendentious version of this report, intended to exaggerate the danger of some open anti-socialist activity by "counter-revolutionary forces" taking place before the upcoming party congress.

The group in league with Moscow was counting on being able to swing a majority of the presidium behind Indra and Kolder's assessment. Piller, Barbírek, and Rigo were to cast the deciding votes. It is true that Piller and Barbírek subsequently did not vote in support of the military intervention, but according to the plan of the pro-Moscow group, that was not the question to be voted on. If Indra and Kolder's paper had been put to a vote, it is very likely that both Piller and Barbírek would have backed them, which would have meant a majority of six to five against Dubček. Of the candidate members, Lenárt and Kapek would vote for the proposal, leaving only Šimon to support Dubček. Of the nonmembers, Indra and Jakeš, and perhaps Voleník, would have sided with the pro-Moscow group, and Císař,

Sádovský, Slavík, and I would have supported Dubček's group—and although this was a formal majority of four to three for Dubček's supporters, the three pro-Moscow men were in fact in a stronger position in the apparatus: they controlled all the departments involved with directing internal party relationships, and they ruled one of the strongest regions—Ostrava. Císař and Slavík had the ideological sections, and Sádovský the agricultural and economic administration. It is true that the sections I was in charge of in the power structure were important in terms of party politics, but for purposes of a putsch, the internal relationships between their political cliques would be the most crucial factor and not the general line of their party activities, for which I was responsible as a Central Committee secretary.

Thus given the balance of power in the 21-member leadership, the vote in the case of a conflict over Indra and Kolder's position could well have been eleven to ten for Indra and Kolder. The twelfth member of the leadership—Evžen Erban, who was a secretariat member and a secretary of the National Front—was not, as far as I recall, present at that meeting. The question is whether this was purely by chance. In Erben's case, however, a leaning towards the conservatives could not be ruled out, although it is more likely he would have tried to remain neutral or support Dubček.

Had Indra and Kolder's proposals been passed by a slender majority, it is probable that that majority would immediately have forced a discussion of Brezhnev's letter. They would then have attempted to formulate a reply that would, in effect, be a letter of request for "fraternal assistance" from Moscow. It is also possible that a slender conservative majority might have tried to split the leadership in a debate over Brezhnev's letter, then contacted Soviet agents in the state organs, people like Pavlovský, Šalgovič, Hoffman, and perhaps several others (particularly in the army), and issued such a request themselves, independently. Immediately following the arrival of the armies, a "revolutionary workers' and peasants' government" would be declared, and its "revolutionary tribunal" would swing into action.

It is known for certain that a Czech version of the unsigned request published in the Moscow *Pravda* on August 21, 1968 and purporting to come from "party and government leaders" actually existed in Prague in those days. One copy was found in the office of Sulek, the director of the Czechoslovak Press Agency, who was also a Soviet agent. It too was unsigned. In my opinion, no signatures existed, and for this reason they cannot be published even today. Even if they existed, the signatures could never be published, because many of the most highly-placed representatives of "normalization," from Husák and Štrougal to Kempný and Colotka, would have been conspicuously absent. Moreover, the names of many extreme Stalinists from the Novotný era who are now unpopular with the Husák regime would have been there, but the Husák leadership has no interest in promoting them. The real reason why there are no signatures on the request, however, is because the whole plan to organize a new leadership along the lines of a "revolutionary workers' and peasants' government" collapsed. It was that new leadership which was supposed to sign the letter, and that leadership never came to pass.

On the afternoon of August 20, the presidium meeting began with a debate—and a very heated one at that—concerning the order of items on the agenda. In the end, proposals relating to the upcoming congress were designated as the first order of business, to be followed by Indra and Kolder's position paper. Dubček himself insisted on this very vehemently. I don't think he suspected any connection between this position paper and Soviet intervention, which began only a few hours later; it was more likely that he suspected that this position paper would lead to a discussion of Brezhnev's letter, which he very correctly sensed would provoke a lot of conflict in the leadership, and he wanted the material for the congress first approved.

Incredible as it may seem, therefore, it was bureaucratic-procedural routine that put a stop to the first stage of the political takeover. The fact that the pro-Moscow group was preparing a bureaucratic putsch made it particularly susceptible to bureaucratic obstructions, but it was also because the pro-Moscow group was genuinely terrified. Once the order of items on the agenda had been changed, the only way it could have saved the situation would have been to come resolutely out into the open and attempt to carry through its scheme without regard for the agenda. It might have succeeded, but only had the chief representatives of the group taken the initiative and acted immediately, without consulting the others. A minute or two elapsed, and it was too late: the meeting had already gotten down to business on the material at hand. What the putschists lacked was the resolution and courage to carry it off.

There were signs of this both before and after the intervention. One such sign was at the Soviet embassy meeting on August 22, and Bilak's wild cry, "All right, lynch me!" on the night of August 20 also indicated fear. Jan Svoboda, one of Novotný's closest associates and head of his secretariat for a time, once recounted, long after August, how a group of Stalinists and Soviet agents had met in Pečky near Nymburk before August 21 to work secretly on plans for the intervention. Representatives of the pro-Moscow group were also to attend the meeting. Svoboda said that they were all so terribly afraid that only Bilak actually showed up. And he was so terrified himself by the whole thing that he could hardly talk.

On the afternoon of August 20, 1968, therefore, the plan to provide political backing for the invasion went awry from the beginning. The stage managers, however, insisted on going ahead according to plan. Towards evening on August 22, it backfired a second time at the Soviet embassy in Prague, due mainly to the Fourteenth Congress, which compelled the chief stage managers in Moscow to agree with the demands to negotiate. They exploited Ludvík Svoboda in this, but they were still compelled to accept as negotiating partners all those who were supposed to have been tried and sentenced by the "revolutionary tribunal": Dubček, Smrkovský, Černík, and the others.

All of these men were interned in KGB barracks in the Carpathian Mountains, but on the morning of Friday August 23 Brezhnev telephoned Dubček, and he and Černík were subsequently taken to Moscow. On the morning of August 25, the other arrested Czechoslovaks (with the exception of Kriegel) joined them, and the delegation led by Ludvík Svoboda, along with the rump of the party leadership, myself included, flew to Moscow. Compelled to negotiate, Moscow had no one else to negotiate with in the end but the Dubček leadership. Its agents had failed to carry off an internal putsch, and it was out of the question for Moscow to deal with the leadership elected by the Fourteenth Congress.

Despite the enormous importance of the Fourteenth Congress for developments after August 22, there were serious political deficiencies from the outset, particularly in the new bodies elected by the congress. I do not mean the "deficiencies" that were subsequently singled out (and still are to this day) in the propaganda of the "normalizers." Their claim that the very proceedings of the congress itself, and therefore its newly-elected leadership, were illegal and against party statutes is nonsense. Any organization that recognizes a congress as its supreme constitutional body must also acknowledge that the assembly of legally-elected delegates in sufficient numbers to form a quo-

During television discussion on the possibilities
for democracy in Czechoslovakia (ca. Feb. 1968).

Z.M., Černík, and Dubček acting as party representatives
in a general conference of the trades union (June 1968).

Z.M. in conversation with graduates of the military
academy.

Z.M. and Dubček in conference with youth movement
functionaries.

August 27, 1968: Czech delegation arriving at Prague airport from Moscow after signing the Moscow Protocol. *Left to right:* Smrkovský, Špaček, Z.M., Dubček.

Husák (left), Dubček (3 from left), and Černík (7 from left) before leaving Moscow after negotiating the "normalization" on Oct. 3–4, 1968.

Central Committee meeting of Nov. 14–16, 1968, at which Z.M. resigned.

rum can constitute an official congress. They are not bound by any previous decisions about the date of their assembly and, ultimately, not even by certain articles in the organization's statutes, for they also have the right to annul or amend those statutes. How can decisions made by a two-thirds majority of a congress—which, according to the party statutes, is the supreme authority for the Central Committee, its presidium, and apparatus—be considered a usurpation of power and in contravention of the party statutes? No, the political weaknesses of the new bodies elected by the Fourteenth Congress were of a different order.

The party leadership elected by the Vysočany congress understood its own role as that of a provisional body, and it was received as such by the public as well. How could it be otherwise when it was those men who were physically absent—Dubček, Černík, Smrkovský, Kriegel, Špaček, and Šimon—who enjoyed the greatest authority in the new presidium? Consequently, both the party organs and organizations and the general public knew that there could be no genuine and lasting solution to the situation until the leaders returned.

The people who now held active functions in the party leadership—including Věněk Šilhán, who was standing in for Dubček—had never been very well known, either to the public or to the party rank-and-file and its apparatuses, and they themselves were well aware that they were only an interim leadership. Thus the Fourteenth Congress only apparently elected a new party leadership: in fact they merely threw their support behind the part of the Dubček leadership that the intervention was meant to topple. The Vysočany Central Committee, practically speaking, placed the fate of the reforms, the entire party, and its own fate as well, in the hands of members of the Dubček leadership who not only were *not* at the congress but were not even on Czechoslovak territory. And when the Soviet politburo began to negotiate with these members, it was dealing with a group of people who, up until August 25, had no idea what was happening in Czechoslovakia and what kind of bargaining position they were in.

The new presidium elected in Vysočany was composed of 28 people. Eighteen of them had already been members of the CPC or CPS (Communist Party of Slovakia) Central Committees, or had held high government functions (Husák and Colotka had been deputy premiers). Of the total presidium membership, fifteen (that is, more than half) were not physically present in Prague and therefore could take no part in the work of that body. In fact, practically all those with any kind of political authority were absent. Apart from the six arrested, they included Ota Šik, who was in Yugoslavia, Gustav Husák, who was in Moscow as a member of the government delegation, and Čestmír Císař, who was hiding somewhere outside of Prague until August 26. In addition, the entire Slovak caucus was in Bratislava—Colotka, Zrak, Ťažky, Pavlenda, and others. Those members of the Vysočany presidium who worked actively from August 23–26, that is, until the party leadership returned from Moscow, were for the most party functionaries from the various regions, districts, and factories (for example, L. Hrdinová, J. Litera, V. Kabrna, Z. Moc, and others), or else they were from outside the party apparatus altogether and consequently lacked the necessary authority within it (V. Šilhán, a professor in the Prague Economic University, and Z. Hejzlar, director of Czechoslovak Radio after June 1968 who had been a high party functionary but fell victim to the repressions after 1951). The main support for the activity of the Vysočany congress came from the apparatus of the Prague municipal party committee and from a portion of the Central Committee apparatus, but the latter was being directed by Martin Vaculík, who had been a candidate member of the presidium under Novotný and was not a member of the Vysočany presidium. Though I was not a member of that presidium either, I worked in Vysočany as a secretary of the Central Committee on August 23 and 24, dealing mostly with people who preferred working with someone who had been a Central Committee secretary before the Vysočany congress. I conferred with leaders of the trades union on the organization and conduct of a strike, with leaders of the Peoples' Militia, with representatives of the National Front, and so on.

In these provisional and uncertain conditions, a large group— about 40 to 50 percent of the party functionaries—took an active part in the business of the Fourteenth Congress, fully aware of the risks involved, and executed the practical tasks laid out in the resolutions and directives passed by the elected organs of the congress. Together with those functionaries who also supported the line of the congress but were a little more circumspect, they formed the vast majority— about 90 percent—of active party members, all of whom opposed the aims of the occupiers and stood behind Dubček and the arrested members of his leadership.

Only a very tiny minority of functionaries and employees of the party apparatus took the opposite position and were willing to collaborate, calculating that the reforms would be definitely defeated and the totalitarian dictatorship restored. Until the party leadership returned from Moscow on August 27, however, many of them merely waited passively for the provisional state of affairs to come to an end, not daring to collaborate openly with the Soviet soldiers or make their opinions known in public. Only a few individuals in the Central Committee apparatus—scarcely more than 20 from a staff of about 500—continued to work in the occupied Central Committee building after August 22, where Drahomír Kolder officiated in the name of "the party leadership." Kolder expressed his feelings about this very succinctly when he telephoned my flat to tell me I was to fly to Moscow with the rest of the leadership. When he was told that I was not home and that it wasn't known where I was, Kolder replied: "Not known? He's in Vysočany, where else would he be? Almost everyone's there, so what are they afraid of? I'm here all alone—I'm the one who should be afraid."

The main Soviet agents in the party apparatus were sitting at that time in Dresden and Moscow working feverishly on the occupiers' slanderous, mendacious, and hackneyed propaganda campaign, which was broadcast from the "Vltava" radio station and printed in the *Zprávy* newspaper and in the press of all five of the countries involved in the intervention, including, of course, the Soviet press. But those agents did not have the courage to go on the air themselves, although there was a desperate need for people who spoke proper Czech; as it was, the announcers' Czech evoked unpleasant memories of the people who addressed the Czech nation in March 1939. One Czech, however, actually did speak on "Vltava"—Pavel Auersperg. I spoke with him on August 31, 1968, at a Central Committee session after our return from Moscow, and he said very openly in his own defense: "They promised to change the modulation of my voice, and then the bastards didn't do it. Anybody could recognize my boozy voice, but what can I do about it now?"

Some members of the pro-Moscow group in the party leadership even waited out these few days of uncertainty in private. This is true, for example, of Antonín Kapek. And this is also true of a representative of reform, Čestmír Císař. On the night of August 20, when Dubček adjourned the meeting of the presidium, Císař was the only one who simply went home. The next morning, Šalgovič's people from the State Security forces went to his home and "took him into custody," as they themselves said afterwards. A few hours later, however, they released him, perhaps because the whole scenario for Indra's "revolutionary tribunal" was beginning to fall apart on the morning of August 21. Until the second-to-last day of the interregnum of the Vysočany congress, he hid out in Kersko u Poděbrad in the cottage of an acquaintance, the dean of the faculty of law, O. Průša. It was from here that he sent a letter that was broadcast and printed on August 24 in which he described his arrest but then went on to say how he "had managed to escape" and that now he was hidden "with good Czech Communists and Czech patriots," whence he was sending everyone these "battle greetings."

The factor that was decisive in making the political success of the Fourteenth Congress, the National Front, and the government possible and which foiled plans to make collaborationist changes in the structure of power, was quite unequivocally the opposition of the entire nation to the Soviet military intervention. Here could be seen the fruits of the Prague Spring, which had grown from an experiment in institutional political reform to become a nationwide democratic and humanistic movement. It is this circumstance that is the main source of my doubts concerning the correctness of my "centrism." For if the reforms had been limited to institutional changes imposed from above—which in all likelihood would have provoked a military intervention anyway—there could not have been such an enormous, intense, and united resistance by the entire nation, coupled with extraordinary discipline and political confidence in Dubček's leadership. In retrospect, it seems most probable that the kind of political reforms I envisioned would have been best only if there had been no Soviet intervention.

The nationwide passive resistance gave rise to thousands of extremely effective acts in the face of which the aggressor's machinery of violence stood helpless. And so the Soviet politburo was soon faced with a fundamental problem: what next? It had the whole country under military control, but it was utterly impotent. And as long as a military power does not resort to acts of mass brutality, the slaughter of large numbers of people, and the imposition by force of its own administration over all aspects of a country's life, it can in fact compel people to do very little. The radio went on broadcasting, the newspapers and leaflets continued to appear; and everything was directed against the occupiers. Moreover, the domestic organs of administration—from the national committees right up to the government itself—continued to function, and these bodies were not only *not* subordinate to the occupation forces they did not even meet or negotiate with them. In everyday life people behaved as though the government had not been overthrown, as though all this were only a temporary episode, after which life would return to normal again.

True, in a way all of this is insignificant in the face of occupation by a foreign army. Yet for the time being, the occupation troops themselves were helpless; as long as they did not use brute force against the civilian population. And in view of its international interests, this is something Moscow could not have permitted.

And so a small nation, invaded by an overwhelmingly superior force, in fact won a brief political victory. The nation knew this, and it was strengthened in its resistance. At the same time, everyone knew that it did not and could not represent a definitive solution. There was a fable that appeared somewhere in the press at the time about an elephant who couldn't crush a needle. It captured the situation quite precisely, not only was the needle invulnerable, but the elephant was, after all, rather large, and some kind of solution for the impasse had to be found. And both the nation and the extraordinary congress of Communists in Vysočany gave a mandate to seek that solution to a handful of people—Dubček, Černík, Svoboda, and Smrkovský—who were in Moscow.

The heroic atmosphere of those days from the 21st to the 26th of August 1968, in the minds both of ordinary people and of the reform Communists who were temporarily in charge, was tied to the sense of provisionality. It also penetrated the awareness of the occupiers and their leadership in Moscow. With a feeling that I was destined to play an important role in the closing stages of that provisional state, I prepared to go to Moscow on the evening of August 25.

I went to Moscow on the initiative of Alexander Dubček, who requested my presence at the negotiations in the Kremlin. Moreover, I was bringing him the endorsement of the Vysočany presidium. I flew with a contingent of the remaining old party leadership—Švestka, Lenárt, Jakeš, Barbírek, and Rigo. Kolder remained in Prague in the occupied Central Committee building; Antonin Kapek was probably hiding somewhere outside Prague; Císař, Sádovský, Slavík, Erban, and Voleník were not invited to Moscow; and the other members of Dubček's leadership were already in the Kremlin. Some of them had gone with Ludvík Svoboda, some had been flown as captives to the Carpathians, as already mentioned.

We were flown from Prague in a military aircraft that, besides ourselves, was carrying only a few army officers and several crates of film shot by Soviet cameramen during the opening days of the occupation in Prague. We sat silently, for after everything we had seen of each other's conduct in the past few days, there was nothing to say. At about nine A.M. Moscow time, on Sunday August 25, 1968, the aircraft touched down at the Vnukovo airport outside Moscow. We were taken in pompous Chayka limousines to some government villas in the Lenin Hills, only a few hundred meters away from the main building of Moscow University.

And so for the first time in thirteen years, I found myself looking at the same panorama of Moscow that I had seen every day as a student. The familiar view, associated in my mind with the generally pleasant memories of those years, became a reality again. And yet I was only a few hours away from the reality of occupied Prague. Moscow lay there in the morning sun, just as it had those many years ago, but the view was eclipsed in my mind's eye with scenes from the streets of Prague, where the light of dawn reflected ominously from the barrels of tank cannons, and soldiers with automatic rifles wandered through the streets like shadows. I was no longer in the Moscow of my youth, I was in the capital city of an occupying power. Instead of friends from university, I was surrounded by polite but professionally alert KGB guards, in uniform and plain clothes. The absurdity of that moment epitomized the absurdity of my entire life up to that point, and very suddenly I was overwhelmed by a wish not to exist at all. However, not only did I exist, I was also expected very shortly to negotiate with a clear head about what was to be done next, about what new absurdity to add to all the preceding ones.

In the Kremlin, they led us into a hall where Svoboda's group were, along with Černík, once more in his capacity as prime minister, and Smrkovský, Špaček, and Šimon. But Dubček, Kriegel, and Indra were missing. I had brought a large briefcase stuffed with material from Prague—newspapers, leaflets, reports from the party leadership in Vysočany—and for all of those who had earlier been arrested I had personal letters from coworkers and in some cases from their families as well. There were also letters from the Vysočany presidium for Dubček and Svoboda. I wanted to talk to Dubček first. Ludvík Svoboda told me he was resting in one of the rooms in the Kremlin assigned to the delegation and could not take part in the negotiations, but that he, Svoboda, would take me to him. He led me through two adjoining rooms, then opened a door, and I saw Dubček.

He was lying in bed, naked to the waist, for it was hot and he had thrown the cover off. He lay there limply, and obviously under sedation. He had a small bandaid on his forehead covering a tiny wound, and his face wore the absent expression of someone who has been drugged. When I entered the room, however, he stirred, opened his eyes, and smiled. I was suddenly reminded of traditional paintings of the martyrdom of St. Stephen, who smiled under torture. Dubček had the same long-suffering expression on his face, and the folds of the pillow radiated outwards from his head like rays from the missing halo. I walked over to him and stroked his face. He spoke incoherently and disconnectedly, and, among other things, said he wasn't up to reading letters just then and asked me to put them under his pillow. This I did, and then I attempted to explain something to him but he was in no fit state to talk about anything specific. I remained sitting on his bed for a while longer, and then left him.

Dubček was in a state of utter nervous collapse. The wound on his forehead had been sustained when he slipped in the bathroom and hit his head on the washbasin. President Svoboda's personal physician was looking after him. That afternoon his condition improved, and Černík and Smrkovský, I believe, spoke with him. I did not talk to him again until the following day, just before we all went to join the official part of the negotiations, in which the notorious Moscow Protocol was to be signed. Dubček did not participate in any of our collective meetings and discussions to prepare the protocol text.

František Kriegel did not take part in these negotiations either, and in fact he was not even present in the Kremlin. We learned the following day that the Soviet leadership had tried to exclude him from the negotiations altogether and, ultimately, even tried to prevent him from returning to Prague. But I shall return to this later.

Alois Indra was also absent from the negotiations. He was ill and was confined to bed somewhere outside the Kremlin, perhaps in a hospital. At the time, it was said that he was suffering from Menier's disease, of which loss of balance is a symptom. Quite apart from the state of his health, Indra had every reason to be unsettled, and he really did not know whether he was up or down. It was only clear that the "revolutionary workers' and peasants' government" was finished.

In addition, two government ministers, Dzúr and Kučera, were not involved in the negotiations over the protocol text. The negotiations were conducted by the presidium of the party; of the other members of the delegation, only Ludvík Svoboda and Gustav Husák played an active part. As we shall see, however, the word "negotiations" is scarcely appropriate. In the first place, until the protocol was actually signed on the evening of August 26, we never met with any official body from the Soviet side but only with various individuals who would present proposals in the form of ultimatums. The Soviets clearly had no intention of negotiating the conditions of capitulation. And, in any case, they had learned in Čierna nad Tisou that even prolonged negotiations would not necessarily result in the achievement of their aims. In the second place, apart from a general meeting on the night of August 25, the Czechoslovak side did not even come to its own position collectively. The Czechoslovak party leadership was split into two factions: those who had tried to form a "revolutionary workers' and peasants' government" and those whom such a government was to have put on trial. And it was clear in advance that the group that had decided to collaborate would be amenable to anything the Moscow politburo proposed. This meant that only the remaining members of the Dubček leadership had an interest in genuine negotiation: Černík, Smrkovský, Špaček, Šimon, and myself, and of course Svoboda and Husák, who at that time did not belong clearly to one side or the other.

When I refer to the negotiations, I have in mind those that took place while I was present, during August 25–26. On the two days previous to my arrival on the morning of August 25, three important questions had already been settled. The first was decided in favor of Dubček's group: the Soviet side agreed to abandon the idea of installing a different leadership. The second and third points, however, were settled in Moscow's favor: the deliberations of the Fourteenth Congress were declared invalid, and the Czechoslovak representatives agreed to withdraw discussion of the Czechoslovak situation from the UN Security Council agenda. I think that Smrkovský, Špaček, and Šimon came in on the negotiations after these points had been settled, whereas Svoboda and those who had accompanied him to Moscow, as well as Dubček and Černík, had all taken part at this stage.

When I returned from first seeing Dubček, I informed everyone present about the situation in Czechoslovakia, or, more precisely, I gave them my own views of the situation. Briefly, as I saw it, the occupation armies were in an impossible quandary as a result of the massive nationwide resistance and had no means to gain control of the situation without resorting to open acts of war against the civilian population. The Vysočany congress had managed to buttress the authority of the party among the population, and both Parliament and the government had recognized the congress and had taken a firm stand against the occupation. All of this had effectively stabilized the structure of power. However, it was only a provisional state of affairs, and it could even be dangerous: only a few simple acts of provocation were necessary to ignite the tense situation. In general, people were looking for a solution to come from here, from the negotiations in the Kremlin. Dubček, Svoboda, Černík, and Smrkovský enjoyed tremendous authority, and as long as they stood firmly united behind the solution reached here in Moscow, the great majority of the people at home would accept it. The compromise with Moscow, however, would have to stipulate the withdrawal of foreign troops from Czechoslovakia, as far as possible within a stated period of time, and, further, the continuation of CPC policy in the spirit of the Action Program. Then I described in some detail the role of the radio and the press and the conditions they were laboring under. I handed out the newspapers and leaflets stuffed in my brief case, which graphically substantiated what I had been saying.

In the discussion that followed, Švestka and Lenárt spoke the most from among the newcomers, as far as I can recall. They played down the nationwide resistance, and, on the contrary, made every effort to emphasize the grave dangers in putting off a solution any further. They talked about the need for cooperation between our state organs and the occupying forces in practical matters, in order to avoid undesirable conflicts with the populace, and the like. On the whole, however, these men did not suggest a different political solution, and they did not object to making the departure of the foreign troops and confirmation of the Action Program necessary conditions in any negotiations with Moscow. Moreover, not a word was mentioned about any necessary "fraternal assistance against the counter-revolution," nor about the political line of the Action Program being "rightwing opportunism," at least not yet.

In a private conversation, I then briefly informed Černík, Smrkovský, Špaček, and Šimon about how Bilak, Indra, Jakeš, and others had tried to form a government at the Soviet embassy and how this had turned out. And they in turn described briefly what had happened to them since we had last seen each other in Dubček's office on August 21. The five of us also agreed on some kind of united approach during the upcoming negotiations, and naturally we also agreed on unity with Dubček as soon as he was able to join in the meetings.

Then Černík told me we had to draft our proposal for the final negotiations and present it as soon as possible to the Soviet politburo. He had already worked out his own conception, which we all discussed, and then Bohumil Špaček and I began to draft the final text. That afternoon I dictated the text of this proposal in Russian to a typist in the Kremlin writing room.

The proposal was in fact a variation of the position adopted by the CPC presidium in July to the Warsaw Letter. Some of the arguments, however, and the general tone of the proposal were adapted to fit the new situation. We acknowledged certain negative features and, in particular, admitted that the powerful political pressure from below had gone beyond the aims and the control of the political leadership. But we still rejected characterizing the situation as "counter-revolutionary" and stressed that the most important thing was the positive socialist and democratic current in the nationwide movement. We admitted that the situation in Czechoslovakia gave reasons for uneasiness in the five neighboring countries and that the CPC leadership had underestimated this factor. Nevertheless, we did not consider the intervention itself as a step that could solve the situation, but rather essentially as a tragic mistake: withdrawing the Warsaw Pact troops from Czechoslovakia was therefore a priority. Put briefly, it was considered necessary to trim the further development of reforms in Czechoslovakia to fit the common interests of all socialist states. In this sense, the conclusions reached in Bratislava provided a possible way out. As far as domestic politics were concerned, our proposals stressed that the Action Program would continue to be the fundamental guide to the party's line. As far as I can recall, Oldřich Černík presented the text of this proposal to the Soviet politburo.

Our proposal enraged the Soviets, and they returned it with the remark that it was an ultimatum and that our delegation should be aware it was in no position to make ultimatums. Perhaps so there should be no misunderstanding, the Soviet side then presented us with a counterproposal that really was an ultimatum. It was from this text that the Moscow Protocol came into existence. At first, everyone in the Czechoslovak delegation rejected the Soviet ultimatum; not even the pro-Moscow group would support it. And Smrkovský then informed the Soviet politburo of our rejection.

Exactly how many versions of the proposals were exchanged and what changes they had I cannot recall. Two or three members of our delegation would always hand over our different proposals and notes to one or two representatives of the Soviet side, who would either be empowered to give us an immediate decision or would return our papers some time later, usually with a rejection and comments. On such occasions, Černík, Smrkovský, Švestka, Lenárt, Šimon, and I would represent our side, and Kosygin, Suslov, and Ponomarev would represent the Soviet politburo. Šimon and I always negotiated with Ponomarev.

While this paper war was going on, the others occupied themselves as they pleased. During the day, Brezhnev and Kosygin also met separately with some members of our delegation. I had no way of checking on what the pro-Moscow group—Bilak, Jakeš, and others—was up to, nor did it interest me very much at that point. Because I was busy formulating various proposals and notes, I was usually absent from the room where our collective sessions, as it were, took place. For the most part, however, only a fraction of our delegation was present in the room at any one time, and they would talk matters over in small groups.

After the Soviet politburo had unequivocally rejected our proposal as an inadmissible "ultimatum," the Soviet proposal became the basis of our discussions. The original version of this proposal differed from what became the Moscow Protocol on three main points: it contained a statement that the military intervention was justified; there was no commitment on the departure of Soviet troops from Czechoslovakia; and, finally, there was no recognition whatsoever of the correctness of the CPC political line. On the contrary, from certain phrases committing the signatories to invalidate the Fourteenth Congress and replace certain functionaries (specifically, Kriegel, Císař, Šik, Minister of the Interior Pavel, and Minister of Foreign Affairs Hájek), a political condemnation of the entire reform politics could be deduced. The protracted negotiations that followed concentrated on changing the wording of these three particular points.

On the whole, the pro-Moscow group in the Dubček leadership behaved passively during all this. They knew that the actual wording of the protocol was not so important. So none of them actually came out in support of the original version of the Soviet proposal, nor did they oppose our efforts to have it changed. But they suggested no changes themselves and merely waited to see how the war of words would turn out. However, there were two people who were not in the party leadership who actively assisted Soviet ends: Ludvík Svoboda and Gustav Husák. Svoboda's position, however one-sided it was, was at least based on the fact that every hour that passed without a solution increased the danger of conflict between the troops and the civilian population. Husák, on the other hand, assisted Soviet ends for less legitimate reasons, insisting that the Fourteenth Congress was unstatutory simply because it took place without the Slovak delegates.

Ludvík Svoboda was not simply not a reform politician, he was not a politician. Rather he was a soldier, an officer in the army of the First Czechoslovak Republic who became commander of the Czechoslovak units fighting in the USSR with the Soviets during the Second World War. It was during the war that he apparently accepted the notion of tying Czechoslovakia to the Soviet Union, with all its ramifications. As minister of defense in the pre-February 1948 government, he was formally a non-Communist but in fact represented the CPC and had a very clearly pro-Soviet outlook, in which the question of national sovereignty was not a real concern. He had a two-dimensional mind that evaluated everything from a simple military perspective, and he may well have been more a pro-Soviet soldier than he was a Communist. The dogmas of the communist ideology were probably quite alien to him, as were Communist practices, but he was convinced that Czechoslovakia's pro-Soviet orientation was necessary.

In this regard, Svoboda's perception of the situation in August 1968 was in accord with the Soviet marshals, for whom the problems of democracy were an issue only insofar as they related to military domination of a geographical area, where Czechoslovakia happened to lie. And Ludvík Svoboda's position on the need for Soviet domination of this area is the key to understanding his politcal attitudes. It is true that after his election as president in March 1968 he placed a wreath on Masaryk's grave in Lany, and he may even have done so with a certain feeling of inner kinship with the founder of the state. He probably wanted to emulate his prewar predecessors in the office more than he did Novotný. Had there been no military intervention, Svoboda might very well have continued to support the development of democracy in Czechoslovakia. But as soon as it was a question of supporting either democracy or the Soviet tendency, he sided unequivocally with Moscow.

Given Svoboda's outlook, his statement on the night of August 22, that he was going to Moscow to arrange for Dubček's return, and that Dubček could then submit his resignation and everything would be all right, was perfectly logical. This did not become clear to me until after I observed him in the Kremlin. I had incorrectly assumed that Svoboda put the interests of the democratic political reforms above those of the Soviet marshals. But, on the contrary, he made the democratic reforms conditional on their compatibility with the marshals' military designs. He was against a Tartar solution, that is, kidnapping and murdering the constitutional leaders. But he was not against Moscow removing unacceptable politicians by more civilized means, such as enforced resignation. He was not a supporter of intervention, because it was barbarian and would lead to bloodshed.

Once, during the deliberations in the Kremlin, Svoboda shouted at the entire Dubček leadership: "There you go, talk, talk, talking again! You've already talked and talked till your country's occupied. So act accordingly and do something! I've seen a lot of dead people in my life and I will not permit thousands to die just because of your jabbering."

Svoboda was not inventing the danger of bloodshed, and it had, in fact, been specified in the letter to him from the Vysočany presidium, the presidium of the National Assembly, and the government, which I had delivered to him personally and which said: "One dangerous factor is the growing weariness and nervous tension of the occupation troops and our citizens." Those who sent the letter, however, placed the interests of the democratic reforms above all else, and therefore they urged Svoboda to break off negotiations in Moscow and return to Prague with Dubček and Černík to help calm down the situation and consult with people at home, and then continue with the negotiations.

Ludvík Svoboda, however, saw things differently. He too wanted to return to Prague as soon as possible but with an agreement in his pocket: his only concern was ending the provisional state of affairs. Besides, I don't suppose he had as many illusions as those who had written him from Prague. He knew that, even if he wanted to, he would not get back to Prague until he had signed the agreement, or rather the *diktat* of the Kremlin. At the same time, this was what he had gone to Moscow to do in the first place, and resistance made no sense to him; it was only the idle talk of politicians.

During the proceedings in the Kremlin, Svoboda continually browbeat our delegation by evoking visions of the potential victims and thousands of dead and urging it to wind the negotiations up as rapidly as possible. As I have mentioned before, I shared these feelings about risking human lives, but Svoboda was unconcerned about including anything in the protocol for continuing the reform policies. He undoubtedly served Soviet ends in this. Nevertheless, I refuse to categorize Ludvík Svoboda with people like Bilak, Indra, Jakeš, and others, who, as representatives of the totalitarian dictatorship, secretly helped to prepare the invasion, or people like Husák, who opportunistically allied himself with the interveners. Svoboda's motives were different. I personally disagree with them as well, but I am only seeking to explain them, not justify them.

The problem of Ludvík Svoboda was not, in my opinion, that he betrayed the democratic reforms of the Prague Spring at a crucial moment. The Prague Spring had in fact made a man head of state who had never been a democratic politician, an old Czechoslovak marshal who in many ways shared the views of the old Moscow marshals. But Czechoslovakia being the small power it is, our marshal did not share the aggressive whims of the great power marshal: as a little marshal he was, on the contrary, obedient to the big marshal with whom he had long since thrown in his lot.

In the following years of the "normalization," Svoboda became utterly bogged down in the anti-reform politics and became an embarrassing stage-prop for that whole process. All this was engendered by his primitive pro-Soviet thinking, his advancing senility, and obvious personal vanity, of the type very few soldiers by profession and nature are spared. In the end, he became an embarrassment to the nation and a liability to the real rulers and was therefore removed from the scene in 1975.

It was at these negotiations in the Kremlin that Gustav Husák quite unmistakably began his great play for the highest position in the CPC. True, he supported both the basic demands of the reform wing of the party leadership: that the final protocol provide a guarantee for the departure of foreign troops from the territory of the Republic, and that it confirm the correctness of the Action Program line. But, at the same time, he consistently and unyieldingly supported the Soviet demand to invalidate the Fourteenth Congress. This question, as I have said, had been provisionally settled before my arrival, but it was reopened for discussion, and ways were sought to find a more politically practicable compromise solution.

I thought it absurd that the Fourteenth Congress, which had played such an important role at home, both in terms of maintaining party authority among the populace and in saving the lives and positions of the arrested leaders, was simply to be swept aside by some agreement with the Moscow politburo. Besides which, I had come to Moscow as a respresentative of the party leadership elected by that congress, and thus I was ultimately responsible to it. True, I was not myself a member of the Vysočany presidium, as Dubček, Černík, Smrkovský, Špaček, Šimon, and Husák were. And, formally speaking, these people were more qualified to defend (or condemn) the position of the Vysočany congress than I was. But they had not, as I had, sat in Vysočany, and they had no idea what the atmosphere was like there and what, even now, the hopes of the delegates representing the party were. On the contrary, I could still see in my mind's eye very real people in those ČKD factory buildings, and I could not help wondering how they would react to having all their efforts during the days of the occupation simply declared "unstatutory."

Smrkovský, Špaček, and Šimon, who had also arrived after the provisional settlement, tried to have the question reopened. They too felt it was unthinkable simply to deny the Fourteenth Congress and its work when it had in fact saved them personally. Therefore the matter was discussed repeatedly, and a new compromise solution was sought. We finally concluded that the best approach lay in invalidating the election of the new Central Committee by the Fourteenth Congress, for this is what Moscow was mainly concerned about, without actually invalidating the congress itself. This solution was feasible because the congress itself had declared that the elections were not definitive and its deliberations were not yet concluded. As soon as possible—at that time we were thinking in terms of about two months—after most of the Soviet troops had been withdrawn from Czechoslovak territory, the congress would then meet again, make adjustments in its resolutions, and elect a new Central Committee. Until that time, the old Central Committee and its presidium would coopt such members of the Vysočany Central Committee as would guarantee a predominance of reform Communists in those organs. In the end, the question of invalidating the congressional proceedings in Vysočany was so worded in the final protocol as to make this solution possible. And the compromise solution was executed at a plenary session of the Central Committee on August 31, after the Dubček leadership had returned to Prague.

In private meetings with members of the Soviet politburo, Husák had evidently promised to press his demands on the CPC delegation to invalidate the Fourteenth Congress. As a result, he made a compromise that much more difficult, but ultimately even he agreed with the compromise proposal, because of serious personal reasons: at the time, he was not even a Central Committee member, and the

Vysočany congress had now elected him to the presidium. The proposed compromise, therefore, guaranteed his cooption into that organ. Originally, Husák had banked on another possible outcome: he was depending on the fact that the CPS congress in Slovakia would elect him as first secretary of the Slovak party, and thus he would enter the leadership independent of the Vysočany congress. This is why he telephoned Bratislava from Moscow and demanded that the CPS congress, scheduled for August 26, be postponed until the delegation returned from Moscow. His people had promised to comply. When I arrived in Moscow, I told him that I knew for a fact that the Bratislava congress was to begin the next day, that it would approve the proceedings of the Vysočany congress and that furthermore a delegation from Vysočany would be present at it. I even told him who would be in that delegation, because it had been determined before I left Vysočany. Husák heard me out, looking at me all the while with a supercilious smile as if to say I was a poor fool who hadn't a clue about how politics really worked, and then he said it was all nonsense: the Bratislava congress would not take place the next day, that he knew it would not, and, after all, he was in charge.

Towards evening, Husák must have discovered that the congress would be taking place next day after all, in his absence. This undermined his self-assurance, and he was more willing to seek a compromise over the Vysočany congress, one that would allow the cooption of some of its elected people into the top party functions, for in his case it could mean a substitute entrée into power. But Husák was ultimately able to realize his original aim as well. The CPS congress did begin on August 26, but Husák arrived on August 27, and he managed to push through a motion invalidating the Vysočany congress, thus discharging his pledge to Moscow. At the same time, by being elected first secretary of the party in Slovakia, he was guaranteed a place on the presidium in Prague quite independent of the Vysočany congress. Still, the Slovak congress did approve on the first evening, before Husák arrived, a resolution condemning the intervention in the same spirit as the Vysočany congress.

During the proceedings in the Kremlin, Husák always conducted himself in such a way that he appeared to be the friend and ally of Dubček's, Svoboda's, and Černík's. In particular, he somehow always managed, directly or indirectly, to support Svoboda. Even then, his behavior towards Smrkovský always betrayed a certain reserve. At the same time, however, he did not join forces with the pro-Moscow group—Bilak, Indra, Jakeš, and others. Even so, he made a good personal impression on the Moscow politburo. Just before flying home from Moscow, Kosygin said to me: "Comrade Husák is such a competent comrade and a wonderful Communist. We didn't know him personally before, but he quite impressed us here."

I was never one of those who harbored any illusions about Gustav Husák. We met personally for the first time at a rather late date—in March 1968—when both of us were working at the Academy of Sciences, he in Bratislava and I in Prague. It was at a meeting of my research team, which was studying problems related to the development of the political system in Czechoslovakia, and we were discussing the constitutional structure of relationships between Czechs and Slovaks.

By that time, I already knew a good deal about Husák from his various friends and enemies, and I was quite prepared to meet an ambitious politician set on making a comeback in the world of power. Even so, he went beyond all my expectations. We were used to speaking concretely, openly, and with tolerance for differences of opinion, but Husák spoke at our meeting like a political boss issuing orders and lecturing us on the correct "line." The substance of what he said was profoundly conservative: he quoted clichés from Lenin's *The State and Revolution* which developments in the Soviet Union and Soviet bloc had long since disproved, and he rejected, out of hand, any thinking tending toward pluralist democratic conceptions. His solution to the question of Czech-Slovak relationships was the creation of a federal state. In short, his performance was dogmatic and, at times, arrogant and demagogic.

Toward the end of the discussion, I told him that his contribution wasn't bad as political speeches went, but that it was completely devoid of any ideas. Husák could hardly contain his rage, and it was clear that I had made an enemy of him. But the impression he made on me was so utterly negative that I had no desire to cultivate his friendship anyway.

Husák, a trained lawyer, had been a member of the Slovak Communist intelligentsia before the war, and he went underground when the war began. During the war, he was an active Stalinist and a supporter of the Soviet-ruled Comintern. At one point, for example, he proposed to Gottwald that a postwar solution lay in annexing Slovakia to the Soviet Union as a Soviet republic, arguing that it was the secret wish of a majority of the Slovak nation. He considered all

Czechs who remained in Slovakia during the war, when Slovakia was formally an independent fascist state, as collaborators with the Germans, and he warned that Jews were an unreliable element in the resistance movement and should be isolated. Such views were typical of the Stalinist outlook, according to which any class, nationality, or faith constituting a doubtful element must be discriminated against or completely liquidated, and which was equally shared by Gottwald's CPC elite.

In the postwar years, until his arrest in 1951, Husák was an active and capable agent of Stalinist policies. In the 1946 Slovak elections, in which the Communists were defeated, he became chairman of the Assembly of Commissioners. Husák, in fact, employed work standards that were a foretaste of those by which the CPC strove to gain complete, monopolistic control of the government after February 1948 irrespective of the election results. As chairman of the Assembly of Commissioners, Husák took an active part in engineering State Security provocations against non-Communist politicians and priests. It is a fact that some people from the anti-Communist opposition in Slovakia had connections with the fascist forces defeated in the war; but Husák, with the aid of police provocations, created the impression that this was true of all non-Communist forces across the board and that everyone but the Communists represented an acute threat to the very existence of a democratic Czechoslovakia. He did not rely on gaining a majority in democratic elections but tried rather to gain positions of power through intrigue, police provocations and the use of dictatorial force.

Husák the Stalinist, however, was not like other Stalinists in Bratislava and Prague. He was genuinely committed to protecting Slovak national interests from Prague centralism. He was not like the men of the power apparatus, whose strength lies in the mediocrity and anonymity of their dictatorial power. He was closer to the highly-trained ruling elite, who exercised intelligent manipulation. Therefore, those who enjoyed the monopolistic power of the Stalinist party and state apparatuses that Husák had helped to create, including the political police, never considered him one of themselves, but rather an alien, individualistic, and ambitious person, whom, in some respects, they even feared. In the apparatus, he was referred to as a "gentleman Communist," and this derogatory label, in various forms, was subsequently circulated by official party propaganda during his imprisonment and later by Novotný's propaganda machine long after his release. Though he made a considerable contribution to the victory of Stalinism in Czechoslovakia, Husák became its victim because he appeared to other Stalinists as a dangerously capable person, and to the defenders of Prague centralism a dangerous representative of Slovak national interests.

Thus Husák is, in fact, an extraordinarily unsuccessful man. In the Slovak National Uprising, he helped bring Slovakia back into the unified Czechoslovak state (abandoning his previous proposals about annexing it to the Soviet Union) in the hope that Slovakia—and thus he, as a Slovak politician—would genuinely have room to realize their national ambitions. In reality, however, a dictatorial centrist regime emerged and a great many social interests got suppressed, including the interests of Slovakia. Between 1945 and 1951, Husák did everything possible to help consolidate the monopolistic power of the CPC and thus establish his own power as a Communist politician. In reality, however, it was that very dictatorship that considered him a dangerous rival and had him arrested and sentenced to life in prison.

To a large extent, Husák's imprisonment resulted directly from his rivalry with V. Široký, a man who in Gottwald's, and later in Novotný's, presidium represented those Slovak Communists who were willing to subordinate all Slovak national interests without exception to the dictatorial centrism of Prague. Husák and Široký were competitors for power in the 1950s; had Husák won out instead of Široký, no doubt Široký would have been the one locked up. But this is not to deny the injustice of Husák's imprisonment for "crimes" he had never committed and suffering for more than ten years the horrors of the Stalinist prisons.

When Husák was finally rehabilitated in 1963, Novotný offered him—as he did Smrkovský—a chance to return to political life, this time as deputy minister of finance. Husák, however, turned the offer down. I think he correctly sensed that Novotný wanted to get him out of Slovakia and into Prague to isolate him from his political home ground. I also think that by this time Husák calculated that bigger and more fundamental changes were in the offing, and that there were better things in store for him.

As a capable and very ambitious politician, Husák could not but have been changed by prison, but in many ways he remained the same. He experienced what a Communist dictatorship can mean to those it spurns, yet he almost certainly did not consider himself a permanent and justifiable outcast. On the contrary, he returned from prison with the conviction that his "rightful" place was somewhere else altogether—at the top. After all, he always had the best of intentions regarding communism, the interests of the working class, and the interests of Slovakia, and, what was more, he was more capable than those in power. He was also convinced that the regime had to be changed, but his notions of what changes were necessary were dominated by his past positions, due partly to his long period of isolation in prison from social developments. Husák did not emerge from prison so much a democratic politician as a powerful political personality convinced of his own messianic mission and eager to show the knaves and fools the proper way to conduct politics.

Miroslav Kusý, one of the foremost reform Communists in Slovakia, told me how he met Husák at dawn on August 21 in front of the Central Committee building in Bratislava, when the tanks were rumbling about and the chaotic atmosphere of those first few hours of occupation reigned. The first thing Husák shouted to him above the roaring of the engines was: "I shall lead the nation out of this catastrophe." Only a person who was deeply persuaded of his messianic role could have said a thing like that at a time like that.

After 1963, Husák made contacts on his own initiative with many reform Communists in Bratislava and Prague, particularly from Communist intellectual circles. For years, he was a consistent critic of Antonín Novotný, and he very skillfully gathered many of the anti-Novotný forces around him, to a point where many influential reform Communists began to think of him as a possible alternative to Novotný. Novotný himself became increasingly fearful of Husák and sought to limit his political influence: by this time, jail was out of the question. But these discriminatory measures merely increased Husák's popularity, and Husák cleverly exploited this.

After the overthrow of Novotný, Husák was once more left out. Neither Dubček, Černík, nor Kolder was very eager to have him in a top party position. In Slovakia, Dubček appointed his friend, Bilak, as first secretary of the Slovak party, and so Husák's hopes were thwarted in Bratislava as well. It was yet another visible rebuff, and, in the end, he had to settle for deputy prime minister.

Husák thought of the Prague Spring as a provisional state of affairs, and he knew that the final distribution of power had yet to be settled. It was an extremely difficult situation for him. Inwardly, he was not at all persuaded that attempts at radical reform aiming at political pluralism were correct, nor did he think they were politically realistic. In private conversations, he referred to radical reform Communists, especially from Prague intellectual circles, as "the gravediggers of the revival process." He considered Dubček and the others in the party leadership to be politically naive and shallow men over whom he towered both in ability and in his sense of political realism. I don't think he had very many illusions about the USSR's foreign policy: after all, he had learned his lesson in the Slovak National Uprising, which because of Stalin's strategic interests was not supported by the Soviet army and was consequently defeated. And he thought it absolutely essential not to let things develop into a conflict with Moscow, partly because he was a convinced Communist, and partly because he was a political realist. But because he was disliked by the pro-Soviet and Stalinist faction in the CPC, he had no choice but to seek alliances with the more radical currents that were demanding more key personnel changes. But in such company he was compelled to disguise his real convictions.

In the 1960s, many reform Communists considered Husák their political ally and, often perhaps, even a personal friend. Husák, however, most likely considered these people at best an essential, if not exactly ideal, instrument for realizing his own messianic visions. Many did not realize this until it was too late, that is, after 1969, when Husák finally reached the pinnacle of power.

Milan Hübl, who was rector of the Central Committee's Party University in 1968, is the best example of this. Hübl was one of those who did everything possible in the final years of Novotný's rule not only to have Husák rehabilitated but to return him to political life. And he cooperated with Husák in his active opposition to Novotný, which, among other things, is why Novotný had him thrown out of the Party University in 1965. Again in April 1969, Hübl was active in swinging the reform Communist votes that enabled Husák to replace Dubček as secretary-general of the Central Committee. He firmly believed that Husák was the best man to salvage what was left of the 1968 reform politics in the new period of "Kadarization." In 1972, Husák repaid Hübl by sending him to prison for six and a half years for "subversion of the state," although Hübl had done nothing more than he had always done. He stood behind preserving the remains of reform communism, working to surround himself with like-minded reform Communists, and to gain the support of the Italian and French Communist parties. Husák, who had himself been unjustly imprisoned once, kept Hübl in prison until the end of 1976, although he was well aware of the degrading conditions that were seriously endangering Hübl's health.

After 1969, Husák in fact liquidated most of those who, through the years, assisted him in reaching the highest position in the party. And he allied himself with many he had dismissed as incompetent flunkeys of the Novotný regime, chief among them Vasil Bilak. It is true that Husák's situation compelled him to take both these actions. He became first party secretary at a time when only a faithful servant of the Kremlin could have done so. And it was the Kremlin's wish to have all his former political friends out of the way and his old enemies raised to positions of power. But Husák is not stupid; he is more intelligent than most of his current presidium cronies. He took over in the full awareness of what it would mean and how he would have to behave.

Installing Gustav Husák in the top party position in May 1969 was an effective move by the Moscow politburo. Precisely because Husák had never been a Soviet agent in the CPC, but rather had been associated in the 1960s with many reform Communists, he temporarily sustained the hope that "the worst would be prevented from happening," that he would represent some kind of "centrist" political position. Many people in Czechoslovakia went on believing this for a long time, and to this day the idea is still touted by Western journalists who continue to write about Husák as a man holding out against extremes. In reality, however, there is no justification whatsoever for such a claim. Husák only does what the Kremlin demands of him. If that means that extremist ideas are sometimes rejected, it is because the Kremlin wants it that way, not because Husák is a moderate. Husák has never had any independent, personal support in the party. He does not belong either to the so-called "healthy core" of the CPC, that is, to those who helped prepare the Soviet intervention in 1968, or to the more pragmatic people in the political and economic apparatuses. He is a figure who has been appointed over their heads and from outside their ranks, at the wish of the Kremlin. That is the source of his strength, but also his weakness. He is not, nor ever will be, anything more than a Soviet viceroy in Czechoslovakia who, when it is the will of his protectors in the Kremlin, will be mercilessly pushed aside.

It is very probable that in August 1968, in the Kremlin, Husák himself had no idea what kind of domestic political situation would arise under his rule in Czechoslovakia. I don't think it was his original intention to liquidate a third of the party membership as "aiders and abettors of the counter-revolution," nor did he imagine that Vasil Bilak, whom he despised, would become his main supporter. Nevertheless, the Kremlin negotiations almost certainly marked the beginning of his deliberate climb towards supreme power in the party and in the land, and he was essentially ready at that point to sacrifice the reform politics of the Prague Spring to his ambitions for power.

Late in the evening on August 25, in Dubček and Kriegel's absence, there were five supporters of democratic reform in the Kremlin—Černík, Smrkovský, Špaček, Šimon, and myself—standing against the pro-Moscow group—Bilak, Jakeš, Švestka, Piller, Lenárt, Barbírek, Rigo. Their eighth member, Alois Indra, was also absent. The five of us were still trying to provide at least slightly more space in the final document for the reform politics, all the while being shouted at by Ludvík Svoboda as well as by Gustav Husák. And it was not difficult to tell—though they were observers taking no part in the deliberations—that the ministers Dzúr and Kučera and the ambassador to Moscow at the time, Vladimír Koucký, would also sign the Soviet proposal without hesitation.

At the same time, constant pressure was being applied by the Soviet politburo. This was done, on the one hand, by privately confronting individual members of our group using intimidation with ingratiation that gave them the hope of obtaining personal Soviet support. But it was also done by creating a generally ominous atmosphere in which two great threats hung in the air.

The first threat lay in knowing we would not leave the Kremlin until we had signed the Soviet ultimatum, regardless of how it might be altered. The Soviet side not only dispensed with trying to disguise this threat, they quite openly stressed it. "If you won't sign it tomorrow, you will in a week," they said. There was no doubt that the Kremlin could carry out such a threat. The six previously-arrested members of the presidium had very clear ideas, indeed, of what this might entail. They had, in essence, already been through the second stage of the inquisition: they had been shown the instruments of torture, literally. I know that they had all reckoned on dying. And they were not exactly anxious to have the experience repeated.

But it was not simply the fact that some members of the Dubček leadership were treated more like objects of gangster-style blackmail than members of a state delegation attending political negotiations; it was also the fact that we knew that on certain serious matters the

Kremlin would not retreat even at the price of massive and politically senseless bloodshed in Czechoslovakia. And that was the second menace the Soviet leadership continually dangled over us, not only via Svoboda, but also directly, in talks with members of our delegation. We were told that if any conflicts with the population erupted, the armies had orders to use their weapons. We had to understand, they said, that they simply could not back down without even reaching some general political agreement. And we would bear responsibility for anything that occurred as a consequence of delay.

Considering the matter in retrospect, it is safe to say that Moscow would never have resorted to such drastic measures, or, if it had, that the international repercussions would have been catastrophic and that there would have been a collective act of heroic resistance against the overwhelmingly powerful aggressor that would have been an historic and moral victory for the nation, finally breaking the long chain of capitulations in its history and straightening the nation's backbone. Of course, we all thought about such things at the time, but it is difficult to accept the responsibility for a bloody massacre on the basis of such considerations. Nor could we console ourselves with the hope that such a massacre might not take place as long as we were unable to reach an agreement in the Kremlin: compelling Moscow to retreat from its original plan and negotiate with the very people who were originally to have been put on trial by a "revolutionary tribunal" was as much as the force of popular passive resistance could hope to achieve. Were the talks to break down, the Kremlin would have had no other choice than to fall back on the original plan in an even more bloody form. It is an illusion to think that a robber who only threatens to use his gun as long as he can get what he wants will not use it if he finds himself in trouble and can see no other way out. And the Soviet politburo was no tyro: the rich tradition of Stalinist mass crimes and Budapest in 1956 both spoke the same language.

Naturally, Moscow too would have found it less acceptable to administer the country itself for a time and thus carry the act of aggression through to its logical conclusion. But the forces that had gone ahead with the occupation could just as easily have gone ahead with establishing a military government, and in certain circumstances they would have had to. In practice, it did not even require the politburo's consent: only the "hawks" among the army chiefs of staff need make the decision. It was within their power to unleash a massacre and then blame it on "unrest" fomented by the "counter-revolution" and Czechoslovak citizens.

We knew that the Soviet leadership, having been compelled to negotiate with Dubček, wanted him and other reformers to do what had proved impossible using Bilak and Indra. But this would nonetheless be a double-edged instrument of Moscow's will, and it raised a number of political possibilities. The route of compromise undeniably gave us certain options, which we could, to some extent, exploit. And compared to the alternative of a military massacre, we felt that compromise was the only acceptable solution in the interests of the reform politics and of the nation.

We also considered the possibility that developments in Czechoslovakia and the failure of military methods might strengthen the position of those who originally resisted intervention. A political compromise with Moscow would have unilaterally benefited the Kremlin in any case, but it would not necessarily have meant the end of the reform politics, for the "hawks" could still have been mollified by suggesting the deployment of a small number of Soviet strategic weapon units, which need not have been a threat to the reform politics, though of course their scope would have to be considerably reduced. In other words, a kind of "Kadarization" was possible, without bloodshed, deportations, or police repressions, and there would be safeguards against the future reestablishment of a totalitarian dictatorship.

This is roughly the way we were all thinking—Černík, Smrkovský, Špaček, Šimon, and I. At the same time, it must have been clear to all of us that it was mere speculation and wishful thinking—as the Czech proverb goes, "the wish is often the father of the thought." We often expressed our doubts to each other and saw our faith, at times, quite ironically; occasionally one of us would succumb to scepticism. I recall how suddenly, in a kind of lightning flash of clear perception, I would feel that all our ideas were utter nonsense, that we were in fact lying to ourselves and that the truth was quite simple: we were about to sign a capitulation, we were renouncing everything, and the nation at home could only see it as treason. At one point, I said to Smrkovský (perhaps Špaček and Šimon were also present) that one unexpected consequence for me of these negotiations was coming to understand Emil Hácha. No one was shocked, for I suppose all of us had thought about Hácha here. The differences between us, however, consisted in the fact that some of us dismissed our doubts more quickly and completely than others. I believe the first one to conclude that we had no choice but simply to sign the Soviet ultimatum was Černík.

This, of course, altered the situation as far as trying to work out various alternatives went. It was clear that the entire pro-Moscow group, which was a majority of the delegation, including the ministers, Dzúr and Kučera, and Ambassador Koucký, would sign the ultimatum no matter what form it took. And it was clear that Svoboda and Husák would also sign it. If Černík were to sign it as well, the only remaining delegate who mattered to the political success of the Soviet strategy was Dubček. Smrkovský's refusal would have complicated the situation, but it would not have been an unmitigated political failure. My signature, along with Špaček's, Šimon's, and Kriegel's, had very little political significance and could scarcely have tipped the balance one way or the other.

Dubček's point of view, however, remained unclear until the ceremonial proceedings on August 26, which were supposed to end in signing the document, and even then it changed. Dubček was still absent from our meeting on the night of August 25. Someone maintained consultation with him, and Dubček always supported our proposed changes and wanted us to continue working on the text and negotiating, but he would not commit himself to sign the document until everything was in its final form.

Later in the night of August 25, the whole Czechoslovak delegation, with the exception of Dubček, Kriegel, and Indra, met around one table. Oldřich Černík chaired the meeting, and each of us was expected to say whether or not he would sign the protocol the next day. The protocol itself had not yet been completed—this was to happen next day in a meeting with the entire Soviet politburo—so there was still time to make changes. So far, the Soviet side had not even accepted the formulation about withdrawing soldiers from Czechoslovak territory that was ultimately contained in the final version of the protocol, and therefore I thought it was premature for everyone to commit himself to sign, even though it was only in principle and did not rule out further attempts at changing the wording. This was the meeting where Ludvík Svoboda yelled at us for talking and talking until our country was occupied. Husák too urged everyone to make his position clear. The atmosphere was very heavy, tense, and overwrought. I refused to give my assurances of a "yes" at this meeting and reserved my decision until the next day, depending on how the final negotiations went. All the rest said they would vote "yes." As far as the absent members of the delegation were concerned, there was naturally no doubt about where Alois Indra stood. Kriegel's position was not known at all, and Dubček too refused to commit himself until the following day. His position was the only one that could still have influenced the situation to any significant extent.

The meeting finished sometime between two and three in the morning, and I did not get back to the government villa in the Lenin Hills until after three a.m. Just as in the Kremlin, the salon had tables laden with vodka, cognac, caviar, sturgeon, and other delicacies. I went to my room and literally collapsed onto the bed from exhaustion. Then I heard a quiet knock on the door. I opened it and saw a young woman in a very attractive negligee, beneath which, it would seem, she was naked. "Is there anything more you'd like, comrade?" chirped the creature with a seductive smile. I didn't know what further services I could ask for as a guest of the Kremlin, but I wasn't interested in finding out. I irritably replied that I only wanted them all to leave me alone, and closed the door.

Since the fateful night of August 20, I had slept only three times, and then for no more than four hours each time. I had smoked hundreds of cigarettes and drunk dozens of cups of black coffee. During my waking hours the tension never once let up, whether it was in Dubček's office with an automatic rifle pointing at the back of my head, at the Soviet embassy in Prague, in Vysočany, or in the Kremlin from the early mornings on. I was so desperately exhausted that sleep refused to come. My head was swarming, not with thoughts, but rather with images and sensations, endless, incoherent films or something like visions. And sometimes, in the intervals between them, I would suddenly have an extraordinarily clear and simple perception.

I opened the window and looked into the garden. The fresh early morning air had a soothing effect on me, and thoughts began to replace the visions. Now, for the first time in fact, my mind began to deal with the situation as a whole and identify what was essential in it. For as long as I had been caught up in the unbroken flow of events, conversations, consultations, decisions about dozens of details, the writing of proposals and notes, translating them into Russian and considering the given options, I had merely been functioning like a programmed computer. I had no time to digest what was happening inside me. Now the accumulating storehouse inside me of experiences, impressions, and feelings bombarded my mind with questions demanding answers. In essence, the questions came down to: what had actually happened and what was my role in all of this? And there was only one possible answer.

The fact that I was now sitting in Moscow, half hostage, half government guest, was the logical outcome of my entire life, of my entire political activity. I had set this situation up myself. The crucial date was not August 20, 1968, but February 25, 1948. For it was then that I had made the unconditional decision, on the basis of my own personal convictions, to join those who had also chosen to submit themselves unconditionally to Moscow and its aims "for eternity." It is no longer material why I or the others did it, whether the motivating ideas and ideals were well-intentioned or not. It happened, and it was my own decision. It is true that for more than ten years I had known Moscow was the headquarters of crime and that I was trying to change this through reforms at home, in Czechoslovakia, hoping all the while that the sincere desire to have done with crimes existed in Moscow as well, and that therefore I would be allowed to proceed. I had certain reasons for believing this was so, but there were also more lasting and persuasive reasons for believing the opposite was true, which I preferred to underestimate or overlook.

There was nothing inconsistent in what had happened a week before. Moscow had merely decided not to let the reform experiment go any further because it seemed too threatening to its real interests. And seen from Moscow's vantage point, it was only logical for them to put me on trial in the Kremlin and ask me: "Well, what's it going to be? Are you with us for "eternity" or not? After all, this is the gist of what you've been saying for the past twenty years." And all they wanted to hear was a yes or a no—the details didn't interest them.

Old General Svoboda was right, after all, when he railed at us and told us to wake up. He understood the situation and was giving Moscow his unequivocal "yes." He asked us all to do the same, and if anyone wanted to disagree then let him say "no," but he should not drag proceedings out any longer. We were caught off guard by the Soviet politburo's gangster tactics. But this too was part of our mistake. Kadar was right to ask Dubček: "Do you *really* not know the kind of people you're dealing with?" He thought it unbelievable that Dubček did not know. We were really fools, but our folly was the ideology of reform communism.

My leg was tingling from leaning against the wide sill of the open window, and so I pulled myself up to sit on it. At that very instant a man in civilian clothes emerged from the shadow of a cedar tree. I had no doubt whatsoever as to his profession. He came up to the window and asked the same question as the young girl at my door: "Is there anything you'd like, comrade?" I said there wasn't, slipped off the sill and lay down on the bed. Even this man in the garden demonstrated that Moscow was in control. Perhaps he was there in the event I jumped out the window, had I chosen that way out of giving a definite answer. He might have blown a whistle and summoned up two more KGB officers on the run. The window was not high, and they could have easily caught me. I doubt whether I'd even have broken a leg.

It was almost six a.m., and at nine the meeting in the Kremlin was to continue. I thought about signing the Soviet ultimatum. I knew it would be signed, and that it would be the logical outcome of the lives of those who signed. Not to sign it would mean beginning an entirely different life. Would I be up to it? I felt that I would like to try. The real consequences of all my political endeavors, including this most recent stage of reform communism, had been catastrophic. Good intentions meant nothing; Dante had known, after all, that they merely paved the road to hell. I decided not to sign the protocol. Then, overcome by weariness, I fell asleep.

After nine o'clock, we all met in the Kremlin again. I announced my decision not to sign the protocol to Černík, and also to Bilak as a representative of the pro-Moscow group. I wanted them all to know. I suggested a conciliatory way of doing it: I would go to the president's physician, whom I knew personally, pretend to be sick and simply not turn up at the final session. To attend and not sign the protocol would certainly have provoked a fury, which I wanted to avoid, nor did I want to put pressure on the others who had already decided. I simply did not want to sign. Bilak said something to the effect that I could do what I wanted but he did not welcome my decision, and he looked gloomy and reproachful. Černík brought Špaček over, and we began to discuss my decision. Then I spoke separately with Smrkovský and Šimon. The result of these talks was that I finally reversed my decision. Why?

All four told me that they had gone through the same phase themselves. In their case, it had been when they went from being prisoners to being government delegates, and they were persuaded by the same feeling—that they were no longer in a position to make responsible decisions. And yet in the end they changed their minds. They saw that this was only a personal solution and that it did nothing to alter the political situation for which they themselves bore responsibility. On the contrary, my arguments the day before had strengthened their conviction that compromise was not hopeless, and that it was still possible to create in Czechoslovakia a better and more promising situation than the Hungarians had been able to do after the intervention in Budapest in 1956. Naturally, they said, it was my own decision, but I had to realize that in rejecting the protocol I would be settling the matter only for myself and my own conscience and would be doing nothing for future political possibilities. If I were to leave the party leadership now, it would make it more difficult for them and jeopardize a great deal that might still be salvaged. Moreover, I would put them all in a bad light by making their signing of the protocol look like a betrayal of personal honor and conscience and not a fulfillment of their duty to seek a political solution. At the same time, I learned that Dubček would be taking part in the final negotiations and would be insisting only on a few as yet unsettled changes in the text, mainly concerning the withdrawal of the troops from Czechoslovakia.

I was standing among the others again, no longer alone with myself and my past life as I had been the night before; I was playing my role again, and once more my brain began functioning like a programmed computer. And quite unrelated to that, I had to admit in my heart of hearts that one of the basic arguments was valid: I too bore political responsibility for everything that had happened, and not to try and find a way out of the situation now meant abdicating that responsibility. Thus I discussed once more with those four men the concrete and detailed aspects of the political solution we sought.

When I had finally changed my mind and agreed to sign the protocol along with the others, I saw the possible political future in approximately the following terms. The protocol, no matter what further adjustments were made, gave Moscow a clear political advantage and the possibility of bringing systematic pressure to bear on the reform politics of the CPC. At the same time, however, it gave us a number of opportunities to preserve some leeway for these policies. In the end, the outcome would not be decided by the words of the protocol anyway, but by the ratio of forces both in Czechoslovakia and Moscow. After returning to Prague the most important and powerful political positions would remain in the hands of reformers. Moreover, the tremendous strength of the nationwide resistance to the occupation would weaken the position of the pro-Moscow group in the entire power structure from top to bottom, despite the fact that the protocol was expressly designed to protect them. It would still be possible to push them into less important positions than their present ones. The most crucial factor would be to achieve the departure of the troops at the very latest by the end of the year, except for a small number of soldiers Moscow had been trying for two years to have posted in Czechoslovakia, something it would now be impossible to prevent. In the same period, it would be necessary to reconvene the Fourteenth Congress and elect a new Central Committee. Both these aims were feasible, we felt, because of the enormous international reaction condemning the occupation and Moscow's consequent interest in cooling things down. On the whole, it was probable that the "hawks" in the Moscow politburo were now on the defensive.

All of this was possible, but by no means inevitable. If by the end of the year it was clear that things were developing otherwise, and it proved impossible to maintain the reform politics, there would be only one thing left to do: the reform leadership would have to relinquish their posts to chosen successors and thus forestall the "revolutionary workers' and peasants' government" from taking power after all and the party leadership from becoming a direct agent of Soviet power. Moscow would agree to such a change because it would mean getting rid of Dubček; and Bilak and Indra had fallen so short in Soviet eyes that a "third group" in power would be acceptable to them. This group, through a process of "Kadarization," would bridge the gap for several years, after which time it would be possible to move into a new period of reform. For this to work, the party cadres that had developed over the years in the spirit of reform would have to be preserved, otherwise a sectarian clique acting as Soviet agents could take over the leadership and destroy any future potential for democratic development in the very heart of the party.

The success of such a scenario would, I felt, depend almost literally on the indivisibility of the reform group around Dubček. And that was what we promised each other at the time. I never had any illusions about the durability of human relationships in the party leadership. It had always been full of intrigue: only a few years ago they were murdering each other; a mere six days ago one part of the leadership had been arrested in the name of the other. But now one part of the Dubček leadership had lived through so much together during those days that I believed it would be possible, even in that particular political circle, to establish some more lasting relationships based on personal confidence, honor, conscience, and solemn promises. Two months later, this too would prove to be just another illusion. And equally illusory was the hope that the Kremlin would settle for anything less than a complete, although gradual, realization of its original aims.

Given that we honestly felt as though we were being held hostage by gangsters, how could we seriously have thought the Kremlin was interested in merely smoothing things over in Czechoslovakia and not in the ultimate and utter elimination of all displeasing political forces? Perhaps there are only two answers: first, wishful thinking; and second, we were still believing Communists, our reform ideas notwithstanding. This, or course, is only an explanation and does not, either politically or morally, justify it.

When I informed the rest, sometime around noon, of my decision to sign the protocol after all, Oldřich Černík embraced me with undisguised and genuine delight. But such delight was very probably selfish. There was no one left in the leadership who differed from him and who could one day say: I did not sign it. His delight was premature, however, for it was soon clouded by František Kriegel.

We had already raised, on the day before, the issue of Kriegel's absence. The Soviet side had made various excuses and, in conversations with us individually, tried to isolate Kriegel from the rest of us. But now, when the document was to be signed, the matter could be put off no longer, and so they brought Kriegel to the Kremlin. First, Smrkovský met with him in another room, and then in the afternoon Kriegel joined us. The situation was demeaning for him and shameful for all the rest of us. Whatever the reasons or excuses, the fact was that we had all gone ahead without Kriegel, and now we were presenting him with a *fait accompli*: there was nothing left to do but sign the protocol. František Kriegel categorically refused. Of course, we had all been through this ourselves, and he was still in the initial phase of things, just as we had been yesterday. The difference was that Kriegel never advanced to the next phase and held fast to his original refusal.

We all tried to persuade him to change his mind. Ludvík Svoboda repeated his performance from the day before and shouted at him so vehemently that Kriegel eventually objected, and Svoboda fell silent. I remember Kriegel saying, "What can they do to me? Send me to Siberia or have me shot. I don't doubt that they will, but I still won't sign." He scarcely listened to our political justifications for the compromise, and he refused to take part in any discussion of them. At that moment he was not a politician but simply a man being threatened with death by bandits who were not demanding his money as ransom but his honor, his children, or his wife. And that man replies, "No! Go ahead and kill me!" I think that Kriegel, who had been in solitary confinement for the past few days, had concluded that he was doomed, and he had come to terms with it. He therefore had no reason to mar his final hours with an act that went against his conscience.

I am not mentioning this to minimize the political significance of Kriegel's refusal in any way. The fact of the matter is that we were genuinely being blackmailed by gangsters and to behave as a politician deliberating with other politicians over political problems and not simply as a man, as Kriegel had done, proved to be folly. František Kriegel then said he would not be a party to any negotiations with the Soviet politburo and allowed himself to be led away again. But an initiative came from the Soviet side to have him present at the negotiations, for whoever was stage-managing the whole affair evidently wanted to have an open breach between the rest of us and Kriegel in front of the Soviet politburo. Dubček, however, resolutely refused to let this happen, and the meeting took place without Kriegel. For the sake of symmetry, Indra was not there either. And so at last, with Dubček this time, we sat down on one side of the huge conference table, with the Soviet politburo on the other.

The meeting began in the late afternoon, and Brezhnev opened the proceedings. In a shamelessly jovial tone, he uttered the standard clichés about comradely relations and common interests that would now form the basis for our agreement on what steps to take next in this complex and serious situation. He spoke about how the Soviet politburo had decided to intervene militarily only with great pain and regret, but that it was unavoidable because the interests of socialism were paramount. He praised the statesmanlike wisdom of Ludvík Svoboda, a faithful friend of the Soviet Union and hero of the Second World War. He professed his great love for Czechoslovakia and was visibly moved by his own rhetoric.

According to the plan, the Czechoslovak side was expected to respond in kind, and then the proposed agreement would be dealt with paragraph by paragraph. Dubček's condition was still very bad, and the doctors had prepared him for the meeting with some injections; therefore, Černík made the opening remarks for the Czech side. On the whole, he spoke concretely, avoiding any empty phrases about comradely relationships and eternal friendship. Very circumspectly, he defended the Action Program and, between the lines, rejected the notion that the military intervention was in the interests of socialism.

Someone from the Soviet politburo reacted to his speech with a provocative remark, and then Brezhnev intervened with a rejection of one of Černík's points. There was a moment or so of tense silence, then Černík finished and Dubček asked to speak—or perhaps he simply began talking, ignoring the procedural formalities. At first, he stammered and slurred his words, but after a few sentences he gradually found his tongue and delivered his speech in fluent Russian. It was an inspired, emotional defense of the "revival process" in Czechoslovakia and it ever more clearly grew into a polemic and an indictment of the interveners. Dubček's speech was improvised; he simply said what he thought, and thus it was more effective both in form and content.

Brezhnev immediately launched into a counteroffensive—also improvised—against Dubček. It was perhaps the only truly interesting speech from the Soviet side during the entire course of the negotiations, for Brezhnev too said what he really thought. He gave concise and intelligible answers to three basic questions: what bothered Moscow most about the Prague Spring; how Moscow regards the sovereignty of the states in its own bloc; and what it considers important in international politics.

Brezhnev did not waste any time on a long official speech about the "counter-revolutionary forces" or the "interests of socialism," but directly blamed Dubček for conducting domestic politics without seeking his, Brezhnev's, prior approval, and even sometimes literally refusing to listen to his suggestions and advice. "From the outset, I wanted to help you out against Novotný," Brezhnev said to Dubček, "and immediately in January I asked you: Are his people threatening you? Do you want to replace them? Do you want to replace the minister of the interior? And the minister of national defense? And is there anyone else you want to replace? But you said no, they're good comrades. And then suddenly I hear that you've replaced the minister of the interior, of national defense, and other ministers, and that you replaced secretaries of the Central Committee.

"In February, I told you what I thought of your speech," Brezhnev continued, "and I pointed out that some of your formulations were incorrect. But even so you didn't change them! Is that any way to do things? Here, even I myself give my speeches to all the members of the politburo in advance for their comments. Isn't that right, comrades?" Brezhnev asked, turning to look at the entire politburo sitting in a row beside him, and with nodding heads and murmurs of agreement they confirmed the truth of the boss's statement. "You see, we have a collective leadership here," continued the speaker, "and that means you have to submit your opinions to the approval of the others."

Brezhnev was personally and sincerely angered that Dubček had betrayed his trust by not having every step he took approved beforehand in the Kremlin. "I believed in you, and I stood up for you against the others," he told Dubček reproachfully. "Our Sasha is a good comrade, I said. And you disappointed us all so terribly." At moments like this Brezhnev's voice would quiver with regret and he spoke haltingly, as though he were close to tears. The impression he made was that of a deeply wronged patriarch who fully believed it was entirely natural and proper that his position as head of the family entitled him to the unconditional subservience and obedience of all its members, for his opinion and his will were, after all, the natural and final authority, and, in any case, he was only thinking of the best interests of all the family. The notion that things could, or even should, be any different was inherently alien to him and quite naturally he saw in it an expression of hostility and betrayal.

According to Brezhnev, all the other sins followed from this main transgression—that Prague did not seek the approval of the Kremlin for everything it did. "Antisocialist tendencies" were rife, the press wrote what it liked, "counter-revolutionary organizations" were formed, and the party leadership was under pressure from these forces, to which it continually gave ground. If Dubček had only acted with Brezhnev's approval or on his advice, if he had cut from his speeches the words and passages Brezhnev had suggested, and if he had appointed the ministers and secretaries Brezhnev had agreed to, none of those horrors could have happened. That, in a nutshell, was Brezhnev's view of the Prague Spring.

Then Brezhnev explained to Dubček that the end result of all this was Moscow's realization that the Dubček leadership could not be depended upon. Even he himself, who had long defended "our Sasha," had to admit that this was so. Because, at this stage, matters of the utmost importance were involved: the results of the Second World War.

Brezhnev spoke at length about the sacrifices of the Soviet Union in the Second World War: the soldiers fallen in battle, the civilians slaughtered, the enormous material losses, the hardships suffered by the Soviet people. At such a cost, the Soviet Union had gained security, and the guarantee of that security was the postwar division of Europe and, specifically, the fact that Czechoslovakia was linked with the Soviet Union, "forever." According to Brezhnev, this was a logical and justifiable result of the fact that thousands of Soviet soldiers sacrificed their lives for Czechoslovak freedom as well, and Czechs and Slovaks should therefore honor their graves, not defile them. Our western borders were not only our own borders, but the common borders of the "socialist camp." The Soviet politburo had no right to allow the results of that war to be jeopardized, for it had no right to dishonor the sacrifices of the Soviet people.

Brezhnev admitted that now, after the military intervention, the situation in Czechoslovakia would be difficult, for people would look at things emotionally. Even Dubček's party leadership could be taken to task for not yet seeing things in the proper light. "Today it might seem impossible for you to accept it all," said Brezhnev. "But look at Gomulka. In 1956, he too was against Soviet military assistance, just as you are. But if I were to tell him today that I was about to withdraw the Soviet army from Poland, Gomulka would jump into a special plane and fly here to plead with me not to do it."

Brezhnev never did produce any proof that the "western imperialists" were posing a genuine threat to Czechoslovakia. He did not trot out any of the official lies that filled the Soviet press at the time, to the effect that the "western revanchists" were on the point of preparing an invasion, that there were American officers among the crowds of tourists in Prague, etc. Brezhnev's logic was simple: We in the Kremlin came to the conclusion that we could not depend on you any longer. You do what you feel like in domestic politics, even things that displease us, and you are not open to positive suggestions. But your country lies on territory where the Soviet soldier trod in the Second World War. We bought that territory at the cost of enormous sacrifices, and we shall never leave it. The borders of that area are our borders as well. Because you do not listen to us, we feel threatened. In the name of the dead in World War Two who laid down their lives for your freedom as well, we are therefore fully justified in sending our soldiers into your country, so that we may feel truly secure within our common borders. It is immaterial whether anyone is actually threatening us or not: it is a matter of principle, independent of external circumstances. And that is how it will be, from the Second World War until "eternity."

Brezhnev pretended to be almost astonished: it was so simple, how could we fail to understand? Words like "sovereignty" and "national independence" did not come up in his speech at all, nor did any of the other clichés that officially justify the "mutual interests of the socialist countries." There was only one simple idea behind everything he said: during the war our soldiers fought their way to the Elbe, and that is where our real Western borders are today.

"For us," Brezhnev went on, "the results of the Second World War are inviolable, and we will defend them even at the cost of risking a new war." And then he said in so many words that they would have undertaken the military intervention in Czechoslovakia even if such a risk had existed. But, he added, there was no such danger. "I asked President Johnson if the American government still fully recognizes the results of the Yalta and Potsdam conferences. And on August 18 I received the reply: as far as Czechoslovakia and Rumania are concerned, it recognizes them without reservation; in the case of Yugoslavia, it would have to be discussed. So what do you think will be done on your behalf? Nothing. There will be no war. Comrade Tito and Comrade Ceauşescu will say their piece, and so will comrade Berlinguer. Well, and what of it? You are counting on the Communist movement in Western Europe, but that won't amount to anything for fifty years."

Once again, his words were very much to the point. Brezhnev was giving us reform Communists a truly invaluable lesson: here we were thinking about a model of socialism for the whole of Europe, and he, the realist, knew that it wouldn't mean a thing for fifty years. Why? Because the borders of socialism, which is to say the borders of the Soviet Union, are for the time being at the Elbe. Even the American president concurred, so that for the next fifty years things will likely continue unchanged. What does a Berlinguer amount to? Does he have any tanks? Can he alter the results of the Second World War?

Brezhnev obviously expected that after such a clear and logical exposition even Dubček would understand the situation he was in, and the protocol, which was to be ceremonially signed, could be discussed. But that did not happen; rather, Dubček began arguing with him. I cannot recall what his exact words were or what points he opposed, but Brezhnev consequently lost all self-control and exploded at Dubček, his face flushed red. At last, he declared angrily: "All the discussions so far have clearly been pointless. It's all just a repetition of Čierná nad Tisou. It's useless, it's getting us nowhere, and therefore," he said, "we are breaking off discussions."

Brezhnev, and with him the entire membership of the Soviet polit-buro, stood up and prepared to walk out. In the ensuing confusion, Ludvík Svoboda began to speak in an attempt to calm the storm. Brezhnev stopped, listened to what he had to say, and then turned again to the exit, saying only that the next step would have to be de-cided upon. Then he walked out, followed by the entire Soviet "col-lective leadership," which left the room behind him like a line of geese.

To this day, I am not certain that this incident took place entirely spontaneously. At the time, it impressed me as a theatrical trick. Brezhnev's reaction and his command to leave the room were quite exaggerated. And if I genuinely cannot recall Dubček's words that apparently so enraged him, they could not have been so provocative, at least no more so than what he'd said already. The subsequent pro-ceedings would seem to confirm my impression that it was a planned move by the Soviet politburo, intended to establish the proper atmo-sphere for approving the protocol, an atmosphere in which the Czech reformists would be on their guard and keep their inapposite remarks to a minimum. But whatever the real reasons for that scene, it caused panic in the room.

Dubček almost collapsed. He was trembling and talked nervously and almost incoherently. The doctors appeared and prepared to give him some injections, but Dubček fended them off, saying he wanted nothing. Suddenly, to everyone's horror, he declared: "I won't sign it then! Let them do what they want, I won't sign it." Some, including Černík, Svoboda and Smrkovský, rushed over to him and all began talking at once to persuade him that he couldn't refuse to sign it now, that there was nothing to be done. I too thought that the negotiations could no longer be turned around in this way, and, moreover, I was convinced that this sudden change of mind was transitory. I spoke with him briefly and told him so. All of us took turns trying to per-suade him to reconsider so the talks could continue. Dubček listened to us, offered no resistance, but stood firm. To all my arguments he merely replied: "Look at them. They have no idea what they've done," and then he repeated, "I won't sign it."

It was Dubček's most clear-headed moment. Perhaps if he had taken part in our meeting the night before and advocated the same position, he might have had a substantial influence on the course of the talks. Now, of course, it was too late. Finally he allowed himself to be given a tranquilizing injection, and, in a second round of exhorta-tions, he finally succumbed.

Meanwhile, there was feverish activity on both sides to try and get the talks started again. Svoboda and Černík, and others from the reform wing, as well as Bilak and Jakeš went into some kind of antechamber where Suslov, Ponomarev, and perhaps some of the others appeared. Svoboda was at last received by Brezhnev, and they worked something out together. This entire incident interrupted the talks for about an hour. When they got under way again, it was already late in the evening.

From this point on, the talks were not very dramatic. The text of the protocol was examined paragraph by paragraph, and in general the Soviet side was more yielding than before. I can't recall precisely everything that was changed in this final phase, but two important formulations were reached: on the departure of the troops after their "temporary" stationing on Czechoslovak soil, contingent upon the progress of "normalization"; and second, on Soviet support for the line expressed in the January and May plenary sessions of the CPC Central Committee. As in Bratislava, Brezhnev rejected on stylistic grounds any suggestion that "January" and "May" be separated by a hyphen rather than an "and." This time, however, he did explain, in the end, that it was the inclusion by implication of the April plenum, where the Action Program was approved, that he opposed. The Soviet politburo considered several formulations in the Action Program incorrect, and, therefore, it would not sign anything implying agreement with it. And, in any case, he said, it must be clear even to us that certain things in the program need changing. The Soviet politburo, on the other hand, expressly supported the May resolution, because—even though it not only recognized the Action Program as correct but also declared it to be the basic party line—it also made concrete references to forces inimical to socialism. The Soviets won their point and thus the Moscow Protocol contained no expressly stated approval of the Action Program.

Sometime around midnight, it was all completed and the moment of signing came. Suddenly a huge door flew open and about ten photographers and cameramen stampeded into the room. As if on command, the entire Soviet politburo simultaneously rose to its feet, and each of them leaned across the table to the Czechoslovak opposite with arms wide, ready to embrace him. It was an absurd scene that the photographers flashguns illuminated: dozens of arms belonging to the Soviet politburo stretched and waved across the table in a row, and I suddenly imagined that a fantastic carniverous plant was trying to entrap us in its sticky tendrils. Instead of standing up and making a reciprocal gesture, I pushed my legs against the trestle of the conference table, and my chair went skidding backwards over the polished parquet flooring towards the wall about three meters behind me. I came to rest beside Ambassador Koucký, who was sitting by the wall along with those for whom there was no room at the table. Koucký had an expression of undisguised alarm, and he hissed at me under his breath: "Have you gone mad?" I admitted that was possible but the main thing was that I didn't want to hug anyone, that I simply couldn't bring myself to do it. Meanwhile, the act of collective embracing had been completed and filmed and photographed.

Then the main representatives of both sides were immortalized as they signed the protocol, after which the photographers and cameramen were ushered out of the room as abruptly as they had been admitted, and the doors closed behind them. Then I heard Podgorny's voice across the table suddenly say, "And Comrade Mlynář is not going to sign?" So he had noticed my escape; indeed he could scarcely have missed it, since I was sitting directly across from him, and it was entirely possible that his embrace had been aimed at me. The others, who had not yet noticed anything amiss, suddenly began looking around to see what the matter with me was. I said I would sign, then stood up and added my own signature to the death sentence for democartic communist reform in Czechoslovakia.

After every suspenseful activity—whether it be tragedy or comedy—there is a sense of relief, but ours was shortlived, quickly reminding us of our situation, which belonged more properly to a gangster novel, though the setting was very civilized.

When the logistics of our departure for Prague were being discussed, someone remarked that František Kriegel had to be brought to the Kremlin so that he could fly back with our delegation. Brezhnev himself replied that it would perhaps be better if Kriegel were not to fly back to Prague with the delegation. "Leave him here for now," Brezhnev said. "He didn't sign the protocol, and he'll make trouble for you." Dubček, and perhaps Svoboda, reacted quite sharply to this and insisted that the delegation would return to Prague in its entirety and that it could not leave without Kriegel. Brezhnev, however, continued to insist and went on about how Kriegel would sabotage the protocol, how he would flaunt the fact that he had not signed it and organize opposition to the "consolidation effort."

Behind all this, there seemed to be a scenario that even Brezhnev was sticking to. Suddenly we all realized that Kriegel was in fact still under arrest, that he was merely a hostage and not a delegate/hostage as we were. Brezhnev himself spoke of Kriegel as though he were unrelated to us. Ludvík Svoboda said that after the return to Prague he would arrange for František Kriegel and his wife to stay in Lany. Brezhnev understood this as an offer to have Kriegel locked up in some fancy prison and remarked: "But he'll escape! Which of you can act as a guarantor for him?" In other words, it was not a ransom the gang leader required, but a personal guarantor, just like in the detective stories. Quite spontaneously, Špaček, Šimon, and I all offered to provide the guarantee. But this was not enough, and private negotiations were necessary. Dubček, Svoboda, Černík, and Smrkovský went into the next room with the leadership of the Soviet politburo. As far as I can recall, even Jakeš—probably through contacts that led right up to the police sector of the group in charge of stage-managing the whole affair—tried to gain Kriegel's release. The result was a shameful agreement that was once again demeaning to Kriegel: the prisoner would be delivered directly to the airport; he would not be allowed back inside the Kremlin.

After all this, the Kremlin potentates now suggested an informal, friendly gathering before we returned to Prague. Jovial behavior and Kosygin do not particularly go together, but he nonetheless began to make jokes and referred to an old Russian custom whereby intimate guests are not allowed to leave until they have sat down together and drunk a glass in parting. This brought to mind something I'd read about a custom among a Mongolian tribe concerning especially dear prisoners: they would pierce the soles of the prisoners' feet with horsehair—after healing, this was quite unnoticeable to the prisoners, until they tried to get up and run away. Seeing that the custom evoked by Kosygin for detaining guests was far more humane, we all sat down with our hosts.

The gathering lasted about an hour, and small conversation groups formed of two or three. It was certainly not uninteresting. Kosygin approached me and after some light conversation asked whether I thought it was realistic to expect the fulfillment of the protocol, where I saw potential problems, and what my view was of certain people in the leadership. The conversation gradually focused on this last point, and I realized that this was Kosygin's way of probing my real attitude. It was simpler and more reliable than a conversation on political ideology. What I thought about "socialism with a human face" was not as revealing as what I thought about Černík, Husák, or Indra.

I told Kosygin very openly that in my opinion it would be disastrous for the future if the Moscow politburo were to depend mostly on those who were connected with the "revolutionary government" in August—and I named Bilak and Indra. "Oh, those people," said Kosygin, waving his hand contemptuously. And then he began to lavish praises on Husák. Perhaps he was trying to make it easier for me to discern which way the wind was blowing in the Kremlin. He in no way disputed my point that the main problem now would be to avoid extremes on both ends of the spectrum. I told him in so many words that Kriegel, Císař, Pavel, Hájek, and others could only be dropped if those on the other side, who had been utterly compromised in August, were to go as well. I got the impression that Kosygin was banking on a rapid defusing of the whole situation, and that therefore his view was consistent with how we saw the possible compromise working.

The next day, however, when we were already back in Prague, I learned from Dubček that Brezhnev had demanded of him, as a condition for any further good relations, that Vasil Bilak and Alois Indra keep their party functions.

Brezhnev and other members of the Soviet politburo accompanied us to the airport, where another official farewell took place, also immortalized by the cameras. František Kriegel was sitting in the waiting aircraft as promised. About two A.M. Moscow time on August 27, the plane took off. Once again, we all sat silently, as we had on the way there, but this time it was for different reasons. Now we were all wondering how the people at home would react to the "Moscow protocol." And I don't think any of us had many rosy illusions about that.

The main roles that each of us would play upon arrival were already assigned. Svoboda would be the first to speak publicly, to be followed by Dubček. Černík would meet that morning with the government, and Smrkovský would speak to parliament. Immediately on arrival, Dubček would meet with the Vysočany presidium of the Central Committee: but because he was to speak to the nation as close to noon as possible, he had to have a speech ready. And so once again, as before August 20, Mlynář and Šimon were assigned the task. We wrote the speech in the aircraft, because those two hours were very probably the quietest we could expect for a while.

I think it was by far the most important speech I had ever written. Dubček then made changes in it, some on paper beforehand but most impromptu, as he was delivering it. It was that famous speech in which, apart from the actual words spoken, most of the political impact came from the tears that Dubček barely managed to hold back. With this speech, Dubček achieved what all of us, in the depths of our souls, feared was impossible: that the nation would believe once again that all was not lost, that there was still hope, and that Dubček was the man who could fulfill it.

EPILOGUE

Events in the fall of 1968 went according to my expectations for little more than a month. At the beginning of October, I began to realize that those expectations were in fact illusions and that things would develop otherwise. The first serious signs of the inevitable disintegration of the Dubček leadership began to appear, precisely among those people whose solidarity was absolutly essential if there was to be any hope at all of realizing the new political line, which was now being applied in the context of a compromise heavily loaded in Moscow's favor.

The only achievement so far had been the admission on August 31, 1968, of a number of new members into the presidium, among them seven who had been elected to the Vysočany presidium. At the same time, with the exception of František Kriegel, all those who had originally been arrested and dragged off to Moscow were on the new presidium; and, on the other side, of the four who voted against condemning the Soviet intervention on August 20, only one, Vasil Bilak, remained in his original position, and that was at Brezhnev's express demand. Alois Indra, for the same reason, was not removed from his secretarial post, but he had not yet returned to Prague and was presumed to be lying ill in a Moscow hospital; it was clear that his political future would be decided later. Piller, Lenart, and Barbírek, who had agreed to become members of the "revolutionary workers' and peasants' government," remained in the party leadership as well. But all of these people together formed only a tiny minority in the 24-member presidium. Of course, Husák and Svoboda were also members now as well.

In September 1968, an emissary from Moscow, then deputy minister of foreign affairs, W. Kuznetsov, arrived in Prague. He had been invested with considerable powers by the CPSU, and he set about his work immediately. He held individual talks with the members of the party leadership, determined what the situation was, took note of all the personal conflicts that emerged in these meetings, and then very cleverly cultivated and encouraged them. From my conversation with him and from what I know of how he dealt with the others, I concluded that his main mission was to recommend to Moscow which members of the leadership should be supported, and which, on the contrary, should be dropped without further delay. He always began these talks by praising his interlocutor personally. For example, at the very beginning of his talk with me, he conveyed the personal greetings of Leonid Brezhnev and said that comrade Brezhnev had thought highly of the article I had written at the time for *Rudé právo*. With Josef Špaček, he assured him that his arrest on August 20 had been a complete mistake, that the comrades in Moscow regretted it and that he, Špaček, enjoyed the full confidence of the Kremlin. Then, in a free and apparently open-minded discussion, Kuznetsov would determine what the person's attitudes were towards various specific questions concerning the interpretation of the Moscow Protocol. At the same time, many of his questions and his apparently personal opinions were formulated very provocatively. And, finally, he would subtly steer the conversation towards personalities: how we personally viewed the various members of the leadership, from Dubček to Indra.

It was probably my opinion on the future of Alois Indra that got me classified as one of those who would definitely have to go. Kuznetsov asked me what I thought "should be done" with Indra. I replied that Indra was, after all, still in Moscow, so there wasn't much of a problem, because as far as I was concerned they could leave him there. Kuznetsov's face, which was never very pleasant at the best of times, froze. Perhaps he understood my remark as a reference to the fate of various Communist functionaries who, in Stalin's time, had never returned from the Kremlin hospital. So I added that I meant Indra could remain in Moscow, for example, as a representative of Comecon, because, as I explained, his role in August, in my opinion, ruled out his return to political life in Prague. I said that I had already discussed this with Kosygin in the Kremlin, and he had in fact accepted my viewpoint. At this point, even the veneer of civility between us had gone, and we soon parted.

I think it was Oldřich Černík who, during his conversations with Kuznetsov, and later during his visits alone to Moscow, was the first to compromise his pledge of solidarity with the leadership. In September, Černík was already beginning to trade off his allegiance to Dubček, Smrkovský, and the others for the hope that Moscow would back him in any eventual power shuffle. For this hope, he sold me out, then Smrkovský, and ultimately Dubček. He formed an alliance with Štrougal, who was his personal friend, and then with Husák and Svoboda, and he was very probably hoping to become first secretary of the party after Dubček. When Dubček was compelled to resign as first secretary under pressure from Moscow in April 1969, he even recommended Černík as his successor, since the last thing Dubček wanted was for Husák to replace him. Dubček was afraid, and rightly so as it turned out, that Husák's unbridled ambition, his thirst for power, and other qualities would be even more catastrophic for the party than what it had already suffered. Černík, despite his weakness of character, did provide a certain guarantee that the rational and pragmatic conception of "normalization" would not surrender entirely to the unbridled fury of the Stalinist riff-raff of the party, which had been deprived of power under Novotný.

During his talks in Moscow, Černík retreated on everything the party leadership had agreed to insist on in the Moscow Protocol, a prime example being the complete withdrawal of the troops. Černík was the first to acquiesce to Moscow on the terms that were ultimately entrenched in the treaty signed in October 1968, which in fact legalized the presence of about 100,000 Soviet soldiers on Czechoslovak territory for a quite unspecified length of time.

By such conduct, Oldřich Černík managed to remain prime minister until January 1970. He survived by several months not only the fall of Dubček, but also the expulsion from the Central Committee of everyone he had embraced in the Kremlin in August 1968 with warm assurances of lasting solidarity. In the end, however, he too was sacrificed, and his personal friend, Lubomír Štrougal, took his place. But before this, Černík publicly denounced the democratic reforms of 1968 and his own role in them. He was the only one of those who were to have been tried by the "revolutionary tribunal" in August 1968 to do so. After his own expulsion from the party in the spring of 1970, he had a moment of lucidity again and in a personal conversation with me said very simply: "I blew both my position and my honor."

Alexander Dubček also relied too heavily after September 1968 on cabinet politics and a personal agreement with Brezhnev to gain Moscow's support and save his position. He did not understand that he was the one Moscow was chiefly interested in removing, that the Kremlin was playing a game, begun with Kuznetsov and continued through other means as well, the whole point of which was to replace him. In January 1969, I tried for the last time to convince him of what was happening. He refused to see it and said that, on the contrary, he had already come out on top in Moscow and that the troops would leave too, as soon as he had managed to persuade Brezhnev he had the situation firmly in hand. "If some reporters and other people who simply don't understand that they are unacceptable to Moscow wouldn't keep spoiling things for me," Dubček said at the time, "I would have been able to arrange an agreement long before this." That was the day after Jan Palach had immolated himself in Prague in protest against the gradual capitulation to the occupiers. Dubček seriously believed that his private meetings with Brezhnev in Moscow or hunting wild boars in Kiev were of decisive importance.

About a week before our discussion, Smrkovský had been compelled to resign as chairman of the National Assembly by pressure from Moscow, executed mainly by Husák. Dubček was still first secretary, but the people in the leadership closest to him had been reduced to Černík, Husák, Štrougal, and Svoboda. Among the Central Committee secretaries, there was only one remaining reformer, Josef Špaček. Otherwise, the only secretaries left were Bilak, Indra, Lenárt, and Josef Kempný, who was quite simply one of Černík's men. All that Moscow had to do now was unseat Dubček, and yet at that moment Dubček believed that he had come out on top! I can't explain it to this day. Most probably, everyone lied to Dubček's face, including Brezhnev. But even so, how could he have believed it?

Dubček had written me off long before this, during talks in Moscow on October 4, 1968. Originally a four-member delegation had been approved to go to this meeting: Dubček, Černík, Husák, and myself. They even entrusted me with the preparation of documents for discussion, which I did, but just before we were to fly to Moscow, Dubček told me I was withdrawn from the delegation, explaining that Brezhnev only wanted a three-member delegation, to correspond to the three members on the Soviet side. Naturally, I didn't take the excuse seriously; I knew I had been withdrawn for other reasons, at the request either of Brezhnev or of Husák and Černík, or perhaps of all three. The Dubček-Černík-Husák trio then returned from Moscow having made additional capitulations beyond the original Moscow Protocol. The delegation accepted the stationing of Soviet troops in

Czechoslovakia for an indefinite period, agreed to postpone the party congress for an indefinite period, and took note of the Soviet politburo's view that the Action Program was, in effect, incorrect.

Dubček did not tell me he had sold me out in Moscow until several weeks later. But it was clear as soon as the delegation returned from Moscow. I spoke privately with Dubček about the fact that the increasing pressure from Moscow was intended to remove eventually all the reformers from the leadership, and that it was therefore time to consider an alternative solution: he and his people should resign in favor of those who would undertake to preserve a minimum of the conditions for reform and forestall an offensive from the Stalinist riffraff and Soviet agents in the party. Bilak, for example, made no secret of the fact that he felt the CPC should have only about a half of its present members to be a truly "Leninist party." At the time, I saw only one possible way to prevent Bilak, Indra, Jakeš, and all those around the "revolutionary workers' and peasants' government" from gaining control of the situation: by opposing them with a new ruling clique. I was thinking specifically of Černík as head of the party and Štrougal as head of the government. These people were not associated with Dubček, Smrkovský, Špaček, Šimon, and myself but rather with the more rational, pragmatic forces in the party, state, and economic apparatus, and thus they could keep Husák in Bratislava, gain the support of Moscow, and keep the Stalinist rabble on a tight leash. It would mean that political reforms would have to be buried for several years, but then, through a somewhat transformed "Kadarization," things could gradually begin developing in roughly the same direction again.

Dubček disagreed with me. His view of the situation was not so dark, either as a whole or as it concerned himself personally. But he did not try to dissuade me from resigning, and from this I deduced that my resignation had probably been discussed in the Kremlin. So I took a two-week vacation; I left Prague, slept for a few days, and then in the fresh air of the woods I pondered the situation. Still, I could come up with no new ideas for what could be done. In signing the Moscow Protocol and accepting the "normalization of conditions" as the official line, we renounced the nationwide democratic movement. In fact, since its return to Prague at the end of August, the Dubček leadership had sought to pacify and sublimate this movement so it would not provoke a new wave of indignation in Moscow and new pressures to expedite the "normalization" process. Popular support could only be tapped by the party leadership in the form of a silent contract, whereby the nation would understand that a great deal was being sacrificed, but only so that strength could be conserved for the future.

In regard to the essential task of conserving these forces for the future, I saw no other course except the one I discussed with Dubček. If we did not proceed accordingly, Moscow would pursue its attack until Dubček and his people were unseated anyway. But to achieve this, they might well mobilize the forces that the party had swept from the scene during the sixties, and thus everything built in the spirit of reform in more than ten years would be utterly wiped out, and a party would emerge in the image of Vasil Bilak. I decided, therefore, to make one more effort to prevail upon Dubček and the others. If I failed, I would resign from all my positions, since I could no longer influence developments by staying on. I couldn't expect to hold onto my posts for more than a few weeks or months anyway. And staying on could only harm the future of reforms.

I returned to Prague at the end of October and talked the matter over with Smrkovský, Špaček, Šimon, and, once again, with Dubček. The first three agreed with me in general, but made their decisions contingent on Dubček's position: without his resignation and the appointment of a new first secretary, their resignations would not have the necessary political impact. Only Bohumil Šimon was inclined to resign alone if necessary. But Dubček's stance remained unchanged. Now, however, in the early days of November, he told me quite explicitly that my resignation would help ease the situation, for they had discussed it in the Kremlin; naturally this would not mean I would cease to have a political role to play: he would continue consulting me, and I would have total access to him and to all the other leadership members. And then he offered me the position of minister of culture.

I told him that I had been offered that position in August at the Soviet embassy, but rejected it. Positions were important to me insofar as they provided me with practical influence on the development of democratic reforms. This was no longer possible, and therefore I said I might as well return to my research work and retire from political office altogether. Dubček accepted my position, and thus we came to terms without difficulty.

My last assignment as secretary of the Central Committee was to prepare, with Josef Špaček, a resolution for endorsement by the plenary session of the Central Committee in November 1968. It was my final attempt to establish a framework within which the reform politics might still be executed. But I no longer believed it was possible. The night before the session of the Central Committee, Dubček (perhaps with Černík and Husák) flew off to Moscow for consultations with Brezhnev. As a result, the passages in our resolution intended to prevent the military intervention from being justified disappeared, and, instead, references appeared to the dangers of "rightwing opportunism" inside the CPC itself. Frankly, however, I no longer cared very much, for I had given up all hope of having any further influence on developments.

On November 16, 1968, the Central Committee accepted my resignation from all my posts in the party leadership. I still remained an ordinary member of the Central Committee, but I actually only participated in one more session—in January 1969. The session began on January 16, the day Jan Palach set himself on fire in Prague. When news of the event reached the meeting, the well-known physician, Dr. Helena Rašková, asked for the floor. She said that she was ashamed of what was being said here, and it occurred to her that Jan Palach had perhaps been driven to make his desperate protest by similar feelings. At this point, she was shouted down by crude yells from the assembly; the Stalinists and Soviet agents in the Central Committee were almost literally barking at her like dogs. Vilém Nový, who later became notorious as a spineless servant of "normalization," immediately followed with a cynical speech on Palach. The death that galvanized the conscience of the entire nation had no effect whatsoever on most of those who were to blame for it.

I experienced the same sudden physical sickness at this session as I did during a meeting of the presidium and the secretariat at which Alois Indra, freshly delivered from Moscow, first showed up. Sitting there with him were all those on whom his "revolutionary tribunal" had meant to pass sentence, with the exception of František Kriegel. And all, including Indra, were behaving as though nothing had happened. Comrade Indra had simply come back. Given this company, one could well imagine party members soon beginning to arrest and perhaps even murder each other again, which might finally persuade the Kremlin that conditions in the CPC were truly back to normal.

This was my last Central Committee meeting; I wasn't present in April, when they elected Gustav Husák as the new party chief, or in September 1969, when they expelled me from that body.

How could I have ever believed that the Prague Spring represented such people's sincere political attitudes? Hadn't I known for more than ten years that Antonín Zápotocký was both a judicious tactician and a man who raised his hand for the death sentence for long-time friends and comrades? These people were no different. In this society, I suppose such behavior really is normal.

Before they expelled me from the Central Committee in September 1969, I was summoned before a presidium commission composed of three people with whom I had sat in the party leadership: Jan Piller, Evžen Erban, and Oldřich Voleník. The meeting began as a friendly conversation among old friends who hadn't seen each other for some time. Then Piller, without further ado, cheerfully read out a proposal of the presidium (which had been led by Husák for some time now): the comrades acknowledged that I had never belonged to the extremists or rightwingers, they even respected this and therefore had all the more reason to hope I would find no difficulty in doing what they required of me. At the upcoming plenary session, I was to take part in the discussion and say two things: that in July 1968 it was incorrect to refuse to meet with the future aggressors in Warsaw, and that back in the summer of 1968 I had already told Smrkovský that his politics changed according to which way the wind was blowing. This was all they asked. If I complied, I could remain a member of the Central Committee. When I asked what would happen if I refused, Piller replied curtly: "Then you can be a member of the Central Committee no longer."

I refused. I told them that I disagreed with the statement about participation in the Warsaw meeting, and as for my alleged statement to Smrkovský, this may have been made but I did not think for a moment it characterized Smrkovský in any way. If we were to sit together once more in the presidium, and I thought that he was not acting correctly, I would say it to him again, but I would say it to his face and not to serve some third party's filthy designs.

To this Piller replied: "You know, I didn't think you'd do it. I like that. It's disgusting now to see how people are changing hats. Císař was just here before you, and I tell you, I felt like vomiting." But Piller was himself, of course, one of those who had changed hats very willingly, if not particularly skillfully. Therefore I told him I was glad to hear that people changing hats made him feel like vomiting, but that it wasn't going to be easy for him from now on. He cut his jovial banter short and quickly brought the meeting to an end. As I learned afterwards, these three later gave the Central Committee a written report in which they wholeheartedly condemned my "rightwing opportunistic activity," which was the reason given for my expulsion from the Central Committee.

Almost all of those who refused to retreat from the political line of the Prague Spring were expelled from the Central Committee along with me, including Josef Smrkovský, whom I was supposed to slander to earn myself another term. Smrkovský, originally a bakery worker, was an old Communist functionary from the pre-Second World War years. He graduated from the Lenin School of the Comintern in Moscow, worked in the underground during the war, and after 1944 was a Central Committee member of the illegal CPC. During the Prague uprising on May 5, 1945, he was vice-president of the Czech National Council, and from then until 1951 a member of the party leadership and deputy minister of agriculture. Between 1951 and 1955 he was unlawfully imprisoned, having received a life sentence. After his rehabilitation in 1963, Novotný brought him back into public political life; he became a minister, a member of Parliament, and in 1966 a Central Committee member. He and Kriegel were the only representatives of the old guard of Communist functionaries in Dubček's leadership, and in a highly expressive way he embodied both their good and bad qualities.

He was a fighting politician, and when he considered a particular position correct, he would defend it obstinately, with a tendency to employ demagogy. He was very quick to grasp the political importance of phenomena and events, and he was also quick to make up his mind. At the same time, his vast experience of life had taught him that a bad decision should not be stubbornly defended and that it was proper to change one's attitude accordingly. In this case, once persuaded, Smrkovský would defend his new position with the same vigor as he had his previous one. To this day, the "normalizers" claim that this demonstrates Smrkovský's lack of character, and they circulate libelous brochures about him with titles like "The Two-faced Politician."

I am convinced that the sometimes quite spectacular reverses in Josef Smrkovský's political positions were never the result of a lack of character. In all critical situations, where not only his career but also his life were on the line, Smrkovský always behaved as a man of staunch character. This was true in his underground activity during the war, it was true in his imprisonment, when he defended himself like very few arrested Communists of the time, and it was still true in August 1968. In such situations, Smrkovský not only did *not* change his point of view, but he defended it tenaciously and with conviction. The Prague Spring for Smrkovský was undeniably the fulfillment of the hopes and the faith of his life, and it was in this knowledge that he served its ideals. It also gave him his last real chance to fulfill himself politically: he was 57 years old, and his health was not good. If, however, today's unscrupulous party careerists have tried to impute careerism as the sole motive force behind his activity, it is one of the basest slanders in the rich repertoire of filthy tactics at their command.

But when the situation was not extreme or critical, Smrkovský could occasionally be indecisive. I have mentioned this once already in connection with the meeting of the party leadership over the "Two Thousand Words" manifesto in June 1968. The incident cited by the Central Committee commission was somewhat similar. When I presented a draft resolution to the presidium for the upcoming Čierná nad Tisou meeting, Smrkovský promised to support me. But then at the meeting he changed his mind. The resolution dealt with the National Front and was designed to ease negotiation with the Soviet politburo. Smrkovský had been persuaded against it by his advisers in radical Communist circles. During a recess, I sat down beside Smrkovský at supper and told him something to the effect that his politics went the way the wind was blowing. I think he felt ashamed that he had gone back on his promise to me, and to defend himself he said something quite embarrassing. "Just look at the popularity charts in the newspapers today," he replied, "I've made it to fifth place already!" I was angry and asked him what he was going to go by when the newspapers could no longer print popularity charts. Smrkovský did not respond and simply went on eating his soup in silence. Those who were sitting close to us overheard the conversation, and I believe Piller was among them.

After 1970, Smrkovský was the first of the expelled party leaders to raise his voice against the politics of "normalization." Dubček, Kriegel, Špaček, Šimon, Slavík, and I were all, each for his own reasons perhaps, completely silent then. And yet surely the point was whether people would submit to the yoke of the old, restored totalitarian dictatorship like cattle going to slaughter, or whether at least some of those who had not so long ago assumed leadership responsibilities would speak up. In September 1971, Smrkovský did speak up: in an interview in the Italian Communist journal, *Vie nuove,* he made the first public statement by someone from the Dubček leadership that was critical of "normalization." Here Smrkovský not only stood firm but once again risked his own neck, as he had done several times before in genuinely grave situations.

Naturally, it made him an authority in the eyes of the entire nation and an object of hatred and harassment of the Husák regime. He remained both things until the end of his life in 1974. Even in death, the regime continued to persecute him: to this day, Smrkovský has no right to a grave in Prague. Soon after he was laid in the family vault, the urn containing his ashes was stolen. The State Security forces then contrived to have the urn found in the toilet of an express-train to Vienna and claimed that Smrkovský was to have been reburied in Austria as a "provocation." True, the police did return the urn to the family, but forbade it to go back to the family plot in Prague to avoid further "provocations." The only other person the Husák regime feared enough to have the body removed from the Prague cemetery was Jan Palach. A regime like Husák's could scarcely bestow a greater honor.

After my expulsion from the Central Committee, I kept my party card for another half a year. In March 1970, precisely 24 years after my membership in the Communist party had begun, I was summoned before Milos Jakeš at the Commission of Supervising and Auditing of the CPC. The largest purges in party history were just getting under way, and they would end with roughly a third of the party members not having their cards renewed. I was in the first wave of expulsions, which was to serve as a model to the other party organs and organizations as to whom to expel from the party and for what reasons. Jakeš himself avoided taking part personally in my expulsion and had O. Mandák, the vice-chairman of the commission, represent him.

What had lasted nearly a quarter of a century was cut short in less than an hour. I did not actually request a membership renewal, on the grounds that I disagreed with the military intervention in August 1968 and with the policies executed by the CPC in the year since then, and because I could no longer fulfill the responsibilities of a party member with conviction. The Communist Party of Czechoslovakia, however, is an organization that you may enter from personal conviction, but one you cannot leave if the leadership does not so desire. And the Husák leadership did not wish me not to have a party card simply because I did not want one, but rather it wished to make my expulsion an exemplary punishment.

Parts of the previously-prepared text justifying my expulsion sounded more like they belonged in an indictment from a political trial of the fifties. I rejected these passages, and it took almost an hour for the commission to strike out or change these parts and write out a new protocol.

After the meeting, I went to the bathroom before leaving the Central Committee building. A moment later, Mandák hurried in, obviously for the same purpose. When he saw me, he stopped, but it was too late. So he stood beside me at the next urinal. "Are we giving you a lot of work?" I asked. "Got three more today," replied Mandák, and again we stood there silently. I was ready to leave but deliberately prolonged the scene. I wanted Mandák to leave first because I was curious how he would take leave of me, a man who had just been expelled from the party, and whether he would use the official party salutation, "Honor to labor!" Mandák was in a rush and could wait no longer, so he chose a compromise. "Goodbye, comrade," he said, and hurried out.

If nearly a quarter of a century before, someone had told me how farcically my membership in that party would end, that person would have made an enemy of me for life. And I would not have thought then that I could survive expulsion from the party. Now, all at once, I felt very clearly that a stage in my life had closed, and that I was beginning a new, in some ways more important, one. Present in all this was a vague sensation of having been liberated.

I subsequently lived seven more years in Czechoslovakia, not among the privileged, but in the ghetto of the outcasts. I had been cast out by the party to which I had dedicated more than half of my life, though I was not forgotten or ignored. But it was now the political police who were assigned the task of looking after me. The experience of those seven years, however, is material for an altogether different narrative.

APPENDIX

Zdeněk Mlynář's Resignation Address to the Plenary
Session of the CPC Central Committee on November 14–16, 1968.

Comrades,

I shall not bother in this brief address to reiterate matters relating
to developments before and after January. Since you elected me to
the secretariat in April and appointed me secretary of the Central
Committee at the May plenary session, my opinions have been familiar enough, and I feel no need to alter them in any way today. I believe that in my official functions—in difficult areas of the state
organs, the National Front, and the social organizations—I have
never done anything that would play into the hands either of liberalistic extremism or conservative sectarianism. For this reason, I won
no laurels from the pseudo-radicals before August, nor could I have
been counted among those who, in my opinion, display tendencies towards sectarianism.

Perhaps the few brief comments I have to offer on the contemporary situation and the tasks confronting the present plenary session
will be discounted. Nevertheless, I must put them forward.

This November plenary session has the task of resolving an extremely contentious political situation that has arisen through a combination of complex and contradictory factors, both domestic and
external. Almost all participants in the discussion here have dwelt exclusively on the domestic factors, and the resolution under consideration reflects this rather one-sided emphasis. I think, however, that the
position of our party must be seen in a somewhat different light.

Today, both the party and the state must implement policies that reflect both the internal and the external factors. Put more simply, on the one hand we must take measures that have either already been accepted by our representatives in Moscow, or will be, and, on the other hand, we have to try and unite a party that is, at the moment, divided, particularly among active functionaries and even in the Central Committee itself. On top of this, we desire the confidence and full support of the working class and of all Czechoslovak people.

However, our partners, the Soviets and others, are operating on the hypothesis that their military intervention was unavoidable for the defense of socialism, both in Czechoslovakia and throughout the Warsaw Pact community. But our people, on the contrary—and I believe this includes a vast majority of the working class as well—are simply not persuaded that this is true.

At the plenary session of the Central Committee on August 31 of this year, and later on television and radio, I defended the notion that the Moscow Protocol of August 26 provides a potential basis for settling this difficult conflict without necessarily provoking an even deeper crisis. My position was based on the interpretation of the protocol that we accepted at that last plenary session and that was presented in speeches by comrades Dubček, Černík, and Svoboda.

On the basis of information received by the presidium concerning the meeting of comrades Dubček, Černík, and Husák in Moscow on October 3 and 4, I have concluded that certain conflicts are continuing to sharpen and that we will scarcely resolve them by a compromise that in effect tries to avoid the issue altogether.

As I see it, the positions that both parties are bound to by mutual negotiations, consultations, and discussions are now both quantitatively and qualitatively different from what we were led to believe at the August 31 plenary session. As the CPSU leadership interprets the Moscow Protocol, it will result in several domestic political and party questions becoming subject to mutual discussion and agreement.

I think the presidium has a responsibility not to conceal this fact from the plenary session and the party as a whole. If I understand correctly what the presidium was told about the Moscow meeting, there are three important political questions in regard to which we cannot act before reaching an understanding with Moscow, if we do not wish once more to increase discord and tension between us and the other five parties.

What are these questions?

First and foremost, what is, and will clearly continue to be, the subject of discussion, controversy, and negotiation is not merely *how* we implemented the party line and the occasional mistakes that encouraged liberalistic extremes, but the political line of the Action Program itself. In reality, there is a fundamental ideological offensive taking place—and this is happening on the pages of the main party newspapers, both in the USSR and in the GDR and Poland. It is an attack on everything in Czechoslovakia and the entire Communist movement that deviates from Soviet ideology. We cannot afford to stick our heads in the sand and ignore the fact that the Action Program itself will most probably soon be under attack as a "revisionist document." Perhaps—and I hope I am right in this—it will change in time, and things will return to normal, but for the time being that is what is happening. One main point of contention here is the concept of the leading role of the party as we have enshrined it in the Action Program.

The second question is the analysis of the relative strength of the social classes in Czechoslovkia, and in this there is clearly no unanimity. We can expect more meetings, debates, and discussions about whether the basis exists in our society for a class struggle. Politically, this means a discussion about whether there was, or was not, a counter-revolutionary situation here that required military intervention.

The third question concerns internal party problems, particularly the possibility of holding both a Czech and a national party congress. Linked with this are the very concrete questions of personnel. The plenary session of the Central Committee has a right to know that the party leadership, or rather its delegation, is discussing these matters too with the Soviet comrades, for this is one of the most crucial aspects of normalization in Czechoslovakia, within the meaning of the Moscow Protocol.

Without wishing to attribute an exaggerated and one-sided significance to the thousands of resolutions we have received from various organizations, I think that everything we have learned "from below," from the party organizations, and everything we know about the attitudes of the other citizens, including the workers, indicates that it is quite impossible to take a position on these points that would satisfy both the Soviet partners and the rank-and-file of our party and working people. Perhaps I am putting it in somewhat extreme terms, but I personally believe that in such a situation it is better to be absolutely clear about the exigencies of the "post-August" politics, which are qualitatively different from the politics of the April Action Program. Quite simply, we will not now be able to implement some of the most important points in this program—which in any case is obvious from the draft resolution—and we must not, therefore, spread illusions about there still being "room" for the Action Program. . . .

At the same time, I would like to stress that the reason we do not have this room is a combination of factors both internal and external in the post-January development, for I want it to be clear that I do not think of it purely as a problem arising from a *diktat* from outside. Internal factors as well have "dictated" our situation. Nevertheless, I do not accept that the entry into our territory of the armies of the five Warsaw Pact states was necessary to defend socialism in Czechoslovakia, and I believe that after the meetings in Čierna and Bratislava we could have handled the difficulties that inevitably arose, including any antisocialist tendencies, with the strength at our own disposal.

This "post-August" politics will have to be conducted with three things in mind. The first is not to allow relations with the five other parties to deteriorate to the point where a new military intervention results. The second, and related, point is to prevent the potential and often inevitable disagreement of Communists and working people with such policies as the leadership shall agree on with the CPSU from leading to politically dangerous conflicts such as strikes, demonstrations, clashes of our young people and workers with the Czechoslovak armed forces, and so on. For any one of these could well result in the same catastrophic development and the same bloodshed as we struggled, successfully, to avert in August. The third thing is to guard against the return of the politics of the fifties, particularly repressions directed against differing opinions inside the party.

I think that at the same time we must be prepared for a number of negative factors, such as a loss of confidence in the party leadership in many organizations, a negative influence on the attitude of the younger generation to the party, an exodus of members from the party, a wave of apathy, political resignation and passivity among many non-Communists, isolated attempts to resist party and state policies, particularly among the young, the passive resistance of many intellectuals, and so on.

I would be glad to be proven over-pessimistic in believing that it will take at least two or three years for those inside and outside the party to absorb this difficult historical experience and begin anew the gradual search for a way to realize what we had set out to do in January and April: develop socialism while fully respecting all the specific conditions that exist in Czechoslovakia. The course we embarked upon in January and attempted to implement through the Action Program has quite simply and clearly been defeated. I repeat, I would be very glad if this were only my subjective pessimism. If I did not say what I felt, however, I would be misleading both honest Communists and citizens.

In this situation, the party requires a leadership composed of comrades who wish to carry out policies on that basis and who will be united in doing so. It is therefore also necessary to allow those who cannot work within the framework of such policies to retire from politics. People associated with the Novotný era or, even worse, with the deformations of the fifties are not the ones to lead the party out of this situation. In terms of the current needs in the party, I personally consider as most realistic the political positions expressed in this plenary session by comrades Černík, Štrougal, and Husák (not to mention the introductory remarks by comrade Dubček and the resolution itself).

Theoretically, of course, another alternative is at least thinkable: to lead the party, the workers, and the people in a way that would risk worsening relations with the five other parties and countries of the Warsaw Pact, that is, by not accepting the limitations on our independence that today are a fact of life. In my opinion, however, this is a path of blood, which, by disregarding certain realities, would be shed in vain. The political consequences would inevitably be a greater and even more profound defeat. It would be the kind of sheer adventurism that we decided we could not accept the responsibility for in August.

I think, therefore, that we are in a situation that can no longer be resolved by undertaking a complex, necessary, fundamental, and qualitative reform of our economic and socio-political system. Such reform, however, is at the heart of the Action Program. A few fragmentary reforms, therefore, can never replace the post-January politics. And realistically speaking, we can do little more than act piecemeal today. This is a painful fact of life for millions of decent people, but what these people deserve least of all are illusions.

For all these reasons, and to improve the confidence of the CPSU leadership in our party leadership, I have requested to be relieved of all my leading functions. My resignation was submitted on October 18 of this year, and the presidium discussed it on November 13 and recommended it to the plenary session of the Central Committee for ratification.

(This text does not contain the concluding passage of the speech, where I formally request that my resignation from all party functions be ratified.)

Zdeněk Mlynář's
Contribution to the Action Program

The Leading Role of the Party:
A Guarantee of Socialist Progress

At present it is most important that the party practice a policy fully justifying its leading role in society. We believe that this is a condition for the socialist development of the country.

The Communist party, as a party of the working class, won the struggle with capitalism and the struggle to carry out revolutionary class changes. With the victory of socialism it became the vanguard of the entire socialist society. During the present development the party has proven its ability to lead this society; from its own initiative it launched the process of democratization and ensured its socialist character. In its political activity the party intends to depend particularly on those who have an understanding of the requirements of society as a whole, who do not see their own personal and group interests as opposed to those of socialism, who use and improve their abilities for the benefit of all, who have a sense for everything new and progressive and are willing to help advance it.

The Communist party enjoys the voluntary support of the people. It does not practice its leading role by ruling society but by most devotedly serving its free, progressive socialist development. The party cannot enforce its authority. Authority must be won again and again by party activity. It cannot force its line through directives. It must depend on the work of its members, on the veracity of its ideals.

In the past, the leading role of the party was often conceived as a monopolistic concentration of power in the hands of party bodies. This concept corresponded to the false thesis that the party is the instrument of the dictatorship of the proletariat. This harmful conception weakened the initiative and responsibility of state, economic and social institutions, damaged the party's authority, and prevented it from carrying out its real functions. The party's goal is not to become a universal "caretaker" of society, to bind all organizations and every step taken in life by its directives. Its mission lies primarily in arousing socialist initiative, showing the ways and real possibilities of Communist perspectives, and in winning over all workers to them through systematic persuasion and the personal example of Communists. This determines the conceptual character of party activity. Party bodies do not deal with all problems; they should encourage activity and suggest solutions to the most important ones. At the same time the party cannot turn into an organization which influences society only by its ideas and program. Through its members and bodies it must develop the practical organizational methods of a political force in society. Political and organizational party activity coordinates the practical efforts of the people to turn the party line and program into reality in the social, economic, and cultural life of society.

As a representative of the interests of the most progressive part of all strata—and thus the representative of the perspective aims of society—the party cannot represent the entire scale of social interests. The political expression of the many-sided interests of society is the National Front, which expresses the unity of the social strata, interest groups, and of the nations and nationalities of this society. The party does not want to, and will not, take the place of social organizations; on the contrary, it must take care that their initiative and political responsibility for the unity of society is revived and flourishes. The role of the party is to seek a way of satisfying the various interests which does not jeopardize the interests of the society as a whole, but promotes them and creates new progressive ones. The party policy must not lead non-Communists to feel that their rights and freedom are limited by the role of the party. On the contrary, they must interpret the activity of the party as a guarantee of their rights, freedom, and interests. We want to achieve, and we must achieve a state of affairs where the party at the basic organizational level will have informal, natural authority based upon its ability to manage and on the moral qualities of Communist functionaries.

Within the framework of democratic rules of a socialist state, Communists must continually strive for the voluntary support of the majority of the people for the party line. Party resolutions and directives must be modified if they fail to express the needs and possibilities of the whole society. The party must try to ensure for its members—the most active workers in their spheres of work—suitable weight and influence in the whole society and posts in state, economic and social bodies. This, however, must not lead to the practice of appointing party members to posts, without regard to the principle that leading representatives of institutions of the whole society are chosen by society itself and by its individual components and that functionaries of these components are responsible to all citizens or to all members of social organizations. We must abolish discrimination and "cadre ceilings" for nonparty members.

The basis for the party's ability to act is its ideological and organizational unity based upon broad inner-party democracy. The most effective weapon against methods of bureaucratic centralism in the party is the consolidation of the influence of party members in forming the political line and the reinforcement of the role of really democratically elected bodies. Elected bodies of the party must first of all guarantee all rights of its members, collective decision making and ensure that all power will not be concentrated in a single pair of hands.

Only down-to-earth discussion and an exchange of views can lead to responsible decision making by collective bodies. The confrontation of views is an essential manifestation of a responsible multilateral attempt to find the best solution, to advance the new against the obsolete. Each member of the party and party bodies has not only the right, but the duty to act according to his conscience, with initiative, criticism, and different views on the matter in question, to oppose any functionary. This practice must become deeply rooted if the party is to avoid subjectivism in its activity. It is impermissible to restrict Communists in these rights, to create an atmosphere of distrust and suspicion of those who voice different opinions, or to persecute the minority under any pretext—as has happened in the past. The party, however, cannot abandon the principle of requiring that resolutions be put into practice once they are approved. Within the party, all its members are equal regardless of whether they hold any post in party bodies or in the bodies of state and economic organizations. Nevertheless, anyone who occupies a higher position also carries greater responsibility. The party realizes that a deeper democracy will not take hold in this society if democratic principles are not consistently applied in the internal life and work of the party and among Communists. Decisions on all important questions and on filling cadre posts must be backed by democratic rules and secret ballot. The democratization of party life also means the strengthening of work contacts between the party and science. In this line we shall make use of consultations and exchanges of opposing and contrary views, since the role of science does not end with the preparation of analyses and documents. It should continue on party grounds by observing the innovations produced by various resolutions and by contributing to their materialization and control in practice.

The Central Committee of the Communist Party of Czechoslovakia set out on this road at its December and January sessions and will make sure that in the months to come questions of the content and democratic methods of party life and relations between elected bodies and the party apparatus are clarified throughout the party and that rules will be elaborated to define the authority and responsibilities of the individual bodies and links of the party mechanism, as well as the principles of the party's cadre policy, which will ensure an effective, regular change of leading officials, guarantee to keep its members well informed, and regulate relations between party bodies and party members in general. In preparing the Fourteenth Party Congress, the party will ensure that party statutes correspond to the present state of its development.

For the Development of Socialist Democracy and a New System of the Political Management of Society

In the past decade, the party has often put forward the demand for the development of socialist democracy. Measures taken by the party were aimed at enhancing the role of elected representative bodies in the state. They emphasized the importance of voluntary social organizations and of all forms of popular activities. Party policy initiated a number of laws which increased the protection of rights of every citizen. It was clearly stated in the theses of the Central Committee of the Communist Party of Czechoslovakia prepared for the Thirteenth Party Congress that "the dictatorship of the working class has fulfilled its main historical mission in our country" and guidelines for further development of our democracy were given no less clearly: "The system of socialist democracy—the state, social organizations, and the party as the leading force—endeavors to bring out the different interests and attitudes of working people to social problems in a democratic way and to settle them within social organizations with regard to nationwide needs and goals. The development of democracy must proceed hand in hand with strengthening the scientific and professional approach to social management."

Nevertheless, *the harmful characteristics of centralized directive decision making and management have survived to the present.* In relations among the party, the state, and social organizations, in internal relations and methods among these components, in the relations of state and other institutions to individuals, in the interpretation of the importance of public opinion and of keeping the people informed, in the practice of cadre policy—in all these fields there are too many elements embittering the life of the people, obstructing professionally competent and scientific decision making, and encouraging highhandedness. The reason may be sought, first and foremost, in the fact that the relations among these bodies in our political system have been built up for years to serve as the instrument for carrying out the orders of the center, and hardly ever made it at all possible for the decision itself to be the outcome of a democratic procedure.

The different interests and needs of people not foreseen by the system of directive decision making were taken as an undesirable obstacle and not as new needs to be respected by politics. The often well-meant words of "an increase in the people's participation in management" were of no avail, because in time "participation of the people" came to mean chiefly help in carrying out orders, not in making the decisions. Thus it was possible that views, measures and interventions were enforced even though they were arbitrary and did not comply with either scientific knowledge, or with the interests of the various strata of the people and individual citizens. Centralized decision making put into effect in this way could not be effective. It led to a number of resolutions not being fulfilled and a weakening of goal-oriented management of social development. This, in turn, has in many cases kept positions occupied by people who were incapable of any other type of "management," who consistently revive old methods and habits, and surround themselves with people who humor them and not with people whose capacities and character would guarantee that they do their jobs successfully. Although we consistently condemn the "personality cult," we are still unable to eradicate certain characteristics of our society which were typical of that period. This undermines the people's confidence in whether the party can change the situation, and old tensions and political nervous strain are revived.

The Central Committee is firmly determined to overcome this state of affairs. As noted above, for the Fourteenth Congress we must cast the fundamental issues of the development of the political system into a concept which meets the demands of life, just as we have established the fundamental concept of the new economic system.

We must reform the whole political system so that it will permit the dynamic development of socialist social relations, combine broad democracy with scientific, highly qualified management, strengthen the social order, stabilize socialist relations and maintain social discipline. The basic structure of the political system must, at the same time, *provide firm guarantees against a return to the old methods of subjectivism and highhandedness from a position of power.* Party activity has not been directed systematically to that end, and in fact, obstacles have frequently been put in the way of such efforts. All these changes necessarily call for the *commencement of work on a new Czechoslovak constitution* so that a draft may be thoroughly discussed among professionals and in public and submitted to the National Assembly shortly after the party congress.

But we consider it indispensable to change the present state of things immediately, even before the Fourteenth Congress, so that the development of socialism and its inner dynamics will not be hampered by outdated factors in the political system. Our democracy must provide more leeway for the activity of every individual, every collective, every link in management, at lower and higher levels and in the center too. People must have more opportunity to think for themselves and express their opinions. We must radically change the practices that allow the people's initiative and critical comments and suggestions from below to meet with the proverbial deaf ear. We must see to it that the incompetent but readily adaptable people are replaced by those who strive for socialism, who are concerned with its fate and progress and the interests and needs of others, not with their own power or privilege. This holds for people both "above" and "below." It is going to be a complicated process, and it will take some time. At all levels of management, in the party, in state and economic bodies and in social organizations, we must ascertain which body, which official, or which worker is really responsible, where to look for guarantees of improvement, where to change institutions, where to introduce new working methods, and where to replace individuals. The attitude of individual party officials to new tasks and methods, their capability of carrying the new policy into practice, must be the basic political criterion.

No Responsibility Without Rights

Which body and which official are responsible for what, and the rights and duties involved, must be perfectly clear in our system of management in the future. It is the basic prerequisite for proper development. To this end, each component part should have its own independent position.

Substitution and interchanging of state bodies and agencies of economic and social organization by party bodies must be stopped. Party resolutions are binding for the Communists working in these bodies, but the policy, managerial activities, and responsibility of the state, economic, and social organizations are independent. The Communists active in these bodies and organizations must take the initiative to see to it that the state and economic bodies as well as social organizations (notably the trades union, the Czechoslovak Union of Youth, etc.) take the problem of their activities and responsibilities into their own hands.

The whole *National Front,* the political parties which form it, and the social organizations will take part in the creation of state policy. *The political parties* of the National Front are partners whose political work is based on the joint political program of the National Front and is naturally bound by the Constitution of the Czechoslovak Socialist Republic. It stems from the socialist character of social relations in our country. The Communist Party of Czechoslovakia considers the National Front to be a political platform which does not separate political parties into government and opposition factions. It does not create opposition to state policy—the policy of the whole National Front—or lead struggles for political power. Possible differences in the viewpoints of individual component parts of the National Front, or divergence of views as to a state policy is to be settled on the basis of the common socialist conception of National Front policy by way of political agreement and unification of all component parts of the National Front. The organization of political forces to negate this concept of the National Front, to remove the National Front as a whole from political power, was ruled out as long ago as 1945 after the tragic experience of both our nations with the prewar political development of the Czechoslovak government; it is naturally unacceptable for our present Republic.

The Communist Party of Czechoslovakia considers the *political leadership* of the Marxist-Leninist concept of the development of socialism as a precondition for the proper development of our socialist society. It will assert the Marxist-Leninist concept as the leading political principle in the National Front and in all our political system by seeking, through the means of political work, such support in all the component parts of our system and *directly among the masses of workers and all working people* that will ensure its leading role in a democratic way.

Voluntary social organizations of the working people cannot replace political parties, *but the contrary is also true. Political parties in our country cannot exclude common-interest organizations of workers and other working people from directly influencing state policy,* its creation and application. Socialist state power cannot be monopolized either by a single party, or by a coalition of parties. It must be open to all political organizations of the people. *The Communist Party of Czechoslovakia will use every means at its disposal to develop such forms of political life that will ensure the expression of the direct voice and will of the working class and all working people in political decision making in our country.*

The whole existing organization, its activities, and incorporation of various organizations into the National Front must be revised and restructured under the new conditions and built up so that the National Front may carry out its qualitatively new tasks. *The National Front as a whole and all its component parts must be granted independent rights and its own responsibility for the management of our country and society.*

Voluntary social organizations must be based on truly voluntary membership and activity. People join these organizations hoping they will express their interests, and they therefore have the right to choose their own officials and representatives, who must not be appointed from outside. These principles should form the foundation of our unified mass organizations. Although their activities are still indispensable, their structure, their working methods, and ties with their members must respect the new social conditions.

The implementation of the *constitutional freedoms of assembly and association* must be ensured this year so that the possibility of setting up voluntary organizations, special-interest associations, societies, etc., is guaranteed by law and the present interests and needs of various strata and categories of our citizens are attended to without bureaucratic interference and without a monopoly by any individual organization. Any restrictions in this respect can be imposed only by law and only the law can stipulate what is antisocial, forbidden, or punishable. Freedoms guaranteed by law and in compliance with the constitution also apply fully to citizens of various creeds and religious denominations.

The effective influence of views and opinions of the working people on the policies and a firm opposition to all tendencies to suppress the criticism and initiative of the people cannot be guaranteed if we do not ensure constitution-based freedom of speech and political and personal rights to all citizens, systematically and consistently, by all legal means available. *Socialism cannot mean only liberation of the working people from the domination of exploiting class relations, but must provide for a greater degree of self-fulfillment than any bourgeois democracy can provide.* The working people, who are no longer ordered about by a class of exploiters, can no longer be dictated to by any arbitrary interpretation from a position of power as to what information they may or may not be given, which of their opinions can or cannot be expressed publicly, where public opinion may play a role and where it may not. Public opinion polls must be systematically used in preparing important decisions and the main results of such research published. Any restriction may be imposed only on the basis of a law stipulating what is antisocial—which in our country is mainly determined by the criminal code. The Central Committee of the Communist Party of Czechoslovakia considers it urgently necessary to define in a press law and more exactly than hitherto in the shortest possible time when a state body can forbid the propagation of certain information (in the press, radio, television, etc.) and exclude the possibility of preliminary factual censorship. It is necessary to overcome the holding up, distortion, and incompleteness of information, to remove any unwarranted secrecy of political and economic facts, to publish the annual balance sheets of enterprises, to publish even alternatives to various suggestions and measures, and to increase the import and sale of foreign newspapers and periodicals. Leading representatives of state, social, and cultural organizations are obliged to organize regular press conferences and give their views on topical issues on television, radio, and in the press. In the press, it is necessary to make a distinction between official standpoints of the state, party organs and journalists. The party press especially must express the party's life and development along with criticisms of various opinions among the Communists, etc., and cannot be made to coincide fully with the official viewpoints of the state.

The party realizes that ideological antagonists of socialism may try to abuse the process of democratization. At the present stage of development and under the conditions of our country, we insist on the principle that bourgeois ideology can be challenged only in open ideological struggle before all of the people. We can win people over to the ideas and policy of the party only by a struggle based on the practical activities of Communists for the benefit of the people, on truthful and complete information, and on scientific analysis. We trust that in such a struggle, all sections of our society will contribute actively towards the victory of truth, which is on the side of socialism.

At present the activity and responsibility of publishing houses and editors in chief, of all party members and progressive staff members of the mass communication media, must be to push through socialist ideals and implement the policy of the party, of the National Front, and of the state.

Legal norms must also provide a more precise guarantee *of the freedom of speech for minority interests and opinions* (again within the framework of socialist laws and in harmony with the principle that decisions are taken in accordance with the will of the majority). The *constitutional freedom of movement,* particularly that of travel abroad for our citizens, *must be precisely guaranteed by law.* In particular, this means that a citizen should have the legal right to long-term or permanent sojourn abroad and that people should not be groundlessly placed in the position of emigrants; at the same time it is necessary to protect by law the interests of the state, for example, as regards the drain of some categories of specialists, etc.

Our entire legal code must gradually solve the problem of how *to protect in a better and more consistent way the personal rights and property of citizens,* and we must especially remove those stipulations that virtually put individual citizens at a disadvantage against the state and other institutions. We must in the future prevent various institutions from disregarding personal rights and the interests of individual citizens as far as personal ownership of family houses, gardens, etc. is concerned. It will be necessary to adopt, in the shortest possible time, the long-prepared law of compensation for any damage caused to any individual or to an organization by an unlawful decision of a state organ.

It is a serious fact *that hitherto the rehabilitation of people*—both Communists and non-Communists—who were the victims of legal violations in the past years, *has not always been carried out in all its political and civic implications.* On the initiative of the Communist party Central Committee bodies, an investigation is under way as to why the respective party resolutions have not been fully carried out, and measures are being taken to ensure that the wrongs of the past are made good wherever it has not been done yet. No one having the slightest personal reason from his own past activity for slowing down the rectification process may serve in the political bodies or prosecutor's and court offices that are to rectify unlawful deeds of the past.

The party realizes that people unlawfully condemned and persecuted cannot regain the lost years of their life. It will, however, do its best to remove any shadow of the mistrust and humiliation to which the families and relatives of those affected were often subjected, and will resolutely ensure that such persecuted people have every opportunity of showing their worth in work, in public life, and in political activities. It goes without saying that even in carrying out full rehabilitation of people, we cannot change the consequences of revolutionary measures made in the past years in accordance with the spirit of class law aimed against the bourgeoisie, its property, and its economic and social supports. The whole problem of the rectification of past repressions must be approached with the full responsibility of the state bodies concerned and based on legal regulations. The Central Committee of the Communist Party of Czechoslovakia supports the proposal that the procedure in these questions and the problems of legal consequences be incorporated in a *special law.*

A broad democratic concept of the *political and personal rights of citizens,* their legal and political safeguards, is considered by the party to be a prerequisite for the necessary strengthening of social discipline and order, for a stabilization of socialist social relations. A selfish understanding of civil rights, an "I'm all right, Jack" attitude toward social property, the policy of placing one's particular interests over those of the whole society—all these are features which Communists will oppose with all their might.

The real purpose of democratization must be the achievement of better results in day to day work due to wider possibilities of purposeful activity and a concern for the interests and needs of the people. Democracy cannot be identified with empty speechmaking. It cannot stand in opposition to discipline, professionalism, and effectiveness of management. But arbitrariness and an obscure definition of rights and duties make such a development impossible. They lead to irresponsibility, to a feeling of uncertainty, and hence also to indifference towards public interests and needs. A more profound democracy and greater measure of civic freedoms will help socialism prove its superiority over limited bourgeois democracy and make it an attractive example for progressive movements even in industrially advanced countries with democratic traditions.

The Power of Elected Bodies Derives from the Will of the Voters

With the coming *elections* begins the onset of implementation of the principles of this Action Program in the work of the elected bodies of the state.

Although efforts were made in the past few months to improve the preparation for elections, it proved impossible to have the elections organized by the originally proposed deadline if we wished to meet the requirements of the principles of an advanced socialist democracy. It is therefore necessary to work out an electoral system that will take the changes in our political life into account. An electoral law must lay down, exactly and clearly, democratic principles for the preparation of the elections, the proposal of candidates and the method of their election. The changes in the electoral system must be based, in particular, on the new political status of the National Front and the elected bodies themselves.

The *national committees* make up the backbone of the whole network of representative bodies in our country, the democratic organs of state power. It must be in the national committees that state policy is formed, especially in districts and regions. In their work the principle of socialist democracy is to be fully applied. The various interests and requirements of the people must be expressed and united in the general, public interest of communities, townships, districts, and regions.

The party regards the national committees as bodies that have to carry on *the progressive traditions of local government and people's self-administration.* They must not be taken for local bureaucratic offices supervising local enterprises. The essential political mission of national committees is to protect the rights and needs of the people, to simplify the process of settling all matters with which the people turn to the national committee, to pursue public interest and oppose efforts of some institutions to dupe the people and ignore their requirements.

The party regards the National Assembly as a socialist parliament with all the scope for activities the parliament of a democratic republic must have. The Communist deputies must see to it that the National Assembly draws up a number of concrete measures before the new electoral period, measures that will put into actual practice the constitutional status of the National Assembly as the supreme organ of state power in the Czechoslovak Socialist Republic. It is necessary to overcome formalism in negotiations and the unconvincing unanimity concealing factual differences in opinions and attitudes of the deputies. From this point of view it is necessary to settle, as soon as possible, the relations between the National Assembly and party bodies and a number of problems regarding internal activities of the National Assembly, particularly those of organization and competence. The result must be a National Assembly which actually decide on laws and important political issues, and not only approves proposals submitted. The party supports a strengthening of the controlling function of the National Assembly in our entire public life and, more concretely, with respect to the government. The controlling machinery must be in the hands of the National Assembly, which will establish it as its own body. Together with closer bonds between the National Assembly and our public opinion, all of this may, in a short time, increase the role and the prestige of the National Assembly in our society.

Separation and Control of Power
Guarantee against Highhandedness

The Communists in the government, too, must ensure as soon as possible that the principle of responsibility of the government towards the National Assembly covering all its activities is worked out in detail. Even under the existing practice of political management, the opportunity afforded for independent activity of the government and of individual ministers was not sufficiently made use of; there was a tendency to shift responsibility on to the party bodies and to evade independence in decision making. The government is not only an organ of economic policy. As the supreme executive organ of the state it must, as a whole, deal systematically with the whole scope of political and administrative problems of the state. It is also up to the government to take care of the rational development of the whole state machinery. The state administrative machinery was often underrated in the past. This machinery must consist of highly qualified people, professionally competent and rationally organized; it must be subject to systematic, democratic supervision; and it must be effective. The oversimplified idea that these could be attained by underrating and decrying the administrative machinery in general has done more harm than good.

Within the whole state and political system, it is necessary for us to create such relations and rules as would, on the one hand, provide *the necessary safeguards to professional officials* in their functions and, on the other hand, enable *the necessary replacement of officials* who can no longer cope with their work by professionally and politically more competent people. This means establishing legal conditions for the recall of responsible officials and providing legal guarantees of decent conditions for those who are leaving their posts through the normal way of replacement, so that their departure does not amount to a "drop" in their material and moral-political standing.

The party policy is based on the principle that no undue concentration of power must occur, throughout the state machinery, in one sector, one body, or a single individual. It is necessary to provide for such a division of power and a system of mutual supervision that can rectify the faults or check encroachments of any of its links on the activities of another link. This principle must be applied not only to relations between the elected and executive bodies, but also to the internal relations of the state administration machinery and to the standing and activities of courts of law.

These principles have been infringed mainly by undue concentration of duties in the existing Ministry of the Interior. The party thinks it necessary to turn it into a department for internal state administration, to which the administration of public security also belongs. All those areas in our state which were traditionally within the jurisdiction of other bodies and with the passage of time have been incorporated into the ministry of the interior must be withdrawn from it. It is necessary to elaborate proposals as soon as possible to transfer the main responsibility for investigation to the courts of law, separating prison administration from the security force, and handing over the administration of press law, archives, etc., to other state bodies.

The party considers the problem of a correct incorporation of the security force in the state as politically very important. The security of our lives will only benefit if everything is eliminated that helps to maintain a public view of the security force marred in the past by violations of law and by the privileged position of the security force in the political system. Thus the progressive traditions of our security force as a force advancing side by side with our people were impaired. These traditions must be renewed. The Central Committee of the Communist Party of Czechoslovakia deems it necessary *to change the organization of the security force* and to split the joint organization into two mutually independent parts—State Security and Public Security. *The State Security* service must have the status, organizational structure, men, equipment, methods, and qualifications which are in keeping with its work of defending the state from the activities of enemy centers abroad. Every citizen who has not been culpable in this respect must know with certainty that his political convictions and opinions, his personal beliefs and activities, cannot be the object of attention of the bodies of the State Security service. The party declares clearly that this apparatus *should not be directed toward, or used to solve, internal political questions* and controversies in socialist society.

The Public Security service will combat crime and keep public order. It is to this end that its organization, men, and methods must be adapted. The Public Security force must be better equipped and strengthened; its precise functions in the defense of public order must be laid down by law and will be directed by the national committees. Legal norms must create clearer relations of control over the security force by the government as a whole and by the National Assembly.

It is necessary to devote the appropriate care to carrying out *the defense policy in our state.* In this connection it is necessary to work for our active share in the conception of the military doctrine of the Warsaw Treaty countries, strengthening the defense potential of our country in harmony with its needs and possibilities, a uniform complex understanding of the problems of defense and all problems of the building of socialism in all our policy, including defense training.

The legal policy of the party is based on the principle that in a dispute over rights (including administrative decisions of state bodies) the basic guarantee of legality is proceedings in court which are independent of political factors and are bound only by law. The application of this principle requires a strengthening of the whole social and political role and importance of courts of law in our society. The Central Committee of the Communist Party of Czechoslovakia will see to it that work on the required proposals and measures proceeds so as to find the answers to all the necessary problems before the next election of judges. In harmony with and parallel to that, it is also necessary to settle the status and duties of the public prosecutor's office, so that it may not be put above the courts of law, and to guarantee full independence of lawyers from state bodies.

The Moscow Protocol

1. During the course of the talks problems were discussed concerning the defense of socialist achievements in the situation which has arisen in Czechoslovakia as well as the most essential measures dictated by the situation and by the stationing of allied troops there. Both sides acted according to all the generally acknowledged norms for relations among fraternal parties and countries and according to the principles affirmed in the documents of the Čierná nad Tisou and Bratislava conferences. There was an affirmation of allegiance to the compacts of the socialist countries for the support, consolidation and defense of socialism and the implacable struggle with counter-revolutionary forces, which is a common international obligation of all socialist countries. Both sides likewise affirmed the strong conviction that in the present situation the most important task is to put into practice the principles and tasks of the conference in Bratislava.

2. The presidium of the CPC Central Committee announced that the so-called Fourteenth Congress, opened August 22, 1968, without the agreement of the Central Committee, violated party statutes. Without the participation of the members of the presidium, secretaries, CPS Central Committee secretaries, most of the delegates from the army and many other organizations, it is invalid. All measures pertinent to this problem will be taken by the presidium of the CPC Central Committee upon its return to Czechoslovakia. A special meeting will be called after the situation has been normalized within the party and the country.

3. The CPC delegation reported that a plenum of the CPC Central Committee would be held within the next six to ten days with the participation of the party's control and revision commission. It will review problems of the normalization of the situation within the country, measures for improving the work of party and state organs, economic problems and problems of living standards, measures for consolidating all links of party and state rule, and it will discharge from their posts those individuals whose further activities would not conform to the needs of consolidating the leading role of the working class and the Communist party. It will carry out the resolution of the

January and May 1968 plenums of the CPC Central Committee concerning consolidation of the position of socialism within the country and further development of relations between Czechoslovakia and countries of the socialist community.

4. The CPC representatives declared the necessity for the speedy implementation of a number of measures fostering the consolidation of socialism and a workers' government, with top priority to measures for controlling the communications media so that they will serve the cause of socialism fully by preventing antisocialist statements on radio and television, putting an end to the activities of various organizations with antisocialist positions, and banning the activities of the anti-Marxist social democratic party. Suitable and effective measures will be taken in the interest of accomplishing these tasks. The party and state organs will remedy the situation in the press, radio and television by means of new laws and measures. In this unusual situation it will be essential, if these tasks are to be accomplished, to take several temporary measures so that the government can have firm control over the ways and means of opposing antisocialist individuals or collectives. Essential personnel changes will be carried out in the leadership of the press and radio and television stations. Here, as at the meeting in Čierná nad Tisou, the representatives of the CPSU expressed full solidarity with these measures, which also conform to the basic interests of the socialist community, its security and unity.

5. Both delegations discussed problems connected with the presence of troops of the five socialist countries and agreed that the troops will not interfere with the internal affairs of Czechoslovakia. As soon as the threat to socialism in Czechoslovakia and to the security of the countries in the socialist community has passed, allied troops will be removed from the territory of Czechoslovakia in stages. The command of the allied troops and the command of the Czechoslovak army will immediately begin discussions concerning the removal and change in position of military units from cities and villages where local organs are able to establish order. Repositioning of the troops is to be effected in barracks, training grounds and other military areas. The problem of the security of the Czechoslovak border with the German Federal Republic will be reviewed. The number of troops, their organization and repositioning will be effected in cooperation with representatives of the Czechoslovak army. Material, technical, medical and other forms of security for the troops temporarily stationed in Czechoslovakia will be determined by special agreement at

the level of the Ministry of National Defense and the Ministry of Foreign Affairs. Problems involving matters of principle will be dealt with by the governments of both countries. A treaty concerning the conditions of the stay and complete removal of allied troops will be concluded between the government of Czechoslovakia and the other governments.

6. The Presidium of the CPC Central Committee and the government will adopt measures in the press, radio, and television to exclude the possibility of conflicts between the troops and citizens on Czechoslovak territory.

7. The CPC Central Committee representatives announced that they would see to it that party workers and officials who struggled for the consolidation of socialist positions against antisocialist forces and for friendly relations with the USSR be dismissed from their posts or suffer reprisals.

8. An agreement was reached regarding the establishment in the near future of negotiations on a number of economic problems with an eye to expanding and intensifying economic and technical cooperation between the USSR and Czechoslovakia, especially concerning the need for further development of the economy of Czechoslovakia in the interest of fulfilling the plan for the development of the national economy according to the CPC Central Committee resolution.

9. There is full agreement that the development of the international situation and the treacherous activities of imperialism, working against peace, the security of nations and socialism, necessitate the further consolidation and increase in effectiveness of the defense system of the Warsaw Pact as well as of other existing organs and forms of cooperation among socialist countries.

10. The leading representatives of the CPSU and CPC affirmed their resolve to scrupulously maintain the principle of coordinated action in international relations fostering the consolidation of unity in the socialist community and of peace and international security. Concerning European problems, the USSR and Czechoslovakia will follow as before a scrupulous policy in conformity with the common as well as the individual interests of the socialist countries and the interests of European security and offer strong resistance to militaristic, anti-Soviet and neonationalistic forces, which follow a policy of revising the results of the Second World War in Europe and existing European borders. Both sides announced that they will scrupulously fulfill all the obligations resulting from the multilateral and bilateral trea-

ties among socialist countries. In close cooperation with the rest of the countries in the socialist community they will continue in the future to struggle against imperialism's treacherous activities, support the national liberation movement, and work toward the easing of international tension.

11. In connection with the discussion of the so-called Czechoslovakia problem in the United Nations Security Council, the leading CPC and government representatives announced that Czechoslovakia did not request the Security Council to discuss this matter. The CPC representatives reported that the Czechoslovak representative in New York had been instructed by the government of the Republic to lodge a categorical protest against the discussion of the Czechoslovakia problem in the Security Council or in any other United Nations organ and make a categorical request for the deletion of this issue from the proceedings.

12. The CPC Central Committee presidium and the government announced that it would review the activities of those members of the government who were outside the country and made statements in the name of the government of Czechoslovakia concerning internal and foreign policy, especially with regard to the maintenance of the policy of the CPC and the government of the Republic. Suitable conclusions will be drawn from this review. In this connection the representatives of the CPC Central Committee consider it necessary to carry out several further personnel changes in party and state organs and organizations in the interest of ensuring complete consolidation within the party and the country. These problems will be considered from all points of view upon the representatives' return to their country. The activities of the Ministry of the Interior will also be examined, and measures will be taken to consolidate its leadership on the basis of the results.

13. An agreement was reached to set up negotiations of party and state delegations within a short period of time to further deepen attempts at resolving the problems which arise in their mutual relations and discussions of contemporary international problems.

14. The delegations agreed in the interest of both communist parties and of friendship between Czechoslovakia and the USSR to regard the contacts between the representatives of the CPC and the representatives of the CPSU as strictly confidential in the period following 20 August 1968, which therefore holds for talks just concluded.

15. Both sides pledged in the name of their parties and governments to promote all efforts of the CPSU and CPC and the governments of these countries to intensify the traditional friendship between the peoples of both countries and their fraternal friendship for time everlasting.

LIST OF NAMES

AUERSPERG, Pavel (1926): for many years functionary of the CPC Central Committee; head of the secretariat of Antonín Novotný, 1964–66; head of the Central Committee ideological division in 1966; party representative on the editorial board of *Questions of Peace and Socialism*, 1967–69; in August 1968, collaborated with the Soviet invaders; head of the Central Committee international division, 1969–73; returned to the editorial board of *Questions of Peace and Socialism* in 1974, where he has remained.

BARÁK, Rudolf (1915): CPC functionary in the Brno district from 1945; minister of the interior and member of the Central Committee presidium, 1953–61; suspected by Novotný of planning a putsch in the party leadership, was tried for "abusing his function" and imprisoned, 1962–68; did not subsequently return to political life.

BARBÍREK, František (1927): Slovak party functionary; secretary of the CPS Central Committee, 1963–66; deputy chairman of the Slovak National Council, 1966–68; member of the presidium of the CPC Central Committee in 1968; since 1969 politically active only in Slovak affairs.

BILAK, Vasil (1917): originally tailor; took part in the Slovak National Uprising of 1944; from 1950, party functionary in Slovakia; party secretary in Prešov, 1954–58; active in the suppression of the Greek Catholic Church in favor of the Orthodox Church as part of the policy to strengthen ties with Soviet Union; CPC Central Committee member from 1954; rose in the party and state ranks in Bratislava following the "liquidation of Slovak nationalists" (including Gustav Husák); first secretary of the CPS Central Committee and presidium member of the CPC Central Committee in 1968; assisted in preparing Soviet intervention; stripped of his positions and replaced by G. Husák on August 26, 1968, but shortly reinstalled to the presidium and secretariat of the CPC Central Committee due to Soviet pressure; after 1969, became leading force for neo-Stalinism in the party.

ČERNÍK, Oldřich (1921): originally machinist; from 1949, member of the party apparatus; chairman of the Ostrava District Committee, 1954–56; secretary, and later minister, of the CPC Central Committee, 1956–61; chairman of the State Planning Commission and deputy prime minister from 1963–68; CPC Central Committee member from 1958 and presidium member from 1966; prime minister, 1968–70, and briefly minister for technology and construction; expelled from CPC and stripped of all functions in 1971; subsequently deputy director of the Office for Normalization.

CHERVONENKO, Stepan Vasilevich (1916): Soviet diplomat; Central Committee member of the CPSU; ambassador to China in early 1960s; ambassador to Czechoslovakia from 1968 and personally took part in forming a new government in August that would collaborate with the Soviet invaders; ambassador to Paris since 1973.

CÍSAŘ, Čestmír (1920): studied in France; insurance company employee, 1939–45; in the CPC apparatus, primarily in the ideological sphere, from 1946; party press editor, 1957–63; CPC Central Committee secretary in 1963; minister of education, 1963–65; ambassador to Rumania, 1965–68; in 1968 returned to the secretariat of the Central Committee and later became chairman of the Czech National Council; stripped of all functions in 1969 and expelled from the party in 1970; subsequently in the government bureau for the care of monuments.

CLEMENTIS, Vladimír (1902–52): Slovak Communist intellectual; in exile in England during the war; deputy foreign minister, 1945–48; foreign minister, 1948–51; arrested in 1951 and executed in 1952 in connection with the Slánský trials; posthumously rehabilitated in 1963.

COLOTKA, Peter (1925): lawyer; in 1946 became law professor in Bratislava; professor of civil rights in 1964; in the higher echelons of the CPC since 1963; deputy prime minister in 1968; became allied with representatives of the "normalization" following the Soviet intervention; presidium member of the CPC Central Committee since 1969; chairman of the Federal Assembly in 1969; chairman of the Slovak Socialist Republic since 1971.

DUBČEK, Alexander (1921): raised in Soviet Central Asia, where his unemployed father emigrated; family returned to Czechoslovakia in 1938; industrial worker, 1938–44; CPC member since 1939; participant in the Slovak National Uprising; CPC functionary in Slovakia from 1949; secretary of the CPC Central Committee, 1960–62; first secretary of the CPS Central Committee and member of the presidium of the CPC Central Committee, 1963–68; first secretary of the CPC Central Committee, 1968–69; chairman of the Federal Assembly from April to September 1969, when he was relieved of all higher functions; served for several months as ambassador to Turkey and in 1970 was expelled from the CPC; subsequently in the district forestry bureau in Bratislava.

DZÚR, Martin (1919): originally technical employee; served in the armed forces of the fascist Slovak state in 1941; deserted to the Red Army in 1943 and fought in the Czechoslovak unit; an officer in the Czechoslovak army since 1945; became minister of defense in 1968.

ERBAN, Evžen (1912): lawyer; trade-union functionary and social democrat from the 1930s; leadership member of the Social Democratic Party, 1945–48; influential in amalgamating his party with the Communists; CPC Central Committee member since 1948 and active in the welfare area of government; Central Committee secretary in 1968 and, since August, chairman of the National Front; Central Committee presidium member, 1968–69; proponent of "normalization"; chairman of the Czech National Council since 1969.

FOJTÍK, Jan (1928): editor of *Rudé právo* from 1951, deputy of the editor in chief,

1966–68, responsible for scientific matters and uninvolved in politics during the Prague Spring; active supporter of "normalization" and secretary of the CPC Central Committee since 1969.

GOLDSTUEKER, Eduard (1913): functionary in the Communist student movement in his youth; in England during the war; a diplomat, 1945–51; sentenced to life imprisonment in 1951; rehabilitated in 1955; professor of German studies at Charles University in Prague from 1956; chairman of the Czechoslovak Union of Writers in 1968; exile in England since 1969.

GOTTWALD, Klement (1894–1953): leader of the CPC since its "Bolshevization" in 1929; in Moscow during the war; prime minister, 1946–48; president of the Republic, 1948–53; he symbolizes the Czechoslovak variety of Stalinism before the war and in the 1950s.

HÁCHA, Emil (1872–1945): lawyer; president of the Czechoslovak Supreme Court until 1938; president of the truncated Republic following the Munich Pact; signed the agreement with Hitler in March 1939 that legalized the completion of the Nazi take-over, and he was president of the Bohemia-Moravia Protectorate during the war; he symbolizes collaboration with the occupation forces.

HÁJEK, Jiří (1913): active in social-democratic politics in the 1930s; concentration camp prisoner during the war; functionary of the Social Democratic Party from 1945–48; professor of history and international affairs following the merger of the Social Democratic Party with the CPC; important Czechoslovak diplomat, 1955–65; minister of education, 1965–68; foreign minister in 1968; stripped of his functions under Soviet pressure in August 1968; expelled from party in 1970; temporarily in the Czechoslovak Academy of Sciences and later pensioned; a spokesman for Charter 77, 1977–78.

HAVEL, Václav (1936): Czech author and dramatist; was a CPC member; prohibited from higher education in the 1950s because of "bad class background," supported himself as manual worker and later as stage hand; in the 1960s wrote several plays, which mirrored the absurdity of contemporary social relations; chairman of the Club of Independent Writers in 1968; his writings have been prohibited reading since 1969; a spokesman for Charter 77 in 1977.

HENDRYCH, Jiří (1913): CPC functionary from the 1930s; concentration camp prisoner during the war; worked in various party posts, mostly in the ideological sphere, 1945–54; secretary of the CPC Central Committee, 1954–68; presidium member from 1958; considered second in power to Novotný; inactive since 1968.

HOFFMAN, Karel (1924): long-time functionary in the CPC apparatus; in the Central Committee apparatus, 1949–59; director-general of Czechoslovak broadcasting, 1959–67; appointed by Novotný as minister of culture, 1967–68, to "strengthen the regime" in the cultural sphere; director of the foreign news section, 1968–71, in which capacity he collaborated with the Soviet invaders; active supporter of "normalization"; chairman of the Central Council of the Trade Unions and member of the CPC presidium since 1971.

HÜBL, Milan (1927): historian and party functionary; rector of the party school of the CPC Central Committee in 1968; expelled from the CPC in 1970; arrested and sentenced to six and a half years in prison in 1971; released in 1976 and employed as janitor.

HUSÁK, Gustáv (1913): lawyer and long-time Slovak Communist functionary; legal assistant, 1938–42; employee of the Association of Furniture Movers in Bratislava and a member of the illegal CPS Central Committee, 1943–44; major participant in the Slovak National Uprising; chairman of the Board of Commissioners (a regional parliament), 1946–50; arrested in 1951 and sentenced in 1954 to life imprisonment as a "Slovak nationalist"; released in 1960 and rehabilitated in 1963; scientific expert with the Academy of Sciences in Bratislava, 1963–68, deputy chairman in 1968; first secretary of the CPS Central Committee and presidium member of the CPC Central Committee after August 1968; secretary-general of the CPC Central Committee after Dubček's fall from power in April 1969, as well as president of the Republic since 1975; epitomizes the pro-Soviet "normalization policy."

INDRA, Alois (1921): originally railroad employee; functionary in the CPC apparatus from 1948; chairman of the State Planning Commission, 1962–63; minister of transportation, 1963–68; secretary of the CPC Central Committee in 1968; leading member of the pro-Soviet faction in the CPC, which prepared the invasion; active in "normalization policy"; presidium member in 1970; chairman of the National Assembly in 1971.

JAGODA, Genrich (1891–1938): head of the Soviet security services (CHEKA, GPU), 1920–36; led the Stalinist repression; was removed in 1937 and executed in 1938.

JAKEŠ, Miloš (1922): long-time functionary in the CPC apparatus; in the Ministry of the Interior, 1958–68, and deputy minister of the interior, 1966–68; chairman of the Party Central Control Commission, 1968–77; member of the party faction that prepared Soviet intervention and a chief representative of the "normalization policy"; active in the party purge in 1970; secretary of the Central Committee and candidate (nonvoting member) of the presidium since 1977.

KAPEK, Antonín (1922): long-time CPC functionary, particularly in the area of economics; employee and later director of the ČKD heavy industrial plants in Prague, 1953–68; candidate of the CPC presidium, 1962–68; member of the pro-Soviet faction during the Prague Spring; afterwards active in promoting "normalization," especially in Prague; executive secretary of the CPC municipal committees in Prague since 1969; presidium member since 1970.

KAPLAN, Karel (1929): historian and CPC functionary; involved in revising the view of the political trials in the 1950s and in rehabilitating their victims; member of the Central Control and Revision Commission of the CPC; principal author of a report on the political trials prepared during the Prague Spring and proscribed following the Soviet occupation; expelled from CPC in 1970 and accused of illegal activity; in exile in Munich since 1976.

KOLDER, Drahomír (1925–72): originally a miner; functionary in the CPC apparatus from 1948; in the Central Committee apparatus and executive secretary in Ostrava from 1954; presidium member and Central Committee secretary, 1961–68; eventually allied with pro-Soviet faction during Prague

Spring; stripped of his functions in August 1968 and ambassador to Bulgaria until 1969; minister for governmental control from fall 1969 until his death.

KOUCKÝ, Vladimír (1920): CPC member since 1938; member of the illegal CPC Central Committee and editor of the illegal *Rudé právo* in 1944; from 1945, Central Committee member and editor, later editor in chief, of *Rudé právo*, also CPC representative on editorial board of the Cominform journal, *For Lasting Peace, For People's Democracy*, published in Bucharest; Central Committee secretary, 1958–68; ambassador to Moscow, 1968–70; ambassador to Belgium, 1970–77; ambassador to Italy since 1978.

KRIEGEL, František (1908): emigrated to Czechoslovakia from Soviet Union; CPC functionary from the 1930s; physician attached to the International Brigade during the Spanish civil war, 1936–39, physician in the Chinese civil war, 1940–45; secretary of the CPC District Committee in Prague, 1945–49; deputy minister of health, 1949–52; active as physician and researcher in 1953; health advisor to the Cuban government, 1960–63; CPC Central Committee member in 1966; presidium member and chairman of the National Front in 1968; refused to sign the Moscow Protocol in August 1968 and under Soviet pressure was stripped of all functions; spoke out in Parliament against treaty permitting presence of Soviet troops and expelled from the party as a leading member of the 1969 Dubček regime; retired since 1970.

LENÁRT, Josef (1923): originally employed in the Baťa shoe works in Slovakia; functionary of the CPS apparatus from 1946; enrolled in Moscow party school, 1953–56; secretary of the CPS Central Committee, 1958–62; prime minister and presidium member of the CPC Central Committee, 1963–68; CPC Central Committee secretary and presidium candidate, 1968–70; first secretary of the CPS Central Committee and CPC presidium member since 1970.

MAMULA, Miroslav (1921): long-time functionary in the CPC apparatus; head of the economic section of the Central Committee, 1952–60, head of the security and defense section, 1960–68; major supporter of Novotný in the power hierarchy; stripped of his functions in January 1968 and never returned to a leading position; works as a "scientist" in the "struggle against anticommunism."

MASARYK, Tomáš Garrigue (1850–1937): Czech philosopher and statesman; university professor in 1882; a leading figure in the struggle abroad against the Austro-Hungarian monarchy, 1915–18; first president of the Czechoslovak Republic, 1918–25; in his philosophy he combined humanism with the ideas of political democracy and social reform; he united the struggle for national rebirth in the nineteenth century with an attempt to integrate Czechoslovakia into European culture and endeavored to give Czechoslovakia a West European cultural and political orientation; he symbolizes national independence and the humanist, democratic traditions of Czech political life.

NEJEDLÝ, Zdeněk (1878–1962): professor of music at the University of Prague in 1908; CPC member from the 1920s; in Moscow during Second World War; minister and a representative of the official communist ideology in the sciences and education after 1945; president of the Academy of Sciences from 1952; he symbolizes the subordination of the sciences to communist ideology.

NĚMCOVÁ, Božena (1820–62): Czech writer from the era of the national rebirth, when Czechs and Slovaks began forming cultural ties in the spirit of Slavic unity against the unfolding antinationalistic forces of German and Hungarian origin.

NOVOTNÝ, Antonín (1904–75): originally a worker; CPC member from 1921; party functionary in Prague and southern Bohemia before the war; in a concentration camp, 1941–43; executive secretary of the Party District Committee in Prague, 1945–51; rose to high positions during the political trials in the 1950s; secretary of the CPC Central Committee and presidium member, 1951–53; first secretary of the Central Committee, 1953–68, and also president of the Republic, 1957–68; stripped of his functions in 1968 and party membership suspended; reinstated in party after Soviet intervention but never returned to political life.

PALACH, Jan (1948–69): student in the philosophical faculty of the University of Prague; immolated himself on Wenceslaus Square in Prague on January 16, 1969, in protest against capitulation to the Soviet invaders; his funeral procession of hundreds of thousands, especially young people, became a manifesto; his grave became a place of pilgrimage, and his remains were removed from the Prague cemetery by the police after 1970.

PAVEL, Josef (1908–73): CPC member since 1929; at the Lenin School of the Comintern in Moscow, 1935–37; commander of the Dmitroff regiment of the International Brigade in Spain, 1937–38; interned in France and North Africa, 1939–42; in the Czechoslovak army stationed in England, 1942–45; party functionary in Aussig and in Pilsen, 1945–47; head of the security and defense section of the CPC Central Committee, 1947–48; commander of the workers' militia in 1948; deputy minister of the interior, 1949–50; arrested in 1951 and sentenced to 25 years in prison; released in 1955; on a committee for promoting health and sport, 1956–65; minister of the interior in 1968; forced to retire under Soviet pressure in August 1968; expelled from the CPC in 1970.

PILLER, Jan (1922): long-time functionary in the CPC apparatus, particularly in the area of economic policy; deputy prime minister, 1962–65; executive secretary of the CPC District Committee for Central Bohemia in 1968; presidium member and chairman of the Central Committee Commission for the Revision of the Political Trials in the 1950s; compelled to join adherents of "normalization" following the Soviet invasion; secretary of the Central Committee Bureau for Bohemian Lands, 1969–70; chairman of the Central Council of the Trade Unions, 1970–71; stripped of all functions in 1971; works as government employee.

PLOJHAR, Josef (1902): Catholic priest and CPC collaborator; chairman of the Czechoslovak Catholic People's Party from 1948, removed in 1968; active supporter of "normalization" following Soviet invasion.

RICHTA, Radovan (1924): active in the illegal communist movement toward end of war, arrested by Gestapo; Communist functionary and theorist from 1945; corresponding member of the Academy of Sciences and director of the

Philosophical Institute in 1968; 1965–68, was head of research team studying conceptions of socialist development during the so-called scientific-technical revolution—this work greatly influenced reform communism; came to support "normalization" following the Soviet invasion; CPC Central Committee member, 1968–71; reappointed director of the Philosophical Institute and a member of the academy's presidium after 1970—assigned to purging the social studies area; named academician and regular member of the Academy of Sciences in 1977.

SÁDOVSKÝ, Štefan (1928): long-time functionary in the Slovak party apparatus; candidate of the CPC presidium in 1966; Central Committee secretary in 1968 and since August full presidium member; attempted to join "normalization" adherents; prime minister of the Slovak Socialist Republic in 1969 and later first secretary of the CPS Central Committee; stripped of functions in 1971; subsequently vice-director of a concern.

ŠIK, Ota (1919): political economist and CPC functionary; concentration camp prisoner during the war; party apparatus official from 1945; lecturer in political economics after 1948; professor at the Central Committee party school and at the party Institute for Political Science until 1962; director of the Economic Institute of the Academy of Sciences and Central Committee member, 1962–69; leading figure in the economic reform of the 1960s; deputy prime minister in 1968; stripped of all functions and expelled from the CPC in 1969; subsequently in exile in Switzerland.

ŠIMON, Bohumil (1920): long-time functionary in the CPC apparatus, particularly in the economics area; head of the Central Committee political economics section, 1963–68; executive secretary of the CPC Municipal Committee in Prague and candidate presidium member in 1968; full presidium member, August 1968–April 1969; deprived of all functions in 1969 and expelled from the party in 1970; subsequently political economist in the Institute for the Reconstruction of Memorable Monuments in Prague.

SLANSKÝ, Rudolf (1901–52): CPC functionary from 1921; high party official since "Bolshevization" in 1929; in Moscow during war; sent to help lead the Slovak National Uprising in 1944; CPC secretary-general, 1945–51; arrested and executed as "leader of the antistate conspiracy center" in 1951; posthumously rehabilitated in 1963, but preparations for his complete rehabilitation at the party level were interrupted by the Soviet invasion and subsequently abandoned.

SLAVÍK, Václav (1920): long-time functionary in the CPC apparatus; editor of the party organ, *Rudé právo*, 1946–53; head of the ideological section of the CPC Central Committee apparatus, 1953–61; Central Committee secretary, 1961–63; CPC representative on the editorial board of *Questions of Peace and Socialism*, 1963–66; director of the Institute for Political Science of the Central Committee in 1967; Central Committee secretary in 1968; presidium member from August 1968 to April 1969; stripped of all functions in September 1969; expelled from party in 1970; subsequently employed in the water supply system.

SMRKOVSKÝ, Josef (1911–74): originally a baker's assistant; leading functionary of the Communist youth organization in 1931; CPC member from 1933; active in the resistance movement during the war; a leader of the Prague uprising of May 1945; deputy chairman of the Czech National Council in 1945; CPC presidium member, 1946–51, while holding various governmental posts; arrested and sentenced to life imprisonment in 1951; conditionally released in 1955 and worked in forestry until 1963, when he was rehabilitated; Central Committee member, 1966–69; presidium member and chairman of Parliament in 1968; under covert Soviet pressure expelled from the Central Committee in September 1969 and from the party in 1970; actively resisted "normalization policy" until his death.

ŠOTOLA, Jiří (1926): Czech writer; secretary of the Czechoslovak Union of Writers in the 1960s; critic of the Novotný regime; on the index of prohibited authors after Soviet invasion; in 1975 publicly recanted and became an adherent of "normalization."

ŠPAČEK, Josef (1927): long-time functionary in the CPC apparatus in Bruenn; executive secretary of the CPC District Committee in Bruenn and Central Committee member from 1966; belonged to the critical co-workers of the party apparatus during the Novotný era; elected to the presidium in January 1968 and later became Central Committee secretary; stripped of all functions in 1969 and expelled from the party in 1970; subsequently employed on a highway project.

ŠTROUGAL, Lubomír (1924): lawyer; district CPC functionary in Budweiss, 1955–59; minister of agriculture, 1959–61; minister of the interior, 1961–65; Central Committee secretary, 1965–68; deputy prime minister in 1968; adopted "normalization policy" following Soviet intervention; chairman of the Central Committee Bureau for Bohemian Lands and Central Committee secretary and presidium member in fall 1968; prime minister since 1970.

ŠTÚR, Ludovít (1815–56): Slovak poet; outstanding figure of the nineteenth century Slovak renaissance; founder of the Slovak literary language; actively promoted ties between Slovaks and Czechs in the spirit of Slavic brotherhood.

ŠVESTKA, Oldřich (1922): long-time CPC functionary and journalist; *Rudé právo* editor from 1945, editor in chief from 1958; presidium member in 1968; became allied with pro-Soviet faction; stripped of his functions in August and named editor in chief of the weekly *Tribuna,* which became a militant instrument for "normalization"; secretary of the Central Committee Bureau for Bohemian Lands in 1969; Central Committee secretary in 1971; returned to *Rudé právo* as editor in chief in 1975.

SVOBODA, Ludvík (1895): officer in the Czechoslovak legions stationed in the Soviet Union, 1915–20; career soldier after return to Czechoslovakia; in Soviet Union during war and commander of the Czechoslovak military units there, 1943–45; defense minister, 1945–50; bookkeeper in an agricultural association, 1953–54; nominated in 1954, on Khrushchev's intercession, as deputy to the National Parliament; commander of the military academy in Prague from 1955; retired in 1959; elected president of the Republic in 1968; presidium member in August 1968; relieved of his functions in 1975 due to serious illness.

VACULÍK, Ludvík (1926): Czech writer; originally a boarding school tutor; later editor for the Czechoslovak broadcasting organization and for *Literární listy;* expelled from the party in 1967 because of his speech at the Writers' Congress, reinstated in 1968; popular and influential publicist during Prague Spring; expelled from party in 1969 and placed on the index of prohibited authors.

VACULÍK, Martin (1922): long-time party functionary from Moravia; party school student in Moscow, 1956–58; in the CPC Central Committee apparatus from 1958; executive secretary of the party municipal committee in Prague, 1962–65; presidium candidate, 1963–68; Central Committee functionary during Prague Spring; opposed Soviet invasion and expelled from the party in 1970; subsequently working in a garage.

YESHOV, Nikolai (1895–1939): head of Soviet security organs during Stalinist repression, 1936–38; was himself finally executed in 1939.

ZAPOTOCKÝ, Antonín (1884–1957): son of a founder of the Czech socialist movement; Social Democratic Party secretary in the mining region of Kladno, 1907–11; CPC member in 1921; secretary-general of the CPC, 1922–25; leader of the Communist trade unions, 1929–38; concentration camp prisoner during war; presidium member from 1945; chairman of the Central Council of the Trade Unions, 1945–48; prime minister, 1948–63; president of the Republic, 1953–57.

INDEX

Note: "Czechoslovakia" is abbreviated to "C." and "Czechoslovak" to "Cz."

Academy of Sciences, Cz. (author's work at), 41, 56, 79, 128, 221
Action Program of CPC, 73, 87ff, 96, 98, 108, 109, 121, 135, 143, 149, 161, 164, 166, 169, 213, 218, 237, 243, 252
Albania, 155, 158
Aleš, V., 34–6
Auersperg, P., 88n, 207

Bacílek, K., 69
Barák, R., 39–40, 58, 68
Barbírek, F., 105, 151, 177, 188, 189, 192, 193, 201, 209, 227, 248
Bartušek, J., 102
Bedřich, Gen. F., 148
Beria, L., 27, 58
Berlinguer, E., 241
Bilak, V., 74, 85, 92, 93, 94, 105, 111, 124, 128, 132, 143, 146–7, 150, 162, 176, 188, 190, 191, 192, 193, 196, 197, 201, 213, 215, 221, 226, 227, 229, 233, 235, 243, 246, 251, 252, 253
Bratislava, six-party meeting at (Aug. 1968), 151ff, 168
Brezhnev, L. I., 70, 71 and n, 86, 91ff, 102, 113, 114, 123, 132, 149–50, 152–55, 160–62, 163, 168, 173, 185, 189, 190, 197, 198, 215, 246; at Moscow meeting (Aug. 1968), 237–45
Brezhnev Doctrine, 154
bureaucracy (Cz.), 80, 117

Ceauşescu, Pres. N., 155, 241
censorship, 64, 97
Central Committee (CPC) headquarters building, 177ff, 190, 201
Černík, O., 51, 65, 69, 77, 91, 92, 104, 110, 111, 112, 113, 120, 124–6, 134, 141, 142, 143, 146, 151, 162,
167, 170, 181, 188, 191, 196, 198, 199, 204, 205, 209, 210, 211, 212, 213, 214, 215, 219, 224, 227, 229, 230, 233, 236, 242, 245, 249–50
Červinka, A., 88n
Charter 77, 7, 38, 76, 143
Chechikvadze, Akad., 86
Chervonenko, S. V. (Soviet ambassador in C.), 92, 161, 179, 189, 190, 191, 192, 193, 194, 195, 196
China, 158, 159, 173
Chudík, M., 69, 91
Cierná nad Tisou (meeting between CPC presidium and Soviet politburo Aug. 1, 1968), 113, 134, 137, 151, 152n, 168, 170, 171, 212, 241, 257
Císař, C., 77, 106–7, 109, 121, 135, 141, 142, 151, 164–5, 188, 201, 202, 206, 207, 209, 215, 246, 255
civil rights, 81
class struggle, 28, 61, 62, 122
Clementis, V., 66
Club of Committed Non-Communists (KAN), 84, 115
Colotka, P., 205
Communist Party of C. (CPC), 1, 7, 10, 21–2, 41, 42–3, 87ff, 93, 94, 95, 96, 99, 112, 113, 115, 116, 117, 118, 132, 138ff, 161, 163, 166, 170, 171, 176, 213, 219–20, 258; effect of Stalin's death, 28–30; expulsions (1970), 63, 256; Central Committee of, 53–5, 60n, 91ff, 100, 104–5, 106ff, 115, 128–9, 132, 137, 142, 147, 161, 165, 172, 188, 202, 205, 219, 235, 253–4, 255, 256, 257; *see also* Action Program, reform Communists, Vysočany
Communist Party of the Soviet Union (CPSU), 248; Twentieth Congress, 24ff, 37, 135, 174

Communist Party of Slovakia (CPS), 205
Communists, reform, *see* reform Communists
Czech National Council, 110, 256
Czechoslovak Press Agency, 176

dictatorship, totalitarian, in C., 50, 51, 62, 84, 99, 100, 144, 207
Dolanský, J., 91, 92
Dubček, Alexander, 51, 64, 65, 69, 75, 85, 91, 92ff, 101–5, 107, 108–11, 113, 114, 115, 120–6, 136, 151, 152 and n, 153, 162, 163, 165, 167, 168, 170, 171, 172, 175, 176ff, 196, 198, 200, 201, 204, 207, 208, 219, 229, 230, 234–5, 247, 248, 249, 250, 251–54; growth in popularity, 120ff; and Warsaw Pact intervention, 146ff; at Bratislava six-party meeting, 151ff; at Kremlin meeting (Aug. 1968), 209–13, 216, 217, 219, 224, 225, 227, 229, 230, 231, 232, 234, 235, 237, 238, 239, 241, 242, 244, 245, 246–47
Dzúr, M., 146, 148, 197, 211, 227, 230

Erban, E., 110, 177, 202, 209, 255

Fojtík, J., 87n
French Communist Party, 225

Galuška, M., 111
German Democratic Republic (GDR), 55, 151, 156, 168
Gešo, L., 34, 35
Goldstueker, E., 96
Gomulka, W., 41, 100, 155, 156, 161, 162, 167, 174, 240
Gosiorovský, M., 95
Gottwald, K., 9, 27, 31, 69, 222
Grechko, Marshal, 162, 163, 186, 191

Hácha, E., 229
Hájek, J., 111, 134, 135, 215, 246
Harus, J., 38
Havel, V., 74
Hendrych, J., 65, 69, 72, 73, 74, 75–6, 89, 91, 92, 96, 97, 108
Hoffman, K., 112, 176, 202
Hübl, M., 225
Hungary, 64, 109, 156–7, 195, 200, 228, 234; Soviet intervention in (1956), 38, 41, 149
Husák, G., 77, 111, 133, 176, 197, 205, 206, 211, 212, 215, 218, 219, 220, 221, 222–7, 230, 245, 248, 250, 251, 252; tried and imprisoned (1954), 28, 34; regime, 7, 63, 64, 109, 203, 258

Indra, A., 51, 74, 92, 93, 94, 106, 128, 133, 134, 135, 143, 150, 176, 177, 183, 187, 188, 189, 190, 192, 193, 196, 197, 201, 211, 213, 221, 229, 230, 235, 237, 245, 246, 248, 249, 251–2
Innemann, K., 40
Italian Communist Party, 74, 225, 258

Jakeš, M., 74, 93, 94, 128, 143, 150, 176, 184, 188, 189, 192, 201, 209, 213, 215, 221, 227, 243, 252, 258
Jakubovsky, Marshal, 148
Johnson, Pres. L. B., 241
journalists, journalism, 52–3, 77, 103, 164

Kadar, J., 155, 156–7, 232
"Kadarization," 64, 225, 229, 235, 252
Kadlec, V., 111
Kapek, A., 105, 111, 135, 150, 176, 184, 201, 207, 209
Kaplan, K., 87n
Kardelj, E., 42
Kašpar, J., 201
Kempný, J., 203, 251
KGB, 55, 114, 119, 189, 190, 194, 210, 233
Khrushchev, N. S., 16, 22, 24, 68, 72, 86, 158–60, 162, 164; criticism of Stalin (1956), 24, 27, 29ff; disposes of "antiparty" group in Moscow, 69; deposed, 70
Knapp, V., 53
Koehler, B., 69
Kolder, D., 69, 73, 87n, 89, 91, 92, 104, 105, 106, 108, 110, 113, 120, 126–8, 131–2, 133, 134, 143, 150, 177, 181, 188, 189, 190, 192, 193, 201, 202, 203, 207, 209, 224
Komsomol, 16
Kopecký, V., 68
Kopřiva, L., 68
Kosygin, A., 162, 164–5, 215, 221, 245–6, 249
Kouba, K., 88n
Koucký, V., 60n, 65, 69, 72, 73, 74, 75, 76, 96, 108, 109, 112, 113, 115, 227, 244
Kriegel, F., 65, 105, 108, 112, 143, 146, 151, 167, 177, 180–3, 188, 204, 205, 210, 211, 215, 227, 230, 236–7, 244–5, 247, 254, 256, 257
Krosnář, J., 65
Kučera, B., 197, 211, 227, 230
Kudrna, J., 93, 102
Kuehnul, K., 42
Kusý, M., 224
Kuznetsov, V., 248, 249, 251

Laštovička, B., 90
law, legal theory, legal studies, 17–18, 44, 60, 62, 81
Lenárt, J., 51, 69, 73, 91, 105, 106, 111, 142, 188, 192, 193, 201, 209, 213, 215, 227, 248, 251
Lenin, Leninism, 5, 13, 14, 15, 17, 19, 45, 104, 122, 141, 164, 199, 221, 252
Literární noviny (later L. listy), 64, 96, 137, 138, 149, 183n, 185

Machačová, B., 196
Mandák, O., 258, 259
Maoists, 3
Marxist philosophy, principles, 2, 5, 13, 14, 15, 16, 17, 44, 45ff, 62, 104, 122, 164, 173
Masaryk, T. G., 72, 110, 111, 118, 122, 132, 216
military intervention in C., see under Soviet Union
Moscow, CPC leaders meet in (Aug. 1968), 204, 209
Moscow University, author at, 17ff, 146, 178, 190
Moscow Protocol, 214ff, 234, 241, 242–3, 246, 250, 252

National Front (of Czechs and Slovaks), 83, 88ff, 115, 170, 197, 208
Nazism, Nazis, 23, 34, 36, 199; occupation of country in Second World War, 1, 12, 14, 65, 118, 178
newspapers, see press
Novotna, B., 66
Novotný, A., and regime, 22, 39, 54, 55, 56, 58, 63, 64, 65–73, 76, 102, 106, 107, 108, 127, 130, 136, 161, 181, 216, 223, 224, 226, 238, 256; fall of, 91–8, 115, 116, 160–1
Nový, V., 254

Palach, J., 251, 254, 258
Pastýřik, M., 102
Pavel, J., 112–13, 170, 215, 246
Pavlovsky, Gen. (Soviet), 191
Pavlovský, O., 93, 188, 191, 192, 202
Piller, J., 105, 135, 142, 177, 188, 191, 192, 196, 197, 201, 227, 248, 255, 257
Podgorny, Pres., 244
Poland, 41, 100, 151, 158, 168, 240
politburo, Soviet, 201, 208, 228, 242, 243
Ponomarev, B., 215, 243
Prague Spring, passim, 63, 73, 76, 78, 103, 105, 111, 118, 119, 121ff, 132, 164, 165, 169, 175, 200, 208, 218,

224, 238, 254, 257; author's attitude to, 45; opponents of reform, 43
Prchlík, V., 105
press, freedom of, 82
private ownership, 61
privileges enjoyed by politicians, 128–31, 178
prosecutor, public (author's work in office of), 33ff
Provazník, S., 88n

Rašková, H., 254
reform Communists,—communism, in C., 45ff, 59, 71, 74, 76, 100, 118, 137, 139, 169, 170, 174, 225, 226, 235
"revolutionary workers' and peasants' government," 93, 195, 202, 212
Richta, R., 77, 87n, 133–4
Rigo, E., 105, 124, 135, 150, 177, 188, 192, 193, 194, 201, 209, 227
Rohan, R., 88
Rudé právo, 7, 53, 56, 72, 107, 109, 116, 176, 249
Rumania, 155, 158, 162, 175, 241
Rytíř, Gen., 188, 191

Sádovský, Š., 151, 187, 188, 191, 192, 195, 202, 209
Šalgovič, V., 112, 114, 167, 176, 191, 202, 207
Samek, J., 40
Second World War, results of and Soviet policy, 239–40
Shchemenko, Gen., 168
Shelepin, 86, 168
Shelest, P., 152
Šik, O., 88n, 105, 111, 128, 206, 215
Šilhán, V., 198, 205
Simon, B., 87n, 88n, 105, 143, 151, 152n, 163, 167, 176, 177, 180, 184, 188, 201, 205, 210, 212, 215, 219, 227, 229–30, 233, 245, 246, 252, 253, 257
Šimůnek, O., 91
Široký, V., 8, 69, 223
Slánský, R., trial of, 8, 9, 34, 58, 65, 106, 178
Slavik, V., 106, 107, 143, 151, 177, 185, 202, 209, 257
Šling, O., 7
Slovakia, Slovaks, 77, 78, 89, 95, 124, 185, 193, 205, 216, 220, 221, 222, 223, 224, 225
Smrkovský, J., 90, 105, 112, 124, 140, 141, 143, 151, 152n, 162, 167, 176, 177, 179, 181, 183, 184, 188, 196, 198, 199, 205, 209, 210, 211, 212, 213, 215, 219, 223, 227, 229–30,

299

233, 236, 242, 245, 250, 252, 253, 255–8

Şolzhenitsyn, A., 16

Şorm, F., 110

Sotola, J., 77

Soviet Union, 2, 8, 9–10, 41, 135; author's studies in, 11ff; living standards, 10; press, 201; superpower foreign policy interests, 158ff; military intervention in C. (1968), 59, 75, 136, 143, 146ff, 157–8, 161, 164ff, 171, 176ff, 208, 240, 241; espionage network in C., 114, 119, 161, 170, 171, 207, 252; embassy in Prague, 93, 161, 187, 188, 189

Špaček, J., 97, 104, 151, 152n, 167, 177, 183, 188, 205, 210, 212, 213, 214, 219, 227, 229–30, 233, 245, 249, 252, 253, 257

Stalin, J. V., 2, 11, 13, 24, 69, 225; writings of, 2; death of, 24–7

Stalinists, Stalinism, 3, 5, 6, 8, 10, 18, 19, 22, 41, 42, 43, 45, 64, 68, 75, 99, 100, 162, 222–3, 225, 228, 252

State Security forces, secret police (Cz.), 112, 117, 167, 170, 176, 183, 207, 222

Štrougal, L., 69, 73, 89, 111, 196, 203, 250, 251, 252

Sucharda, B., 111

Sulek, J., 176

Şuslov, M., 215, 243

Švach, E., 122

Švermová, M., 7, 34

Svestka, O., 105, 108, 132, 133, 134, 143, 150, 176, 177, 188, 192, 201, 209, 213, 215, 227

Svoboda, J., 204

Svoboda, L., 110, 146, 149, 194, 195, 196, 197–8, 204, 209, 211, 212, 213, 215, 216, 228, 230, 232, 236, 242, 244, 245, 246, 250, 251; personal background of, 216

Tito, Pres. J. B., 155, 171, 241

trades union, 62, 81, 144

treaty, Cz.-Soviet (1970), 154

trials, political, in C., 7, 8, 17, 28, 127

"Two Thousand Words" manifesto, 137, 138–43, 161, 166, 170, 257

Udaltsov, I., 161

Ulbricht, W., 153, 154, 155, 156, 161, 162, 167, 174

United Nations, 212

United States, Americans, 158, 169, 170, 199, 240, 241

Urválek, J., 34

Vaculík, L., 137, 138, 139, 143, 167

Vaculík, M., 69, 105, 206

Vlasák, F., 111

Vodsloň, F., 105

Voleník, O., 106, 177, 188, 209, 255

Vysočany, Fourteenth CPC Congress at, 176, 187, 188, 191–2, 197, 198, 200, 205, 207–8, 209, 212, 217, 218, 219, 231, 246

"Warsaw Letter," 139, 153, 167, 168, 214

Warsaw Pact, 71, 118, 168, 172, 200; forces in C., 146ff, 186, 214

Yugoslavia, 155, 158, 171, 173, 241

youth organizations, 62; and see Komsomol

Zápotocký, A., 9, 68, 255

Zhivkov, T., 156

Zprávy, 207